The Practice of Spatial Thinking:
Differentiation Processes – Second Editi

Publishing Info

The Practice of Spatial Thinking: Differentiation
Processes — Second Edition

Leon van Schaik, SueAnne Ware,
Colin Fudge, Geoffrey London

Second Edition:
   Benedict Anderson (2005)
   Suzie Attiwill (2013)
   Nigel Bertram (2013)
   Richard Black (2009)
   Stephen Collier (2009)
   Graham Crist (2010)
   Lucas Devriendt (2015)
   Harold Fallon (2013)
   Arnaud Hendrickx (2013)
   Tom Holbrook (2014)
   CJ Lim (2014)
   Paul Minifie (2010)
   Vivian Mitsogianni (2009)
   Stephen Neille (2007)
   Deborah Saunt (2014)
   Jon Tarry (2012)
   Jo Van Den Berghe (2013)
   Gretchen Wilkins (2012)

ISBN: 9 781948 765350
Library of Congress Control Number:2019951131

Revisions to the Second Edition: Leon van Schaik
and Ian Nazareth

Research conducted by Leon van Schaik and Sue Anne
Ware was supported under the Australian Research
Council's Discovery Projects funding scheme
(DP110100939). The views expressed herein are those
of the authors and are not necessarily those of the
Australian Research Council.

We gratefully thank all the contributors for
providing their research text and images for
inclusion in this publication.

Cover: Leon van Schaik, Differentiation in Vital
Practice v3, 15 March 2013
Chapter covers: Ramesh Ayyar, Marc Morel,
Christine Scott-Young
Case Study Paul Morgan: Drawings Paul Morgan,
Photography Leon van Schaik
Case Study TCL: Drawings and renders TCL,
Photography John Gollings
Book design: Stuart Geddes and Kim Mumm Hansen

Table of Contents

Preface to the Second Edition

This second edition of The Black Book sees a change of publisher as Professor Martyn Hook, the Dean of the School of Architecture and Urban Design at RMIT, moves to secure international access to the intellectual property generated by our practice reflection research program. Martyn is himself a graduate of the program, in which he and his partners in iredale pedersen hook architects examined the nature of the mastery that they had established in their first decade. Martyn has supervised many of the practitioners who have joined the program, an activity that he continues to give priority.

The Black book documents research conducted in the acquittal of an Australian Research Council Discovery grant (ARC DP 110100939). It also takes its place in a lineage of publications[1] including ten page digests of the research conducted within the design practice reflective research program in RMIT's School of Architecture and Urban Design and its predecessors.

Included in this volume are digests of the research of the following practitioners:

Benedict Anderson (2005)
Suzie Attiwill (2013)
Nigel Bertram (2013)
Richard Black (2009)
Stephen Collier (2009)
Graham Crist (2010)
Lucas Devriendt (2015)
Harold Fallon (2013)
Arnaud Hendrickx (2013)
Tom Holbrook (2014)
CJ Lim (2014)
Paul Minifie (2010)
Vivian Mitsogianni (2009)
Stephen Neille (2007)
Deborah Saunt (2014)
Jon Tarry (2012)
Jo Van Den Berghe (2013)
Gretchen Wilkins (2012)

In addition, their work can be seen in full on the research repository at RMIT: https://practice-research.com/ and their examinations can be viewed on vimeo at https://vimeo.com/user3911530

Leon van Schaik AO,
School of Architecture and Urban Design, RMIT
MELBOURNE

1 *Fin de Siecle and the twenty first century: Architectures of Melbourne*, RMIT, 1993, Melbourne; *Transfiguring the Ordinary*, Printed Books, 1995, Melbourne Interstitial Modernism, RMIT, 2000, Melbourne; *The Practice of Practice - research in the medium of design*, RMIT UP, 2003, Melbourne; *The Practice of Practice 2: Research in the Medium of Design*, onepointsixone, 2010, Melbourne

Foreword

The research presented in this first volume and carried out in Australia as part of an Australian Research Council Discovery Program is of major significance for design practice, review, and our deeper understanding of the design of space and spaces. In continuing the exploration of "spatial intelligence,"[1] this research, and the work contained in the second volume further develop our understanding of designers, how they work and what they draw on through their lives that shapes their spatial thinking, and their practice.

The research also provides broader insights into a more public understanding and acknowledgement of our collective spatial intelligence. It shows how this could be developed and enhanced to provide more spatial and design literacy in our communities, and how these can engage with their changing environments.

In 1999, I was appointed to a new UK Government Agency entitled the "Commission for Architecture and the Built Environment" (CABE). I was responsible for South West England, and with a small permanent staff and the new regional "ambassadors," we commenced the process of turning the ideas contained in the *Urban Task Force Report* (Richard Rogers)[2] into an operational agency both nationally and within all the regions of England. With others, I was involved in the development of the national and regional *Design Review* processes, *Design Enabling*, *Urban Design Approaches*, *Urban Design Education*, *Design Research* and the communication of these ideas and operational systems to the property development and built environment worlds, as well as to the general public.

One of the first tasks we completed for the Minister, the Deputy Prime Minister and the Treasury was to promote the understanding of the *Value of Design*. This was done to provide an important set of arguments for the operation of CABE but also to pose a strong challenge to the "doubters," particularly in the property business world. Led by Professor Matthew Carmona at the Bartlett School of Planning, UCL, this work proved very helpful in supporting our early work with CABE[3]. And had it been available at the time, the research contained in this ARC, Discovery Project would have been equally as valuable.

In this volume, the design practice research of fourteen practices is introduced and summarised. These case studies are examined to understand the differentation in their spatial thinking. As an introduction, Leon Van Schaik uses a methodological tool to examine a project by Architect Paul Morgan, and SueAnne Ware examines the work of Landscape Architects Taylor Cullity Lethlean through the lens of a further case study. The content is framed in an essay from Geoffrey London reporting on *Design Review* in Australia, the practice of which stems from the earlier work by CABE in the UK and is introduced here. Finally, Leon Van Schaik and SueAnne Ware conclude this volume explaining that the research contained herein presents: "a pioneering investigation into the ways in which spatial-thinking is differentiated in the mastering of practice," and how this understanding informs "the design review processes that are so central to creating upward spirals in the quality of designing."

Further practice case studies are being documented for future publication. The volume concludes with an overall discussion refinining the complete research program including the implications for policy, practice, education and further research.

Given the significance of this research in understanding design practice and the use of this interpretation for more public processes of design review, it is interesting to note that in the UK, a further impetus to this type of understanding and public policy responses has just been published. The Farrell Review, released in the UK in March of 2014,[4] is a comprehensive appraisal commisioned by the current Government and Minister Ed Vaizey and led by Sir Terry Farrell of our collective efforts to plan and design our

1 Schaik, Leon van, (2008) *Spatial Intelligence: New Futures for Architecture*, John Wiley & Sons, Chichester.

2 *Towards an Urban Renaissance* (1999) Final report of the Urban Task Force, Chaired by Lord Richard Rogers of Riverside, London

3 CABE (2002) *The Value of Good Design*, London.

4 'Our Future in Place' (2014) in *The Farrell Review of Architecture and the Built Environment*, www.farrellreview.co.uk

future built environment, which, in turn, shapes the way we live our lives. It comes after a significant period of mourning following the demise of CABE in its original form at the hands of the same and current government. The Review contains five broad recommendations: understanding place-based planning and design; better connectedness between all stakeholders; improved public engagement through education and outreach; a sustainable and low carbon future; and a commitment to improving the everyday built environment and making the ordinary better. It emphasises the critical importance of architecture and design, design literacy and the civic value of good design and well-designed public spaces. It focuses on the future of place, and places design in the "urban age".

The research reported in this volume, and in the one to follow, provide a rich seam of evidence in the complex field of design that links our heightened understanding of design practice and innovation with the more public development of processes for design review and improving design quality[5]. This research could foreseeably impact on the policy response of governments to independent studies such as the *Farrell Review* in the UK, but, significantly, could also act as the stimulus for new thinking and innovate opportunities involving education, policy, practice and research initiatives for Australia and the Asia Pacific Region.

Professor Colin Fudge

5 This research, when added to the earlier studies over the last 25 years at RMIT University, knowingly or not, also reflects a longitudinal study of a professional occupation, that of the architect. It occurs to me that this is similar to the great tradition of the mostly American sociologists focussing on the understanding of occupations in the 1940s–1960s. For example, "Boys in White", a study of how interns became doctors by Howard Becker, Blanche Geer, Everett Hughes and Anselm Strauss (1961).

Summary

Introduction to The Practice of Spatial Thinking: Differentiation Processes:

How do designers in research-driven practices differentiate themselves from each other and form distinctive platforms for future practice?

Guide to this Volume:

This is a documentation of research conducted under the aegis of ARC PROJECT ID: DP110100939, beginning in 2011 and concluding in 2014. The summary of the proposal reads as follows:

Spatial Intelligence (SI) is the human capacity upon which architects, landscape architects and urban designers build their capacity for spatial thinking, their unique skill base. This research will extend our understanding of this aspect of their professional design practice, enabling a more deft application and analysis, greater public benefit and wellbeing. A new conceptualisation of SI as the core knowledge base of thee professions enables a new evaluation of techniques used by architects, landscape architects, and urban designers when they deploy their spatial intelligence in the design of spaces and places.

This project will result in the identification and methodical analysis of Spatial Intelligence as deployed by architects, landscape architects and urban design practitioners. It will also explore improvements in, and invention of new design policies and design procurement procedures that are informed by deeper understandings of Spatial Intelligence.

The Chief Investigators are Leon van Schaik, SueAnne Ware, Colin Fudge (RMIT) and Geoffrey London (UWA).

Background and Objectives:
Spatial Intelligence is one of the seven human intelligences defined by Howard Gardner (1999), and it is developed from the capability that enables us to orientate and navigate spatially. Gardner writes,
   An increasing number of researchers believe … that there exists a multitude of intelligences, quite independent of each other; that each intelligence has its own strengths and constraints; that the mind is far from unencumbered at birth; and that it is unexpectedly difficult to teach things that go against early 'naive' theories that challenge the natural lines of force within an intelligence and its matching domains. (1999, xxiii)

Twenty years of research by neuroscientists has helped us to critically understand SI and the ways designers employ/use it (van Schaik 2008). This new understanding provides the opportunity for research that will help redefine the role design can play in promoting the wellbeing of communities through the design of spaces and places. The evidence based research into the positive impact of good design on therapeutic outcomes in healthcare buildings conducted by Professor Robert Ulrich (Texas A&M) refers. Our research examines the need for conscious use of SI by designers as they deal with different stakeholders, clients, and contexts.

Further aims of this research are to:
→ *Enable designers to become aware of deeply understood structures of their design judgements, which, in practice, become a form of intuition. (Halpern 2005);*

→ *Improve the efficacy of design review processes used in the curation and procurement of high quality design by clients (both governmental and private);*

→ *Extend the analytical tools the CIs have developed – through twenty years of design practice research (van Schaik 2005; van Schaik, London & George 2010; Ware 2009) – to enable practitioners to improve their design practice.*

The outcomes will be as follows:

→ *The first systematic analysis of procedures and techniques for deploying SI in design since the public emergence of new knowledge about SI (van Schaik 2008).*

→ *The surfacing of tacit methods of deploying SI inclusively in design.*

→ *Improved procedures and techniques in designing, and in managing design.*

→ *An articulation of SI as a driver of excellence in design that will enhance the contribution already made through the Design Practice Research Lab's work on the 'natural history' of the creative innovator, and on the public behaviours that sustain creative innovation.*

→ *Redesign of design review processes that are currently being used to steer strategically significant design projects. This approach was pioneered by CABE (UK) and has been deployed by the Government Architects in Western Australia, Victoria (van Schaik, London & George 2010) and South Australia based on a design review process franchised from CABE.*

→ *Proposals for the 're-professionalisation' of design professions.*

→ *The findings will be published in book form.*

Colin Fudge and Geoffrey London frame the research in the context of the work of commissioning agencies, such as the UK Commission for Architecture and the Built Environment (CABE). Colin Fudge served on CABE design review panels and in Australian Government Architect offices. Geoffrey London introduced formal design review processes in West Australia and Victoria. The book *Procuring Innovative Architecture*[1] provides a background, with the opening essay by Geoffrey London framing the relevance of the research into spatial thinking to design review processes, and this is at the core of the commissioning agencies' approaches to improving commissioned designs.

Spatial thinking has been a particular research interest of Leon van Schaik. The book *Spatial Intelligence*[2] documents this work, where van Schaik describes the tool for identifying differentiation in spatial thinking developed in the research. The publications produced in the process of that development are listed, followed by a case study using the tool to examine a project by architect Paul Morgan. SueAnne Ware then presents a further case study working with Landscape Architects Taylor Cullity Lethlean. The research is conducted through the distinguished practices research program initiated at RMIT twenty-five years ago.[3] In Volume One, the design practice research of fourteen practices is introduced and summarised in ten page sections with a final conclusion. An additional sixteen practices are documented in Volume Two. Whilst it was envisaged that the respective research would be captured in electronic journals, researchers have preferred to use a mixture of means to record their design processes.

1 Schaik, van Leon and Geoffrey London (with an essay by Beth George) (2010) *Procuring Innovative Architecture*, Routledge, London

2 Schaik, van Leon (2008) *Spatial Intelligence: New Futures for Architecture*, John Wiley & Sons, Chichester

3 Schaik, van Leon and A. Johnson (2011) *Architecture & Design, By Practice, By Invitation: Design Practice Research at RMIT*, onepointsixone, Melbourne

Reviewing Design Review

This paper documents the outcomes of draft policy work:

→ *The draft policy work will focus on design reviews. Design review is increasingly used in project delivery management, ubiquitous in England's Commission for Architecture and the Built Environment (CABE), and was used by the Government Architect in Western Australia, and is being used in Victoria. The following questions will be addressed: What does understanding the role of Spatial Intelligence in designing mean for design review?*

→ *Does it indicate better times for performing reviews? Are there better ways of doing reviews and achieving improved design outcomes?*

→ *The effects of this draft policy will be evaluated by Government Architects from Australia and Europe, and by outstanding commissioners of innovative design identified in our research into the procuring of innovative architecture. (van Schaik, London & George [2010])*

Professor Geoffrey London, October 2013

The process of design review is well known to architects. It underscores design studio teaching and the use of juries at schools of architecture. Architectural practices use in-house reviews as a means of advancing design thinking on projects by bringing to them a wider range of critical response than that provided by the project team. Design review, while widely acknowledged as a productive process, has not had an entirely benign history in schools of architecture. Too often design reviews, juries or critiques have been vehicles for powerful egos with stridently expressed positions, sometimes jousting with one another, rather than assisting the presenting student and their design.

In 1999, the Commission for Architecture and the Built Environment (CABE) in the UK set up a design review panel and sought to formalise its operations with a tightly controlled structure and set of review guidelines. Their intention was to develop a well-respected, design-focused process that enabled constructive critique to improve quality and add value to a project.

The CABE panel drew on expertise from a breadth of multi-disciplinary built environment professionals. They promoted their reviews as independent, constructive and supportive of good design intentions. The review findings were recorded in a written report made public after planning approval was achieved. The reviews were, until recently, at no cost to proponents and CABE strongly encouraged review as early in the design process as possible. Although the CABE design reviews were advisory only, without regulatory power, their authority increased once the UK Chief Planner advised local authorities that the CABE review reports should be regarded as material evidence in their planning determinations. This often had the result of speeding up approvals in the planning process.

The CABE process became an international benchmark and has been drawn on extensively by those states in Australia that use formalised design review.

I've been asked to reflect on this formalised process and will do so through my experience of the Victorian Design Review Panel (VDRP), which has been operating since early 2012. The Office of the Victorian Government Architect (OVGA) had been developing the plan for such a panel as a key strategy in its proposed Victorian Policy for Architecture and the Built Environment. The establishment of VDRP became possible as the incoming Victorian government had made an election commitment able to be immediately covered by the OVGA plan.

Expressions of interest were sought publicly for places on the Panel and one hundred and thirty submissions were received across the disciplines of architecture, landscape architecture, urban design and planning. Sixty were selected to be interviewed for the twenty-five member Panel.The lengthy process proved worthwhile because, in addition to asking a standard set of questions, each of the sixty was invited to conduct a brief review of a selected project via a set of drawings. We looked for their capacity to recognise issues quickly and clearly describe them. There was no checklist of issues to be covered and we were often surprised by what people could extract from the previously unseen drawings: the speed of reading the drawings and making astute assessments was impressive in many candidates.

Twenty-five finalists were selected for the Panel who then went through a process of appointment by Cabinet. In addition to the Panel, eight technical specialists were appointed covering the areas of sustainability, feasibility, public art, master planning, universal design, and economic development, together with a small number of government design specialists. The VDRP is directed and managed by the OVGA: the Panel is co-chaired by the Government Architect and the Associate Government Architect. In its first year of operation, only government-funded projects were reviewed, but at the invitation of the Minister for Planning, the VDRP now accepts projects directed to it by local authorities.

To prepare for design review, the OVGA visits the sites and works directly with the clients and design teams. A team of three, with a mix of skills in landscape architecture, planning and architecture carry out this important up front work. They prepare comprehensive written project briefings for Panel members, provide a verbal briefing before each review, and prepare a letter of advice following the review. Clients, design teams and other key decision-makers are invited to the review sessions.

A full day is set aside each month for two sessions of Panel reviews with between four and six projects seen during the day. Members of the Panel are drawn on in rotation to form, together with the technical specialists and government experts, panels of up to six reviewers. At the end of each review, the Chair summarises the assessments set out by the reviewers and a letter of advice is sent. In addition, out-of-session, full reviews and less formalised desktop reviews can be conducted as required.

Since April 2012, the VDRP has conducted eighty reviews across an extraordinary variety of project types at a total project value in excess of $3.5 billion. More than six hundred people have attended proceedings. A number of the projects have returned for second, third and fourth reviews, with clear evidence of the response to earlier reviews and subsequent improvement. The VDRP was funded as a three-year pilot project and the OVGA is commissioning a review to present the case for its continuation.

From the evidence of CABE and the VDRP thus far, the great worth of conducting such a process is that it does raise design quality, it does add value to projects and it foregrounds design as important. It allows clients, local authorities and other stakeholders to hear informed discussion about design. It gives design intelligence a public airing, allowing the complexity and rigour of designing to be openly discussed and, as a result, better understood by those outside the design disciplines. In the case of well-considered design proposals, the process has helped project architects by endorsing their design strategy.

I am regularly surprised by what Panel members are able to read into plans – their capacity to visualise and comprehend three dimensionally can astonish. Their experience and skill allows swift assessment of the architectural idea driving the project, its strengths and weaknesses, and the ability to suggest how the strengths may be enhanced and the weaknesses diminished.

There is clear evidence of spatial intelligence in practice, a topic about which Leon van Schaik has written (van Schaik 2008).

At a recent review session, a senior bureaucrat in attendance was sufficiently intrigued by this exercising of spatial intelligence to cancel all her subsequent meetings and stay on for the full day of reviews.

Difference rather than shared competence

Over the period of the ADAPTr program we have developed a tool[1] that helps design practitioners understand how what they do when they are designing is different to what other practitioners do. Why focus on the difference? Isn't it the shared competency that defines the service that a profession offers? A profession offers services on the basis of "knowing, doing and helping.[2]" So we agree that a basic competency of professional knowledge, of professional modes of doing and of helping is necessary. This is what is known[3] as "mastery" in a discipline. After four or five years of study, this takes between seven and ten years of practice to achieve. During that time some exceptionally creative designers push the boundary of what is thought of as basic competence. These are the designers that interest us. They have differentiated themselves from the norms of competence, and they have differentiated themselves from their equally adventurous peers.

Who are these exceptionally creative designers? There have been very few empirical studies, but the handful conducted before we began our work identified a spread of operational modes within the architectural profession[4]. The majority of practitioners focus their mastery on concepts of 'service'. They join (or found) large practices, construction companies or tract builders. They thrive in matrix organisations, often global in reach, often similar in their values to the global corporations that they tend to serve. A smaller number focus their mastery on aspects of the delivery of design. They often concentrate on innovating systems of construction, and gravitate to or create linear, command-structures in their firms. An even smaller number are the innovators who concentrate on new ideas and whose firms have adhoc organisational structures that change to suit each project they undertake. "*Small and incompletely rationalised offices, though handicapped by diseconomies of scale, are the seedbed of ideas that produce high quality work. And when they venture beyond the limits of their scale and flaunt their diseconomies, they do exceptionally good work.*"[5] While we have worked with all three kinds of practices, and can demonstrate[6] that all of them can benefit from this approach to PhD research, the driver of our research is the design practice of the smaller, nimbler, ideas-driven firm.

The schema set out here is itself a differentiation 'fan' of choice. Choices fan out in front of a designer at every turn in the life of their practices and in the genesis of every project. Our aim is to make those choices conscious. So we avoid wilful templates thrust upon practice. The *service/matrix, delivery/linear, idea/adhoc* practice sphere/practice organisation model comes from research into the sociology of architectural practice.[7] We derive all of the 'fans' that we use from our own research but have validated our findings by cross checking with the work of others, as noted.

The most unconscious choices made by designers are those that are closest to 'home'[8]. The unfolding of our spatial intelligence in the world colours our spatial thinking in ways of which we are largely unconscious. Becoming aware of this colouring is crucial to the development of exceptional, ideas-driven practice. Designers who work in large bureaucratic organisations tend to subsume the individuality of their spatial histories to a corporate norm[9]. We use analytical fans that are derived from research into spatial intelligence[10] to help practitioners unlock their spatial histories and become spatially aware. Have they not thought of their spatial history at all? It is subconscious. Have they grown up in one place, are aware of that place, and have not felt challenged by other spatial histories? They are conscious but subliminally. Or have they, through experience in other communities, become acutely aware of space as a cultural construct with discernible borders? They are conscious of being self-constructing constructs.

1 This tool is an engine for enabling 'slow thinking'. Practice necessarily operates in 'fast thinking' mode. As Kahneman has shown, fast thinking is effective most of the time, but fails us in critical understanding of the deep processes at work in practice. Daniel Kahneman, Thinking, fast and slow, Allen Lane, 2011, London

2 McCaughey, Davis, Piecing Together a Shared Vision: 1987 Boyer Lectures, ABC Enterprises, 1988, Crow's Nest, NSW

3 Howard Gardner, The Disciplined Mind What all students should understand Simon & Schuster 1999, Penguin Books, 2000, New York

4 Blau, Judith R., Architects and Firms, MIT Press, 1987, Camb., Mass. Gutman, Robert, Architectural Practice -A Critical Review, Princeton Arch. Press, 1988, Princeton

5 Blau, Judith R., pp 3–4, 144

6 We have worked with the design active staff of a few large firms with a global reach, including EDAW (as it was) in Australia and at an international gathering in Los Angeles, and design ginger groups lead by Andrew Lee, most recently at Ong and Ong, Singapore. Also in 2015 with Peddle Thorpe NZ in Auckland.

7 John Heintz and Guillermo Aranda-Mena, Business Strategies for Architectural Firms: Type Versus Capabilities, International Conference Management of Construction — Research to Practice. (Montreal, Canada), 26–29 June 2012.

8 This concept is derived from the thinking of philosopher of space, O. F. Bollnow, Human Space, Hyphen Press, 2011, London

9 Rowan Moore on Foster, Rowan Moore 2002 Norman's Conquest Prospect, March 2002 pp 52–56

10 See Schaik, Leon van, Spatial Intelligence: New Futures for Architecture, John Wiley & Sons, 2008, Chichester

What is their spatial focus for a project? So near and so shared with nearby peers that it is difficult to see a need for articulation? In the middle-ground (where experience causes spatial histories to intersect with the experience of new found peers and thus become more readily visible)? Or at the horizon (where spatial history often becomes evident as it encounters regional and national difference)?

Our research into design practice captures the benefits of being or becoming aware of the workings of spatial intelligence. Jo Van Den Berghe, a notable Belgian practitioner involved in this research, states in this regard: "You don't know what you know until you know what you know." But there is another layer of consciousness that becomes available when designers are aware of their spatial histories. They can begin to differentiate between their observational stances and those of their audiences (clients and users) just as writers and their critics do. They can be 'naïve' – direct, fresh and child-like in their designing. They can be 'sentimental' – layering emotional intent onto their design, though – given the immense critical opprobrium for this[11] they probably adopt this posture only when overt and ironic theatricality is what they seek. For example Peter Corrigan's RMIT Building 8 refers ironically to the Harvard Business School and to Melbourne's off-North grid. Or they can aim for an accurate and fresh 'poetic' or eidetic, Proustian observational stance, the more reflective obverse of naïve immediacy. For example Allan Powell's entry courtyard to Tarrawarra Museum of Art is a space designed to transport the visitor into a new state of mind before entering the gallery. These stances inflect the modes of expression that they then adopt: Phatic – 'the direct blow to the eye' as Allan Powell pejoratively describes it; Stock – the deliberate use of cliché, as in 'a pornography of modernism' as Ignazi Sola de Morales described it in an early stage of this research. This is the difference between Post Modern referencing by Charles Moore in his Piazza D'Italia, and the banal assemblage of angled porticos, 'V' poles and arced facias that has flowed through commercial work. The Delayed[12] stance describes a layered designing where the intent unfolds in time. These modes can be deployed abstractly creating a 'mood' or a 'state of affairs' –a term adopted by architects from Wittgenstein, that architect philosopher; and surfacing in Allan Powell's language again as 'sunny or umbracious, fragile or ponderous platforms for being'[13]; or by creating an 'emotionally intelligent'[14] order with a rational and parsimonious arrangement of plan and construction as in Sean Godsell's RMIT Design Hub[15]; or by means of a deliberate scenography or narrative as in Toby Reed's design for the Co-generation plant at Dandenong.[16].

Perhaps the most underplayed fan of differentiation in design, at least in the Anglophone world, is the ideological. Professions seem to seek an apolitical position so that they can seem able to serve all clients – we see this at its extreme in the legal profession, where you are trained to take on any brief, whatever its morality, and advocate for it the best possible case. But designers take on a political position either project by project, or at the base of their entire practice. The long debate between Rationalists and Contextualists[17] resonates with the idealist and realist aesthetical dispute between Whig and Tory architects in enlightenment England[18]. Silent in these debates, but only I suspect because of the Hegelian dualist habit of mind, was the ever-present Populist position. Every design adopts or reveals a political position: Realist in that it accepts a flawed world and does what it can to ameliorate that with the means at hand thus producing one-off, unrepeatable designs[19]; Idealist in that it postulates a system for reforming the class of design being tackled, a system that the designers believe should be widely replicated[20]; or Populist in that it seeks to place the tools of design in the hands of the user/client.

Once a practitioner has achieved mastery in their field, the culture of practice they have established can be assessed. The preferred mode, manner and regime of care in and of designing can be consciously

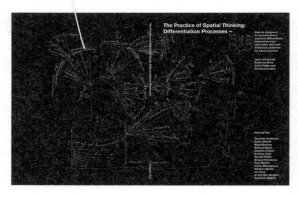

Fig 1. The cover of PRS Black Book (first edition) showing the differentiation tool diagram

11 Richards I.A., Practical Criticism: A Study of Literary Judgment, first published 1929

12 Mohsen Mostafavi Homa Fardjadi, Delayed Space: the Work of Homa Fardjadi & Mohsen Mostafavi, Princeton Arch Press, 1994, Cambridge, Massachusetts

13 Allan Powell, Forgotten Zones: A Matiere for Architecture, in Schaik, Leon van (Ed.) Fin de Siecle and the twenty first century: Architectures of Melbourne, RMIT A+D, 1993, Melbourne pp 89-110

14 Goleman, Daniel, Working with Emotional Intelligence, Bloomsbury, 1999, London

15 Sean Godsell, RMIT Design Hub, Melbourne 2012 see Schaik, van L., Practical Poetics in Architecture, Wiley, 2015, Chichester pp 115-123

16 Peter Hogg and Toby Reed Architects, Precinct Energy Project, Dandenong, Australia see Schaik, van L., Practical Poetics in Architecture, Wiley, 2015, Chichester pp 94-100

17 Shane, D. G., At the Rally — Contextualism, in Spring, Martin and Beck, Haig (Eds) AD XLVI 11 Andreas Papadakis, 1976, London

18 Li Shiqiao, Power and Virtue Architecture and Intellectual Change in England 1660-1730 Routledge, 2007, Abingdon

19 This is the default mode for designers.

20 Habraken's Supports is a case in point, as are various 'extrudable' urban designs (Plan Voisin, Hilbersheimer, etc. But some architects embody an ideal world in the smallest of projects, see Sean Godsell's park shelters.

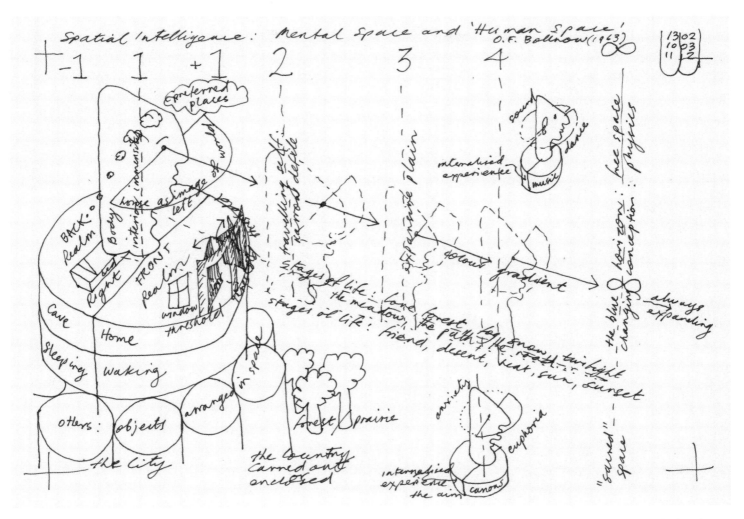

Fig 2. This ideogram describes the O.F. Bollnow's spatial organisation of mental space, from the subconscious (Cave/sleeping) to the conscious (Home/waking) on to the nearby (narrow defile- German space is carved out of forest), then to the middle ground (the expansive plain), the unfamiliar distance and finally to the ever receding horizon.

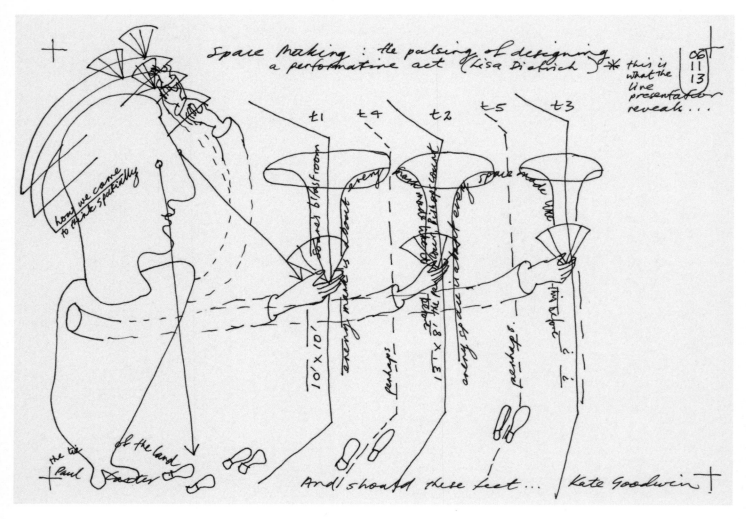

Fig 3. This ideogram insists that space making is a physical act as well as a mental act. It involves our touching and measuring arms and hands, our pacing and choreographing feet…

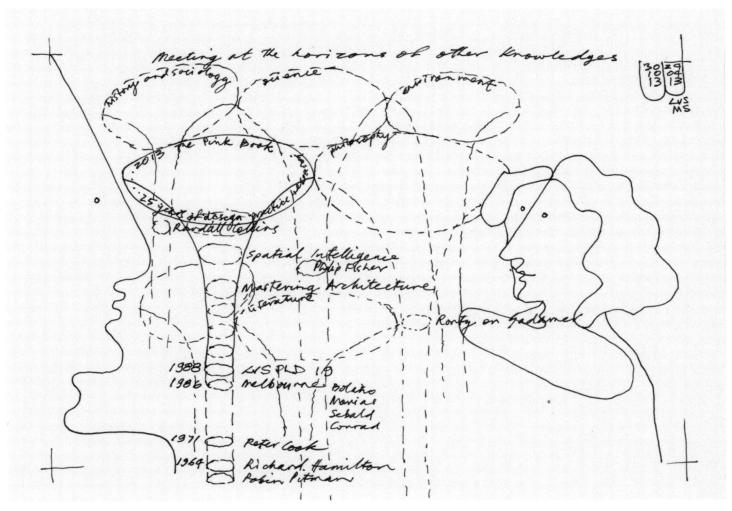

Fig 4. Mastery is established through a process here depicted as the construction of a rising and expanding funnel of knowing doing and helping. Full mastery brings the possibility of conversing with other masteries—at their horizons.

determined and acted on. The 'mode' fan we use, based on research conducted in the 1990s, differentiates between rigorous but contrasting approaches[21]: working 1:1, full scale, prototyping often on site, or abstract mathematically based simulation in virtual space, sometimes in real time. These in turn contrast with a bricoleur approach, in which traditional skills are augmented on a project by project basis with skills from adjacent disciplines such as film-making. The design 'manner', following research into current practice in China[22], differentiates between 'figuration' — in which a designer, after absorbing the brief, envisages a complete solution and then works to bring that to fruition, and 'mimesis'- in which a designer deploys a process without pre-figuring the final design. This has some overlap with the third position[23], usually digital, in which a mathematical or biological engine is set in motion around certain parameters of the design, and then is 'stopped' to make a design. At this moment this manner begins to share the characteristics of the figuration manner in that a preferred formal outcome is identified and then pursued. Regimes of care[24] are present in the minds of designers as they design: is this a design that is intended to look always new, always maintained as new (fast)? Is it intended to age and weather continuously, with maintenance at a minimum (medium)? Does it embody the long term morphing that a landscape necessarily has, including the eventual replanting of an avenue or the repeated rebuilding of temples in Kyoto (slow)?

The fifth fan is the fan of enchainments[25]. No one works alone, everyone works in the context of what others are doing, have done. People are aligned with or opposed to a constellation[26] of peers, mentors and challengers. Mapping these helps designers articulate their positions. We now know that 'tri-polar' environments of practice are the most fruitful environments for intellectual change and therefor for exceptional creative practice that pushes the boundaries of a discipline. Being aware of the tri-polarities of your discipline and of the design culture of your city region is now essential for conscious practice. Embedded in this are awarenesses of the natural history of the creative individual, the public or group behaviours that sustain individual creative practice, and the integrated scholarships of Discovery, Integration, Application and Dissemination that thread through all practices (see Scholarship cube Fig 5). The concluding and archetypal triad is the ancient Vitruvian formulation that defines the three fundamental components of (architectural) design; Firmness, Commodity and Delight. While everyone aims for all three, invariably one or other is in front of mind, and takes the lead.

All of these operational fans are subject to further attitudinal framing.

Understanding that as a designer you have always in your mind an implied audience for your designing helps the charting through these fans. But as in a newly articulated concept[27], it is also the case that you can deliberately assume an authorial position suited to a project. The power of this becomes more evident when a designer charts the kind of awareness[28] that they are utilising in a design. Survival-thinking/power-thinking/ordering/reasoning/systems-thinking/transcendant thinking (using all the below), are all used by designers. Being aware of the characteristics and limitations of these ways of thinking enables designers to deploy them deliberately during a design process[29].

Each of the fans of differentiation discussed here has a history of development. They have come into being through the research that we have conducted with designers in our design practice research program. They are being refined as our research reach widens. And new fans may well emerge as we—the research sponsors and the individual researching practitioners—move ahead.

A word about the evolution of these triads: (Fig 6 refers) defining them is a work in progress, but each of them has strong lineages. The triadic fans emanating from the spatial history (1a) of each designer are articulated in response to the concept 'mental space' (Schaik, L van,

21 This three pole practice approach was the result of analysis of practice modes conducted by LvS at Harvard GSD in 1994, and implemented and tested at RMIT over the following decade

22 Li Shiqiao William S.W. Lim, Mimesis and Figuration Large Screens, Cultural Creativity and the Global City Asian Design Culture AA Asia, 2009, Singapore pp 18-24

23 First fully tested by Greg Lynn who identified 'the stopping problem' — what determines the stopping moment? An aesthetic preference?

24 Term appropriated from medical use and applied to landscape practice during work on a Monetfiore home in Melbourne, 1989.

25 Schaik, Leon van, Mastering Architecture: Becoming a Creative Innovator in Practice Wiley Academy, 2005 Chichester, p 106, 234

26 As Dr Marcelo Stamm puts it

27 Schaik, L van, Tides of ambition: Who architects design for, and who they are when they design Momentum: New Victorian Architecture, The Megunyah Press, 2012, Melbourne pp. 42-52

28 Clare Graves Spiral of awareness is the basis of this. See Don Edward Beck Christopher C. Cowan, Spiral Dynamics: Mastering Values, Leadership, and Change: Exploring the new science of Memetics, Blackwell (Business), 1996, Camb. (Mass.), Oxford, p 28 Maslow's hierarchy: physiological need, safety and security, social needs, esteem, self-actualisation, is a forerunner.

29 Deborah Saunt tuning her design team

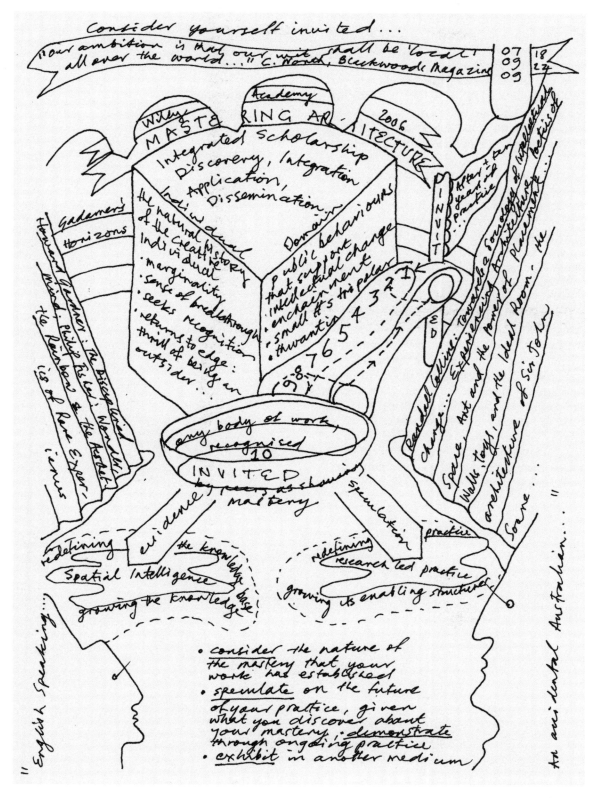

Fig 5. The design practice research scholarship cube drawn on the stage in this ideogram reconciles three major areas of research: on the left face the natural history of creative individuals, on the right the public behaviours that sustain (or thwart) creative practice, on the top face the complementary scholarships of Discovery, Integration, Application and Dissemination that dissolve the separations between research and practice.

2008); of spatial intelligence – subconscious/home/aware (1b) (Schaik, L van, 2008); home and near/middleground/horizon (1c) (Bolnow 2011, Rorty 2000). The observational strategies (1d) and expressions resulting (1e) are dependent on spatial history awareness—naïve/sentimental/poetic, phatic/stock/—and are part of a continuing discourse begun in the first half of the twentieth century (Richards, I A 1929, Pamuk, O 2006). Delayed expression, the third in the phatic/stock/delayed triad, has its origins in the thinking of Mohsen Mostafavi and Homer Fardjadi (1994); while the choreographic intentions – mood/emotion/scenography stem from film theory (Vlada 1987).

The more conscious, forward thrusting triads: idea/delivery/service (2) and adhoc/linear/matrix (2a) have their origins in the work of Blau (1987) and Gutman (1988), but have on-going developments (2012). The ideology triad (3)– real/ideal/pop – was developed in conversation around his book (2007) with Dr Li Shiqiao, which identified anew the impact of the first two positions on design. The early work of Shane also refers (1976). Regimes of care (4c)– fast/medium/slow – are based on a concept used in an RMIT Landscape Architecture and Psychology studio working on a garden for people with advanced Alzheimer's disease (Schaik Montefiore Project 1992) in writings about landscape. The practice culture 'mode' triad (4a) – 1:1 (full scale, fieldwork, prototyping)/abstraction (math based, digital)/bricoleur (varied assemblages of existing skills) derives from a decade of academic leadership in the fields of design and social science, while the 'manner' triad (4b) evolved in conversation with Li Shiqiao (2009). The enchainment triad (5) – peers/mentors/challengers – stems from integrating research by Collins (2000) into our design practice research (Schaik 2005). Firmness/commodity/delight (6) is the ancient Vitruvian triad (Kruft 1994). Finally, the spiral of kinds of awareness (7) is derived from psychologist Graves, who was building on Maslow, who was building on Piaget (Beck 1996), but is applied without hierarchy – which most current research debunks, suggesting that all are modes concurrently available.

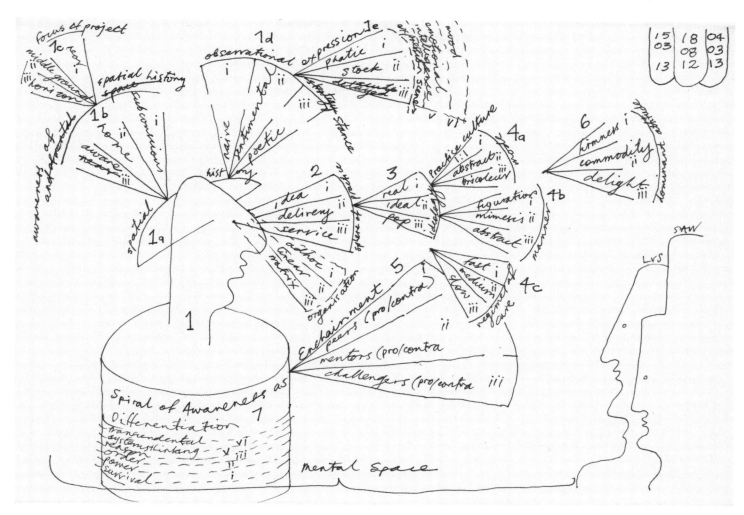

Fig 6. The Differentiation triads or fans:

1 = the architect/landscape architect	4 = practice culture — mode: 1:1, full scale, prototyping, field work / abstraction (mathematical modelling) / bricoleur, using traditional skills in various assemblages
1a = the spatial history of the architect/s	4 = practice culture — manner: figuration (typological) / mimesis (replicating processes) / abstraction (rule based, algorithmic)
1b = the awareness of that history: subconscious only/at 'home'in as in generally aware of a history/ aware as in has conducted a structured investigation of	4 — practice culture — regimes of care: fast / medium / slow.
1c = spatial focus of project/s: near and personal/ middle ground and regional / horizon as in connected to other horizons (ref Illustration xx)	5 = pro and con enchainment: peers / mentors / challengers
1d = observational strategy: Naïve as in direct, spontaneous / sentimental as in referencing standards / poetic as in freshly observed	6 = dominant architectural focus: firmness / commodity / delight
1e = mode of expression: phatic or visceral / stock or cliché / delayed or slow dawning & serial or scenographic / expecting emotional intelligence / engaging in a state of affairs, a mood.	7 = differentiation via modes of awareness deployed: Survival / power / order / reason / system(ic) eco thinking / transcendental (all combined)
2 = sphere of practice: idea-based, adhoc structure / delivery based, linear structure / service based, matrix structure	
3 = ideology, political stance: realist / idealist / populist.	

References

→ Don Edward Beck, Christopher C. Cowan (1996). Spiral Dynamics: Mastering Values, Leadership, and Change. Exploring the new science of Memetics. Blackwell (Business). Camb. (Mass.), Oxford

→ Blau, Judith R. (1987). Architects and Firms. MIT Press. Camb., Mass.

→ O. F. Bollnow (2011). Human Space. Hyphen Press. London

→ Randall Collins (2000). The Sociology of Philosophies. A Global Theory of Intellectual Change. Harvard University Press. Camb. Mass.

→ Geertz, C.:1973, The Interpretation of Culture, Basic Books, New York.

→ Gutman, Robert (1988). Architectural Practice - Critical Review. Princeton Arch. Press. Princeton

→ Kruft, Hanno-Walter (1994). A History of Architectural Theory. From Vitruvius to the Present. Princeon Architectural Press & Zwemmer. New York/London. p233-234 Christopher Wren (1632—1723) Tracts I-IV first published in Parentalia by Stephen Wren (1750), Architecture has its Political Use; publick Buildings being the ornament of a country; it establishes a Nation, draws People and Commerce. He believes in the validity for architecture of the laws of Nature, and in timeless principles of architecture taking over Vitruvius' principles of Beauty, Firmness and Convenience, and adding like the scientist he was: the first two depend upon geometrical Reasons of Opticks and Staticks; the third only makes variety. (Tract I (1942) the Wren Society.

→ Li Shiqiao (2007). Power and Virtue. Architecture and Intellectual Change in England 1660-1730. Routledge. Abingdon Li Shiqiao (2007). Power and Virtue. Architecture and Intellectual Change in England 1660-1730. Routledge. Abingdon

→ Li Shiqiao (2009). Mimesis and Figuration Large Screens, Cultural Creativity and the Global City. In William S.W. Lim (Ed.) Asian Design Culture. AA Asia. Singapore pp 18-24

→ Mohsen Mostafavi, Homa Fardjadi (1994). Delayed Space. Work of Homa Fardjadi & Mohsen Mostafavi. Princeton Arch Press. Cambridge, Massachusetts

→ Orhan Pamuk (2006). Implied Author. In Translated by Maureen Freely (Ed.) The Saturday Guardian. The Guardian. London (28 October) pp 4-7

→ Orhan Pamuk (2011). The Naive and the Sentimental Novelist. Faber and faber. London

→ Pask, G.:1987, Conversation Theory, in J.B. de Jong (ed), Addenda & Errata: The OOC Ockham Coffee Table Book, Thesis Publishers.

→ Richards I.A. (1956). Practical Criticism. A Study of Literary Judgment. Harcourt Brace and World. NY (First published 1929) pp. 228-240 Stock Responses

→ Rorty, Richard (2000). Being that can be understood is language: Richard Rorty on H. G. Gadamer. London Review of Books. London 22, 6 (16 March) pp 23-25

→ Schaik, van L,:2008,. Spatial Intelligence: New Futures for Architecture, John Wiley & Sons, Chichester.

→ Schaik, van L, Practice Makes Perfect, Architectural Review October 2013, Education Issue, London, pp 81-82,

→ Schaik, van L. and Blythe, R., 2013, What if Design Practice Research Matters in M Fraser (ed), Design Research in Architecture, Ashgate, London.

→ Schaik, van L. and Johnson, A.: 2011, Architecture & Design, By Practice, By Invitation: Design Practice Research at RMIT, onepointsixone, Melbourne.

→ Schaik, van L. and Spooner, M.: 2010, The Practice of Practice 2: Research in the Medium of Design, onepointsixone, Melbourne.

→ Schaik, van L., Black, R., Burne, R., Garner, J., Godsell, S., Helsel, S., Irving, J., Lowe, J., Mills, J., Neille, S., Pringle, T., Ramus, R., Thompson, K., Westbrook, N.: 2000, L van Schaik (ed), Interstitial Modernism, RMIT A+D, Melbourne.

→ Schaik, van L., Bruns, A., Giannini, E., Lyon, C., McBride, R., McDougal, I., Murray, S.:2005, L van Schaik (ed), Transfiguring the Ordinary, Printed Books, Melbourne

→ Schaik, van L., Day, N., Elliott, P., Katsalidis, N., Powell, A., Raggatt, H., Rijavec, I., Selenitsch, A., Trudgeon, M.:1993, L van Schaik (ed), Fin de Siecle and the twenty first century: Architectures of Melbourne, RMIT A+D. Melbourne.

→ Schaik, van L., Glanville, R., Craig, T., Gollings, J., Goodwin, R., Hassell, R., Holland, L., Jones, J., Kovac, T., Ling, F., Look, B.G., Moore, I., Tarry, J., Varady, J., Wardle, J., Warn, G., Weller, R.:2003, L van Schaik (ed), The Practice of Practice - research in the medium of design, RMIT A+D. Melbourne.

→ Schaik, van L.: 2013, Differentiation In Vital Practice in P. Ednie Brown, M. Burry and A. Burrow (eds), The Innovation Imperative: Architectures of Vitality, Architectural Design, London, pp.106-113.

→ Schaik, van L.:2005, Mastering Architecture: Becoming a Creative Innovator in Practice. Wiley Academy. Chichester.

→ Schaik, van L.:2008, Spatial Intelligence and Place-Making in P Brislin (ed), Unified Design, Arup Associates,. John Wiley & Sons, Chichester, pp. 129-146.

→ Schaik, van L.:2013, A conversation with Sean Godsell, El Croquis, 165, pp. 6-18.

→ Shane, D G (1976). AD. In Spring, Martin, Beck, Haig (Ed.) At the Rally - Contextualism. Andreas Papadakis. London XLVI, 11

→ Vlada Petric (1987). Construction in Film: The Man with the Movie Camera, A Cimematic Analysis. Cambridge UP. Cambridge

→ Zeldin, T.:1998, An Intimate History of Humanity, Vintage, London.

Publications and Events Disseminating the Research: 2011–2019

The major impact of work of the Design Practice Research Lab has been on the subsequent practice of practitioners who have engaged in the research. All have made significant advances in the excellence and the growth of their respective practices, as measured by peer review

This work has spread by word of mouth, practitioner to practitioner, through books (van Schaik 2008 & 2005; van Schaik, London George 2010; Ware 2007 & 2002) and through conferences and seminars (van Schaik, CV08, RAIA Sydney, 2008; Ware AILA Melbourne, 2009).

Monographs and reviews in professional journals represent the other major dissemination route. The spatial intelligence research will be communicated in the same way and will specifically include:

→ Work in progress papers prepared and submitted to recognised journals for publication. Including: AD (Wiley UK), *Landscape Review*, *Architectural Design Theory*, *A+U*, *Fabrications*, etc.

→ Seminars and forums with State Government Architects and others who develop design policy and procurement policy will expose high level government agencies to research findings.

→ Practitioner case studies will be published by internationally recognised publishers in monographs and professional journal articles.

→ A book publication will follow completion of the research.

2011–2019 – Recent Books, Chapters, Journals, Reviews, Exhibitions, Lectures

→ Schaik, van Leon (2014) 'The Pace of Landscape: Slow Drifting, the Freeway and Suburban Dreams,' in Gini Lee and SueAnne Ware (Eds) *Making Sense of Landscape: Taylor Cullity Lethlean*, Spacemaker Press, East Hampton, USA

→ Schaik, van Leon and Richard Blythe (2013) 'What if Design Practice Matters?' In Murray Fraser (Ed) *Design Research in Architecture*, Ashgate, London

→ Schaik, van Leon (2013) 'Differentiation in Vital Practice: An Analysis using RMIT University of Technology and Design Interfaces with Architects,' in Pia Ednie-Brown, Mark Burry, and Andrew Burrow (Eds) *The Innovativation Imperative: Architectures of Vitality*, Architectural Design, London, Vol: 83 No 1, p106

→ Schaik, van Leon (2013) 'A Conversation with Sean Godsell' in *El Croquis* No. 165: Sean Godsell 1997–2013, Digital Edition, http://www.elcroquis.es/Shop/Issue/Details/79?ptID=1

→ Schaik, van Leon, Tom Holbrook and Deborah Saunt (2013) 'Practice Makes Perfect,' in *The Architectural Review*, Emap, London, October, 2013: Vol CCXXXIV I400, pp82–86

→ Schaik, van Leon (2013) 'View Hill House – Denton Corker Marshall' in *Architecture Australia*, Vol: 102, No: 4, July 2013

→ Schaik, van Leon (2013) 'Precinct Energy Project – PHTR Architects,' in *Architectural Review* (Australia), No. 131

→ Schaik, van Leon (2013) 'La Plage Du Pacifique – Kristen Green Architects' in *Architecture Australia*, Vol 102, No: 5, September 2013

→ Schaik, van Leon (2013) 'Lavender Bay Boatshed – Stephen Collier Architects,' in *Architectural Review* (Australia), Issue 132

→ Schaik, van Leon (2013) 'Procuring Innovative Architecture exhibition' at *Convergence: Transforming Our Future*, RMIT Design Hub, Melbourne, May 3–25, 2013

→ Schaik, van Leon (2013) 'Procuring Innovative Architecture exhibition.' WOHA Architects Gallery, Singapore, September 25–October 5, 2013

→ Schaik, van Leon (2013) 'Design Matters lecture', University of Calgary, Faculty of Environmental Design, Calgary, Alberta, Canada, April 3, 2013

→ Schaik, van Leon (2013) 'Design Practice Research: How We Release the Sealed Cognitive Capital in Established and Successful Creative Practice' lecture, Victoria University, School of Architecture, Wellington, New Zealand, August 22, 2013

→ Schaik, van Leon (2013) 'Terrain Vague in the Work of Jeffrey Smart: Lessons for Urban Design' lecture. Reprinted in *Architecture Australia*, online edition: architectureau.com/articles/jeffrey-smart/, August, 19, 2013

→ Ware, SueAnne and Gini Lee (Eds) (2013) *Making Sense of Landscape: The Practice of Taylor Cullity Lethlean*, Spacemaker Press, East Hampton, USA

→ Ware, SueAnne (2013) 'Parables in an Activist Practice', in *Exposure: Design Research Practice in Landscape Architecture*, Melbourne Books, Melbourne, Australia

→ Ware, SueAnne (2013) 'On Site, Place and Specificity,' in Bruhn, Cameron (Ed) *Multitudes: Hassell Studios 1938-2013*, URO Media, Melbourne, Australia

→ Ware, SueAnne (2013) 'New Acton Precinct,' in Landscape *Architecture Australia*, No. 138, May 2013

→ Ware, SueAnne (2013) 'Design Practice Research: Theoretical Framing and Practical Examples from RMIT' lecture, Sveriges lantbruksuniversitet (SLU) Alnarp, Malmo, Sweden

→ Ware, SueAnne (2013) 'Differentiation Models and Tri-polarity: Complex Positioning in Design Research', Architecture, Design and Art Practice Training Research (ADAPTr-) ITN Marie Curie Practice Research Symposium, Ghent, Belgium

→ Schaik, van Leon (2012) 'Tides of Ambition: Who Architects Design For, And Who They Are When They Design,' in Geoffrey London (Ed) *Momentum: New Victorian Architecture*, The Miegunyah Press (Imprint of MUP), Melbourne, Australia

→ Schaik, van Leon (2012) 'On Lyons. In Lyons' Practice' in Justine Clark and Juliana Engberg (Eds) *More: The Architecture of Lyons 1996-2011*, Thames & Hudson, Melbourne, Australia

→ Schaik, van Leon (2012) 'The Ambition to "Make the Culture"' Essay in Conrad Hamman (Author) and Fleur Watson (Ed) *Cities of Hope Remembered/Rehearsed: Australian Architecture by Edmond and Corrigan 1962-2012*, Thames & Hudson, Melbourne, Australia

→ Schaik, van Leon (2012) 'The Need for the Conscious: Use of Mental Space in Designing with People' in Melanie Dodd, Fiona Harrison and Esther Charlesworth (Eds) *Live Projects: Designing with People*, RMIT University Press, Melbourne, Australia, pp12–20

→ Schaik, van Leon (2012) 'Cloud House — McBride Charles Ryan' in *Houses*, No. 86, June 2012

→ Schaik, van Leon (2012) *Procuring Innovative Architecture*, exhibition, DESSA Gallery Ljubljana, Slovenia November 23–December 24, 2013

→ Schaik, van Leon (2012) 'Spatial Intelligence' lecture, University of Technology, School of Architecture, Sydney, Australia, October 9, 2013

→ Ware, SueAnne (2012) 'Post-Industrial Public: Auckland's North Wharf Promenade, the Jellicoe Street Precinct and Silo Park' in *Topos 8: Water Landscapes*, December 2012

→ Ware, SueAnne (2012) *Design Practice Research and Landscape Architectural Contributions*, ENSP-V, Versailles, France

→ Schaik, van Leon with Anna Johnson (2011) *Architecture & Design, By Practice By Invitation, Design Practice Research at RMIT*, onepointsixone, Melbourne, Australia

→ Schaik, van Leon (2011) *Meaning in Space: Housing the Visual Arts, or, Architectures for Private Collections*, Lyon Housemuseum, Kew, Australia

→ Schaik, van Leon (2011) 'Overview: Architecture and a Sustainable City' in Esther Charlesworth (Ed), *The EcoEdge: Design Challenges in Building in Sustainable Cities*, Informa/Routledge, London

→ Schaik, van Leon (2011) 'Modernism & Contemporaneity in Architecture: Peripheries & Centres' in William S. Lim and Jiat-Hwee, Chang, (Eds), *Non West Modernist Past: On Architecture & Modernities*, World Scientific Publishing, Singapore

→ Schaik, van Leon (2011) Foreword, in William S. Lim (Ed), *Incomplete Urbanism: Critical Urban Strategy for Emerging Economies*, World Scientific Publishing, Singapore

→ Schaik, van Leon (2011) 'Etching Time Into Design: Law Street House — Muir Mendes Architects' in *Architectural Review* (Australia), No. 122

→ Schaik, van Leon (2011) 'Free Form: White House Duback Block Architects' in *Architectural Review* (Australia), No. 118

→ Schaik, van Leon (2011) 'Heart of Gold: Myer Flagship Store — NH Architecture' in *Architectural Review* (Australia), No.120

→ Schaik, van Leon (2011) 'Shed Space: Greeves Street House — Robert Simeoni Architects' in *Architectural Review* (Australia), No. 119.

→ Schaik, van Leon (2011) 'Design Practice Research' lecture, University College Dublin, School of Architecture, Dublin, Ireland, April 1, 2011

→ Schaik, van Leon (2011) 'Design Practice Research' lecture, Welsh School of Architecture & Design, Cardiff, Wales, April 27, 2011

→ Schaik, van Leon (2011) 'Spatial Intelligence' lecture, Monash University, Faculty of Art & Design, Caulfield, Victoria, Australia, August 10, 2011

→ Ware, SueAnne, Julian Raxworthy, Richard Weller, Jo Russell-Clarke, Elizabeth Meyer and Gini Lee (2011) *Sunburnt: Australian Practices of Landscape Architecture*, Sun Architectural Publishing, Amsterdam, The Netherlands

→ Ware, SueAnne (2011) 'Franklin Wharf Improvements' in *Landscape Architecture Australia*, No 131, August 2011

→ Schaik, van Leon, Spanning Continuums, Addressing the Separation of Research and Practice in Architecture, in Deborah Saunt, Tom Greenall and Roberta Maraccacio (Ed.s) The Business of Research: Knowledge and Learning Redefined in Architectural Practice, AD 03 Vol 89, 2019, pp 38-48

→ Schaik, van Leon (2018) Architecture in its Continuums, URO Melbourne

→ Schaik, van Leon (2015) Practical Poetics in Architecture, Wiley Chichester

→ Schaik, van Leon (2011) Meaning in Space: Housing the Visual Arts, or, Architectures for Private Collections. Lyon Housemuseum Kew, Victoria

Earlier Books, Reviews & Exhibitions
(Prior To 2011)

→ Schaik, van Leon and Geoffrey London (2010) *Procuring Innovative Architecture*, Routledge, London

→ Schaik, van Leon and Michael Spooner (2010) *The Practice of Practice 2*, Onepointsixone, Melbourne, Australia

→ Schaik, van Leon (2010) 'Framing Paradise — WOHA' in *Architectural Review* (Australia), No. 115

→ Schaik, van Leon (2010) 'Grace Darling House — Iredale Pedersen Hook' in *Houses*, No 76

→ Schaik, van Leon (2010) *Thinking about Architecture: Thinking About Architects* exhibition, RMIT University Building 45 Melbourne, Australia, July 9-15, 2010

→ Schaik, van Leon (2009) 'Kensington House — Tandem Design Studio' in *Architectural Review* (Australia), No. 112

→ Schaik, van Leon (2009) *Thinking about Architecture: Thinking About Architects* exhibition, DESSA Gallery Ljubjlana, Slovernia, March 23–April 17, 2009.

→ Schaik, van Leon (2009) *Thinking about Architecture: Thinking About Architects* exhibition, WOHA Gallery, Singapore, September 12–26, 2009

→ Schaik, van Leon (2009) *Thinking about Architecture: Thinking About Architects* exhibition, Westminster University Bridge Gallery, London, UK, November 1–30, 2009

→ Ware, SueAnne (2009) 'The Thickened Edge: St Kilda Foreshore Promenade' in *Scape: The International Magazine for Landscape Architecture and Urbanism*, No. 2, Birkhauser, Berlin, Germany

→ Ware, SueAnne and Julian Raxworthy (2009) *Sunburnt: Australian Practices of Landscape Architecture* exhibition, Gallery of Australian Design, Canberra, ACT, Australia, September 16–October 24, 2009

→ Schaik, van Leon (2008) *Spatial Intelligence: New Futures for Architecture*, John Wiley & Sons, London

→ Schaik, van Leon (2008) 'A High Point — Terroir Architects' in *Monument*, Melbourne, Australia, No. 83

→ Schaik, van Leon (2008) 'Glenburn House — Sean Godsell Architects' in *Architectural Record*, New York, USA, No. 04, April 2008

→ Schaik, van Leon (2008) 'Commonwealth Place Kiosks — Terroir Architects in *Architectural Review* (Australia), No. 105

→ Schaik, van Leon (2008) 'Life Saving Club — Robert Simeoni Architects' in *Architecture Review* (Australia), No. 108

→ Ware, SueAnne (2008) 'Brett Milligan, An Emerging Practitioner' in *Landscape Architecture Australia*, No. 119

→ Ware, SueAnne (2008) 'Teaching and Researching Landscape Architecture in the Global South' lecture, University of Cape Town, Cape Town, South Africa

→ Ware, SueAnne (2008) 'Practice based Research and Reflectivity through Design Research' lecture, Victoria University, Wellington, New Zealand

→ Schaik, van Leon (2007) 'Visiting the Australian Garden — Kerstin Thompson Architects' in *Architecture Australia*, Vol 96 No 1

→ Schaik, van Leon (2007) 'Contour Line — Sean Godsell Architects' in *Monument*, Melbourne, Australia, No. 82

→ Schaik, van Leon (2007) 'On Museum Architecture — Architectus' in *Art & Australia*, Vol 44, No. 3

→ Schaik, van Leon (2007) 'Trojan Horse: Acton Park House (Terroir)' in *Monument*, Melbourne, Australia , No. 79

→ Ware, SueAnne and Rosalea Monacella (Eds) (2007) *Fluctuating Borders: Memory and the Emergent, New Possibilities for International Borders*, RMIT Press, Melbourne, Australia

→ Schaik, van Leon (2006) *Design City Melbourne*, Wiley Academy, London

→ Schaik, van Leon (2006) 'Cape Schank House — Paul Morgan Architects' in *Architectural Review* (Australia), No. 99

→ Schaik, van Leon (2006) 'Fullagar residence — Stephen Varady Architects' in *Architectural Review* (Australia), No. 97

→ Schaik, van Leon (2006) 'Sheep House — Iredale Pederson Hook' in *Monument*, Melbourne, Australia, No. 75

→ Schaik, van Leon (2006) 'Wunderkamer — Robert Morris Nunn' in *Monument*, Melbourne, Australia, No. 74

→ Schaik, van Leon (2006) 'St Andrews Beach House — Sean Godsell' in *Architecture Australia*, Vol 95, No 5

→ Schaik, van Leon (2005) *Mastering Architecture: Becoming a Creative Innovator in Practice*, Wiley Academy, London

→ Schaik, van Leon (2005) 'A Place for Intelligence — Garner Davis Library' in *Architectural Review* (Australia), No. 92

→ Schaik, van Leon (2005) 'Queenscliff Centre — Lyons' in
  Architecture Australia, Vol 94, No1

→ Schaik, van Leon (2005) 'Craigieburn Bypass — Taylor Cullity
  Lethlean, Tonkin Zulaikha Greer and Robert Owen' in *Architecture
  Australia*, Vol 94, No 4

→ Schaik, van Leon (2005) 'The Footscray House — Geoff Crosby'
  in *Architectural Review* (Australia), No. 94

→ Schaik, van Leon (2005) 'Out of the Past — Donaldson + Warn'
  in *Monument*, Melbourne, Australia, No. 70

→ Schaik, van Leon (2004) *Sean Godsell* (Italian edition),
  Mondadori Electa spa, Milano, Italy

→ Schaik, van Leon (2004) 'Emergence: Morphogenetic Design
  Strategies — Practice Profile Dale Jones-Evans' in *Architectural
  Design*, Vol. 74, No. 3

→ Schaik, van Leon (2004) 'Peppermint Bay — Terroir' in
  Architectural Review (Australia), No. 87

→ Schaik, van Leon (2004) 'The Shrine of Remembrance — ARM'
  in *Architectural Review* (Australia), No. 91

→ Schaik, van Leon (2004) 'Newman College — Edmond & Corrigan'
  in *Monument*, Melbourne, Australia No. 64

→ Schaik, van Leon (2004) 'Ugly Duckling — Terroir' in *Monument*,
  Melbourne, Australia, No. 63

→ Schaik, van Leon (2004) 'New Frontiers — Durbach Block'
  in *Monument*, Melbourne, Australia, No. 62

→ Schaik, van Leon (2004) 'Tropical Dream — Architron'
  in *Monument*, Melbourne, Australia, No. 61

→ Schaik, van Leon (2004) 'Back to the Future — Tom Kovac'
  in *Monument*, Melbourne, Australia, No. 60

→ Schaik, van Leon (2004) 'Architectures Non Standard — Kovac'
  in *Monument*, Melbourne, Australia, No. 59

→ Schaik, van Leon (2004) *Melbourne Masters Architecture*
  exhibition & catalogue, TarraWarra Museum of Art, Healesville,
  Victoria, Australia, November 14–April, 2004

→ Schaik, van Leon (2003) 'Flinders — John Wardle Architects'
  in *Architectural Review* (Australia), No. 85

→ Schaik, van Leon (2003) 'Three Tasmanian Homes — Terroir'
  in *Architectural Review* (Australia), No. 86

→ Schaik, van Leon (2003) 'Luminous Energy — Leigh Woolley'
  in *Monument*, Melbourne, Australia, No. 57

→ Schaik, van Leon (2003) 'High Art — Nicholas Murray'
  in *Monument*, Melbourne, Australia, No. 58

→ Schaik, van Leon (2003) 'Scienzae e Accademia — John Wardle
  Architects' in *Domus*, No. 863, October 2003

→ Schaik, van Leon (2003) 'Magical Realism — Allan Powell'
  in *Monument*, Residential Special issue Melbourne, Australia

→ Schaik, van Leon (2003) 'A Room With a View — Introduction:
  Landscape Coastal section (various practices)' in *Monument*,
  Residential Special issue Melbourne, Australia

→ Schaik, van Leon (2002). 'Young House — Two Times Architects'
  in *Monument*, Melbourne, Australia, No. 49

→ Ware, SueAnne (2002) 'LA_Boratory RMIT' in Peter Connolly and
  Rene Van der Velde (Eds), *Technique: Landscape Architecture
  Graduate Design Research at RMIT University 1995-2002*, RMIT
  University Press, Melbourne, Australia

→ Schaik, van Leon (2001) 'Asymptote & Drome' in *Architectural
  Review* (Australia), No. 74

→ Schaik, van Leon (2000) 'Number 5 Gemmill Lane — Look
  Architects' in *Singapore Architecture*, Issue 208

→ Schaik, van Leon (2000) 'The High Life — Nonda Katsalidis'
  in *World Architecture*, Issue 86

→ Schaik, van Leon (2000) 'The Prince — Allan Powell' in *Inside:
  Interior Design Review*, Annual

→ Schaik, van Leon (2000) 'In Print — John Wardle'
  in *Architectural Review* (Australia), No 71

→ Schaik, van Leon (2000) 'Working Drawing House — Nervegna Reed'
  in *Monument*, Melbourne, Australia No 38

Case Study
Paul Morgan's Trunk House

In my abstract, I describe current thinking, with the main body of the text capturing a conversation as it traverses these concerns, showing in parentheses how it relates to each triad of positioning depicted in the ideogram.

At 9am on a hot Monday morning, 25th February 2013, Paul Morgan collected me from outside the Victoria State Library in central Melbourne and drove me westwards for an hour and a half into a forested area. On a wooded, two hectare block, falling from a ridge to a creek bed to the sun-giving north, he has created a country retreat for a couple of medical academics who have an attachment to Ballarat, the nearest town. Paul has completed three second-home retreats at similar distances from central Melbourne, resonating as a 'type' in the consciousness of established Melburnians). As we drove, threading our way through spaghetti freeways and progressively onto smaller and smaller roads, we discussed the project, the state of Paul's practice, and how he sees his work in relation to that of his peers.

I have known Paul for some time. He was a pioneer researcher in our design practice research. He helped me compile and edit one issue of 38 South[1], the first of three monographs on our Urban Architecture Laboratory's investigation into the nature of this city. When I was chair of the editorial board, it was he who, having edited the journal in 1985 and 1986, rescued Transition from a crisis by editing the 1987 issues. I have studied his work since, writing a detailed review of his Cape Schank House (AR Australia Nov. 2006); and RMIT has commissioned him to provide innovative learning landscapes for RMIT, an area of practice in which he has an extensive reputation.

Paul spent his formative architecture years as a student at RMIT in the 1970s and early 80s. He was at the centre of an earlier blossoming of the school of architecture, during the years in which students wrote 'learning contracts' every year, and self-assessed the extent to which they met those contracts. Paul was the legendary student who failed himself three times! Melbourne architect Norman Day failed him once in 1982 during a period when Paul contracted to edit and produce an architectural magazine and design two houses but managed to complete only one house. For the magazine, he secured an interview with the then relatively unknown Frank Gehry, with a reputation resting on his own house alone. While looming on the mental horizon was Peter Corrigan, with his theatrical set designs and St Josephs Church complex, together with the modernist Case Study House inspired houses of Chancellor and also of Patrick McIntyre Senior. In addition, all students were taken to the hills around Melbourne to see the mud brick architecture of Alistair Knox, and the house by Mori Shaw that had a floor that followed the contours of the ridge upon which it perches.

As I document in Design City Melbourne (Wiley 2006), there was a ferment of interdisciplinary activity then on the go. Artists, lawyers, architects, theatre set-designers and fashion designers founded the Fashion Design Council. Paul was there and dressed in a black suit with slashed pockets designed by his friend Martin Grant (now in Paris) and subsequently married artist Rosalind Drummond.

While teaching a studio at RMIT, Paul introduced me to artist David Noonan, and we organised an exhibition of a work that consisted of 58 paintings of models by Alvar Aalto. Soon after this, Noonan painted two very large canvasses of Lubetkin's Penguin Pool, which appeared as a continuation of the cross-fertilisation between art and architecture that Paul encouraged. This reprisal of Paul's early contributions to the culture

1 Schaik, van Leon, Morgan, Paul (Eds) (1991) 38 South, RMIT, Melbourne

of architecture had taken us one third of the way on our car journey. We passed through an exurban fringe where Robin Boyd had built innovative country retreats in the 1950s and 60s. As we conversed, our discussion turned to the formidable depth of Paul's history in Melbourne. At every twist and turn in the development of the city's architectural culture since the 70s, he was there; at the meetings of the Half Time Club; and at the completions of the first works of architects Ian MacDougall and Howard Raggatt together with others of their generation. He heard via historian Conrad Hamann that Alistair Knox, who though all thought he was a backwoodsman with no architectural apprenticeship, described working for Sir Roy Grounds, and remarking on that architect's nostrum: 'plaster covers a multitude of sins'.

As we talk, I remark that he has a nuanced stance on every incident in the history of the architectural culture since his early student days. In contrast, my knowledge is second hand and removed; his is that of a participant; mine that of an observer. I talk to him of Nikos Papastergiadis and Paul Carter, and their writings on being migrants; and of the way the city is all surface to someone who hasn't exercised their history in those places their families have known and mythologised.

Paul acknowledges his fairly privileged position in the established culture of the city, and gives, as an example, that until he met his partner, the daughter of Maltese immigrants, he would not have declared the city racist. Subsequently, he now knows that there is indeed an ugly thread of racism in the old settler subculture, which is virulently xenophobic, but, he observes, despite that and without irony, the city is described as 'the world's most liveable city'.

We talk of the designing of the Trunk House; the dialogue of mental spaces he set up after the project was passed to him by the recently retired architect father of one of his students; how he met the clients and told them that he was not going to impose a vision on them, but that he was going to take a brief from them and respond to it professionally, as he assumed they did in their own medical practices. He invited them to spend a weekend on their own at Cape Schank House (2006), a weekender Paul designed for himself, his partner and child, and that they convey frankly what they liked about it, and what they did not. Finally, how he carefully recorded, in his deadpan, unemotional way, what they liked, what they did not.

We discussed his design approach. In part, he defined this by triangulating himself with other architects of his generation. At school at Xavier, which architect Peter Brew also attended, Paul was within a year of Sean Godsell, two peers with formidably rigorous, somewhat minimalist, practices. Subsequently, he aligns them with other practices, Simeoni, KTA and NMBW. In Vitruvian terms, these are all architects who privilege firmness above commodity and delight. While he admires the work of Simeoni and NMBW, he sees them as inspired by an Aldo Rossi pursuit of idealised types adapted to the Melbourne situation. We touch on a third school in Melbourne, the Allan Powell/Wood Marsh/Wardle cluster, who put delight and wonder ahead of other values, but who also design to or from pre-visualised architectural forms.

His own approach is 'open-system form-finding' and in this he sees himself allied to Minifie van Schaik[2]. He has an intellectual appreciation for what the pursuit of firmness produces, but avers that his heart has been won by the theatrical expressionism of Peter Corrigan, whose St Josephs at Keysborough (1978) was being completed when he was a student. This is an architecture that sets out to honour the popular culture of the city: to express its icons literally and lusciously. It celebrates commodity. Inspired by this, but not in imitation, Paul retains his idealist political stance, if respectful of popular culture. 'If you can't experiment in a young, low density city like Melbourne, where can you experiment?' Paul asks rhetorically.

His method of designing, rather like that of Wardle (in whose case I have described the process as a 'laminar flow'[3]), is to set up the site, its

2 I discuss the differentiation of Minifie van Schaik in 'Differentiation in Vital Practice: An Analysis using RMIT University of Technology and Design Interfaces with Architects,' in Pia Ednie-Brown, Mark Burry, and Andrew Burrow (Eds) (2013) *The Innovativation Imperative: Architectures of Vitality, Architectural Design*, London, Vol: 83 No 1, p106

microclimate, the program and client preferences in an overlapping of 'fluid dynamics', enabling him to hover over the parameters and edit until he can ensure an integrated ground plane and coax an expressive, theatrical form to emerge above. Paul works closely with landscape architects to achieve the basis of the 'fluid dynamic' and here, the Trunk House seems to perch magically on undisturbed ground that has found exactly the right levels for interacting with each component: store, carport, outdoor dining terrace, entry platform, and viewing deck. The landscape architect Cath Stutterheim has set up these levels and used small dry-stone walls (endemic to the region) to anchor the arrival platform in place, and with the clients she has created a path edged only in small fallen branches, that flows gently up and down the contours between the cabin and the creek bed below. These careful moves barely impinge on the forest but manage water run-off and avoid erosion. Collaborating with the different intelligence of a landscape architect enables Paul to ground his fluidly developing design.

Inside, the cabin is lined with timber sawn from the few trees that were felled to make room for its eighty square metre footprint. The planning approvals from state and local authorities took eighteen months, which gave time to accommodate the fluid dynamic design process and the dovetailing with the processes of other consultants. Planning approval included an arborealist testing every one of 283 trees for structural soundness, revealing which trees were unsafe and might fall to crush a cabin. Recycled timbers form the floors, and bedroom and bathroom walls are in plywood. The kitchen is an 'L' shape in the main room of the cabin, the oven is part of a wood burning stove: more than enough fuel drops in the forest, and needs to be removed to reduce fuel load in the bush fire-prone area. The lighting is chiefly by inset up-lights shining through translucent panels in the joinery. Where you might expect a fireplace, the focus of a large inbuilt sofa, there is a large TV screen. There are two bedrooms: the couple has a university age daughter. They retreat to this cabin from busy professional lives to read and to sing.

What is the expression of the cabin? It is embedded in a forest of 'Stringybark' eucaplypts, most of which branch into a 'Y' shape. Paul's 'fluid dynamics' gave rise to a figure: a structure that made use of these 'Y's to both express and to camouflage being in a forest where the only view is indeed of tree trunks, and in which most conventional structures assert their unsympathetic presence with flat walls and pitched roofs that deny the sinuous flow of this uniquely Australian form of space – as artist Wm. Robinson has shown it to be. The clients, having purchased the site because of a childhood attachment to these forest ranges, were captivated by this idea, and Paul set out to realise it, working with innovating engineer Peter Felicetti. Felicetti pointed out that there is a weakness at the branching point, and Paul realised he would need someone with a particular eye to match and meld the many 'Y' posts needed. He approached the sculptor/furniture-maker Mike Conole, who had made works for Melbourne and Los Angeles artist Ricky Swallow. Felicetti then collected fallen tree forks from the area, and connected these in a structural lattice. As the fallen timber was already weathered the structural strength proved to be several times greater than anticipated, and the slenderness of the frame far more pronounced than expected. Paul's view was that matching the irregular set of 'Y's required a special visual intelligence, and indeed Mark Conole's efforts in selecting the 'Y's and dowelling them together created the beguiling zigzag frame that supports the big over-sailing roof. Its size gauged to collect enough rainwater to supply the house and a fire tank. It has its own organic profile, beginning thickly where it springs from the ground and encases the store rooms, then tapers out as it covers the cabin and becomes the verandah overhanging the forest glade. Karsten Poulson, a builder who has worked with many innovative architects undertook the construction, meeting exactly the clients' budget.

Opposite top left: Elevations

Opposite top right: The driveway

Opposite centre right: A weekend cabin positioned amongst the trees

Opposite bottom: Floorplan

3 Schaik, van Leon (2008) Essay on some works of John Wardle Architects, *Volume: John Wardle Architects*, Thames & Hudson. Melbourne pp17—37

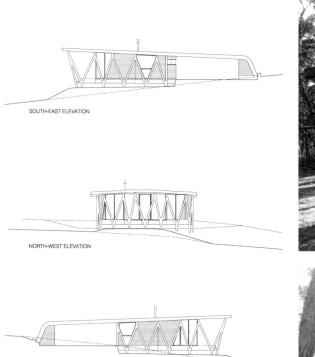

SOUTH-EAST ELEVATION

NORTH-WEST ELEVATION

NORTH-EAST ELEVATION

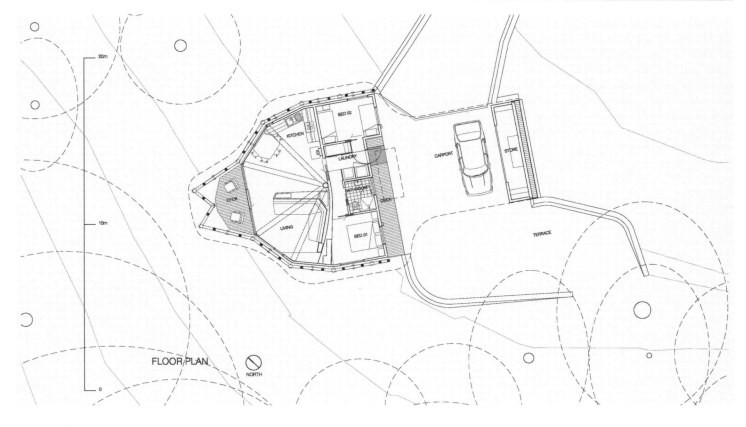

FLOOR PLAN

NORTH

This account of the design is very cool, instrumental, almost an engineering account of parameter-by-parameter solving and balancing of requirements. However—as we have seen—in the architect's mind's eye, the design sits in counterpoint to, or in alliance with, houses around Melbourne by Boyd, Grounds, Chancellor and Patrick, Shaw and Kevin Borland. All were produced by the generation that influenced his teachers and the houses by his teachers. For example, the Athan House (1986-8) by Peter Corrigan, a house that expresses every cultural pursuit of the family that commissioned it, with an externally expressed library, music room and dining kitchen. Having these precedents, these haunting presences in Paul's mental space, all have their doppelgangers in the Case Study Houses in what might be thought of as Melbourne's 'companion city' – Los Angeles. But Paul is not tied to this sparse coupling. He designed the interior of the Cape Schanck House, and is designing in his mind the second stage of the Trunk House, with a 'mise-en-scene' approach, a considered scenography of inhabitation, hour-by-hour, season-by-season, that makes sure that the whole is more than the sum of its parts. It is significant that Melbourne has a vibrant film culture, and the relationship between film theory and architecture has been strongly pursued there by Antonia Bruns (PhD RMIT 2000–4) amongst others.

An unconscious echoing of John Lautner's houses arose at Cape Schanck. Once pointed out, Lautner's work has become a sounding board for Paul, the once invisible doppelganger embraced and enfolded. Australian topography does not afford the dramatic overviews that Lautner could exploit, with Los Angeles lying like a carpet a thousand feet below, evoking in MacDonald's detective novel the exclamation: "I had to admit I lived for nights like these. I thought that if I could link up all the lights the city might come alive like a Frankenstein monster."[4]

Here, in the countryside in the hinterland of Melbourne, the fluid dynamics have to work in a minor key. The house visitor senses how this happens as he or she finds that the deck is just high enough for you to sit swinging your heels as you look into the forest, and that with a slight shift of your backside, you can slip off the floating timber plane of the cabin floor and wander towards whatever it is that has caught your eye in the bush surrounding you.

Paul's major reputation lies in his work in creating learning landscapes for tertiary education institutes and universities. The forest has infiltrated his latest project, which punctuates a vast space with 'huddle points' – hot spots of Wi-Fi and information technology. These are inspired by the information clusters in the NYSE (Asymptote brought these into architectural play with their Virtual Stock Exchange, reviewed by the author in *Architecture Review Australia* N0. 74, 2001, pp 42–45), and in addition, carrying something over from Paul's crafted understanding of the forest around the Trunk House.

4 Ross MacDonald (1968)
The Instant Enemy, Knopf
New York

Case Study:
Taylor Cullity Lethlean

As a part of uncovering and articulating a designer's Spatial Intelligence,[1] we spend a great deal of time examining and surfacing in detail anecdotal evidence of the spatial preferences of our collaborative research designers. Often our conversations revolve around which landscapes, buildings, interiors, paintings, and other cultural artefacts have strong spatial memories attached to them. We also explore with designers where they were educated and key influences in terms of who taught them (whether they 'rebelled' or 'embraced' these mentors and their ways of working). Additionally, many senior practitioners often consider their university cohorts … and if they still have various modes of practice in common, or is there a point of difference amongst their colleagues? Hence, part of our approach to this research is about designers communicating understandings of their spatial histories and intelligences, their previous and current communities of practice, thus situating their practice through various lenses and modes of practice.

When we map Taylor, Cullity and Lethlean (TCL)'s *Australian Garden* at Cranbourne onto our differentiation model, we consciously note each of the three individual practitioner's contributions (Kevin Taylor (d. 2011)[2], Kate Cullity, and Perry Lethlean). We explore their spatial histories, preferences and modes of design practice in general and through a particular project – the *Australian Garden*, which is a collective design project derived by the team. For example, Perry Lethlean speaks of the early influences of his mother's bush painting practice; and an intense period of studying gardens in Japan when he describes his proclivities towards spatial composition and careful arrangement in designing landscapes. Kate Cullity's intense focus on the cultivation of care; exploring detailed material qualities through designed landscapes influenced by her childhood wanderings through Perth's Kings Park; while spending a great deal of time in the garden with her mother paying close attention to the Australian deserts' material presence in her early journeys. Kevin Taylor's deep relationship with site emanated from his early teenage night-fishing excursions to Southern Ocean beaches at Waipinga and the Coorong in South Australia; while being very open, sensitive, and vulnerable after his father's untimely death. Early in his practice career, Kevin worked with Wendy Sarkissian and Greg Burgess, who foster deep community participation and engagement in their approach to design. This experience subsequently influenced his interests in notions of civic space and the public nature of design. These individual spatial histories map into our differentiation model and reveal an interesting complementary set of spatial intelligences. Perry was not very conscious of his spatial awareness and this process was part revelation and a surfacing of his subconscious. Kate was comfortably at home discussing and describing her spatial awareness but not overly interested in dissecting it or comparing it with others. Kevin was the most acutely aware and articulate about the influence of spatial awareness on his practice and beyond. Through uncovering and discussing their spatial histories further, we then understand their complementary approaches within their individual project foci. More specifically, Perry is significantly influenced by the urban mappings of Mario Gandelsonas, who he encountered when he studied urban design after completing his landscape architecture studies and he concentrates his design efforts on the *horizon*. He prefers to design strategically through a series of key moves at an urban scale, always designing within a larger framework of key adjacencies and relationships with their contexts. Kate, who studied botany, is enthralled

1 Leon van Schaik (2008) discusses Howard Gardner's conceptions of human capabilities focusing on spatial intelligence and architecture in *Spatial Intelligence: New Futures for Architecture*, Wiley & Sons, London

2 Kevin Taylor passed away in November 2011, (see http://architectureau.com/articles/a-tribute-to-kevin-taylor/ Accessed 21 January 2014)

by examining cells and organisms closely through microscopes. She also practices as a fine artist creating sculptural works, preferring to work at a *near scale* where site detail, crafting and care of the landscape and its tactility are of the utmost importance. Kevin, who studied architecture as well as landscape architecture, had a fascination for intertwining and siting architecture fittingly within its landscapes. Additionally, Kevin's ability to read, open up, and make sense of landscapes allowed him to find common ground with community groups during their consultations. Kevin's primary focus is on the *middle ground* and the site where he is able to connect Perry's urban gestures to Kate's attention to fine detail. Collectively, their observational stances are more towards the *sentimental* and the *poetic*, whereas Kate and Perry share an expressionistic regard for *phatic* moments, while Kate and Kevin shared a layered or *delayed* experiential mode where aspects of the design unfold, or are revealed upon a closer reading.

In the *Australian Garden*, the designers present us with an initial, awe-inspiring view of the 'Red Sand Garden' — a garden which can be seen but only entered visually and mentally and is both *phatic* and *scenographic*. The metaphor of the Red Centre and the interior landscapes of Australia are understood by experiencing them through looking *into* the landscape, not being in it, and is similar to the situated objects of Japanese gardens. Visual composition and plan figuration are essential in the manner and modes of designing at play here. This is in contrast to the Eucalypt Walk and the Cultivar Gardens where close attention to detail, mood or ambience is characteristically set through being amongst and within the garden spaces. These gardens are approached sensually where *poetics* and rationality (*emotional intelligence*) combine to make kinesthetic and bodily experiences. Visitors are immersed into landscapes of wafting scents of eucalypts, wattles, and boronias, as sunlight dapples and streams across the gardens, and as a result, learn about the vegetation's ecological preferences and preferred growth conditions. Even though each designer has a different focus, all three regimes of care, fast (*immediate*), *medium* and *slow*, are inextricably engaged within these gardens, as they are in the case of most landscape designs.

When examining the *Australian Garden* further, TCL's varied spatial approaches and spheres of practice play themselves out in very interesting ways. While all three designers tend to design well within plan compositions using *figuration*, their dominant attitudes towards Vitruvian principals of Commodity, Firmness, and Delight are bi-polar. Delight is quite evident from larger landscape topographic gestures, intertwining paths and detailed material selections. The exuberance of their material palettes is vividly expressed through slate monoliths carefully situated next to Boab trees and the leathery textures of shrub masses in the 'Weird and Wonderful Garden', together with the exquisitely and intricately layered planting patterning in the 'Dry River Bed Garden'. Pedestrian paths, where visitors step across gigantic lily pads, wind down serpentine and scribbly paths, and in addition, the playful and exaggerated topographies at Gibson and Hawson Hills enchant and amuse. However, behind the playful gestures and garden follies there lies firmness, in that the garden is about Australia's unique landscape conditions, which include water, temperature and soils. Firmness lies in the landscape infrastructures behind the garden and the expertise of the designers who understand how gardens and space change seasonally, annually, and over decades. Each of TCL's ambitions is embedded in durational regimes of care: Perry has a tendency to gravitate towards the immediate impact of a design, arguing that the work needs to look good when first planted. Kate and Kevin are better placed in the medium and slow side, preferring to see their works inhabited through time, as the landscape evolves. The *Australian Garden* balances this, the 'Red Centre Garden' and the 'Rock Pool Waterway' being *immediate* and fast, while the 'Forest Garden,' 'Melaleuca Spits'

Opposite top left and right:
The *Weird and Wonderful Garden* is host to some of Australia's more unusual floristic forms. Its meandering pathways lead to hidden gardens of textured intensity.

Opposite centre left:
Tilted slabs of Pyrenees quartzite provide a range of micro-climates for a diverse collection of rare and unusual flora.

Opposite centre right:
Australia is often described as a country either in drought or flood. Water, or its absence, is the principal organising structure within the garden. Water pathways within Stage 2 of the Australian Garden take visitors on an imagined journey to our continent's fertile coastal edges. Formally arranged display gardens on the eastern edge contrast with more immersive informally arranged compositions on its Western boundary.

Opposite bottom:
Australian Garden Plan. Quintessential Australian landscape experiences are interpreted, abstracted and distilled to inspire visitors to see Australian flora in a new way. A *Sand Garden* forms the centrepiece with a *Rockpool Waterway* and Display Gardens to the east and a *Eucalyptus Walk* to the west. Visitors are led along a metaphorical journey through the Australian landscape to encounter gardens inspired by meandering rivers, coastal edges and more formal urban experiences.

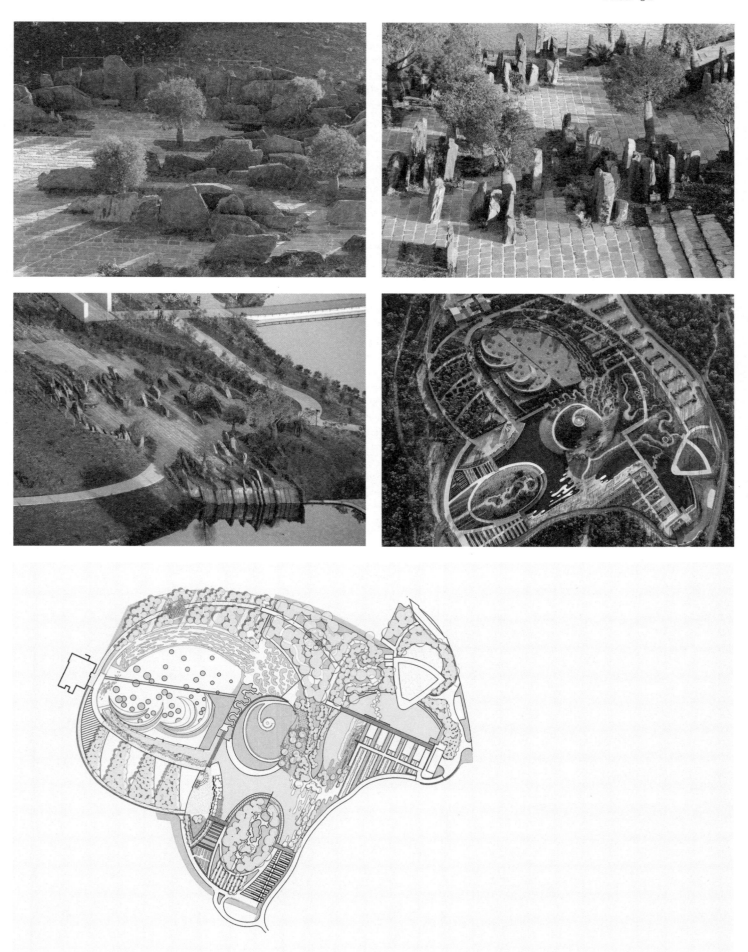

and 'Eucalypt Walk' take time. Each garden within the whole has various explorations of pattern, repetition and geometric abstraction; these speak to their collective modes of practice. Kate works at 1:1 *full scale* where Perry and Kevin tend towards the *bricoleur*. All three are inspired by, and actively collaborate with allied disciplines in art and architecture. However, Perry tends to utilise spatial juxtapositions and visual montages in his landscapes, whereas Kevin was overtly concerned with how visitors would inhabit and read the landscapes that they have created. The *Australian Garden* is a distillation of these positions where Kate and Perry share a passion for the poetic idea of their design concepts, while Kevin focused intensely on how the design services its inhabitants, be they humans or ecologies. This matches their overriding political ideologies that lie behind the public nature of most of TCL's projects. Kate and Perry are *idealists* and somewhat utopian while Kevin was firmly *populist* and sometimes deeply pragmatic. Using this same critical distance and thinking about the organisation of the practice across it breadth of seminal works and amongst the three principals, we again see a balancing and symbiotic approach. Kate's approach appears *adhoc* and scattered but fundamentally, when she finds her threads and interests, she allows it to remain open for things to pass in and out. Materials, planting regimes, and processes churn about until she is ready to test it in the landscape at 1:1 full-size. Perry arrives at his design work in a somewhat *linear* process of diagraming big ideas and gestures, then transforming this onto sites in formal and spatial sequences. He tends to hand his design ideas over to the others once he is satisfied with its spatial compositions. Kevin was prosaic in his matrix-like approach to making sure each of his, the clients', and the users' concerns, as well as the landscape's own needs were embedded at a range of scales and through a range of formal gestures in the design work. He knitted needs, wants, and desires into sites, ambiances and distinct places. Overall, the practice morphs its organisation to suit the ad hoc needs of each project undertaken. TCL differentiates themselves from their peers by uniquely combining spatial arrangements and compositions with public cultivation of care and in making sense of landscape.

Introduction to PhD Case studies

The outcomes will be:
→ *The first systematic analysis of procedures and techniques for deploying Spatial Intelligence in design since the public emergence of new knowledge about Spatial Intelligence (van Schaik 2008).*
→ *The surfacing of tacit methods of deploying Spatial Intelligence inclusively in design.*
→ *Improved procedures and techniques in designing and in managing design.*
→ *An articulation of Spatial Intelligence as a driver of excellence in design that will enhance the contribution already made through the Design Practice Research Lab's work on the 'natural history' of the creative innovator and on the public behaviours that sustain creative innovation.*

Introductions to the PhD abstracts follow the detailed case studies. The introductions capture the key insights of the design practice research of each researcher, all of whom have been involved in the process of the research as proposed:
In our Design Practice Research 'Lab', Terroir have evolved (under our supervision) an electronic journal that records the interactions between the members of a design team, capturing conversations, verbal descriptions of concepts, sketches of concepts, sketch models of concepts, source images influencing concepts, computer modeling of concepts.
→ *A journal process (amended text) will be adapted by all twenty (the proposal indicated four only) practices as they conduct new design projects. A research associate will assist in the application of the system.*
→ *The practices will then use a record of peer reviewed presentations to the research symposiums (see below) (amended text) to fully record their design processes in a first compilation of project work in their practices.*
→ *The data collection will be monitored by CIs at our laboratory bases in Melbourne (Australia) and Brussels (Belgium).*
→ *At the end of the first year, we will analyse the data with the design practitioners, identifying the 'natural history' factors and the 'public behaviour' factors (van Schaik 2005)*
→ *We will also extract the Spatial Intelligence factors (van Schaik 2008)*

While every design is based on uncovered facts, and is to that extent 'constructivist,' every design is a unique invention that reconciles a complex array of competing factors and is thus necessarily 'relativist'. Tracing the decisions made as invention takes place is best conducted through "rich description" (Goffman 1961; Geertz 2001, Harrison & Madge 1986) and subsequently analysed for patterns of consistency. In the trial conducted in our Design Practice Research 'Lab' with Terroir, we could trace the following patterns:
→ *spatial memories triggered in each design participant by the project and its context;*
→ *fragments of films, books, paintings and music triggered by the project and the subsequent interaction with these materials by design participants to extend their ideas further;*
→ *spatial exemplars ranging from the canonical, the kinetic to the natural;*
→ *spatial 'games', analogous to punning, in which individual memories triggered cascades of incremental and serendipitous inventions*

In this way, we could discern patterns of using SI that ranged from personal exposure to design canons, personal experience of particular spaces, spatial anecdotes derived from films, books, paintings and music. Tracking and understanding these made explicit to the design team what had previously merely been asserted through the raw input of designers (sketches, models, computer renderings.)

→ *Twice yearly, the firms will give feedback on these analyses through presentations at our research conferences in Melbourne and Brussels.*

→ *The practices will then embark on a second tranche of project work, armed with this new knowledge about their design processes. This work will be recorded as above (amended text).*

→ *Again the data collection will be monitored and analysed, and the firms will give feedback twice yearly. We will evaluate the difference in their design practice consequent upon their new awareness of the operation of their Spatial Intelligence through the research symposiums (amended text), where findings will be presented to invited panellists and to peers.*

→ *In the third year, a draft design procurement policy informed by the research into the operation of Spatial Intelligence will be tested in the context of a third tranche of projects conducted by the firms.*

In the following introductions, terms used in the analytical tool described in the chapter 'Developing a Differentiation Tool' are in italics. These introductions should be read in conjunction with the ideogram of the tool, illustrated overleaf.

Benedict Anderson
The Architectural Flaw: Speculations on the Reconstructed City, 2005

Benedict Anderson is a designer, film-maker, and writer. Not trained in the discipline, he has used his practices as the platform from which to arrogate the teaching of architecture. Based in Berlin and Northern Europe, he made a comparative study of the rebuilding of the Frauenkirche in Dresden and the stripping and eventual demolition of the DDR's People's Palace in Berlin. He documented the histories of these buildings, filmed the Frauenkirche in its ruined state, the camera caressing the long scaffolding tables on which every intact piece of carved stonework was laid out, identified, named and eventually tagged with its position in the walls or the dome by its original x,y and z coordinates. When the reconstruction was completed, he filmed the rebuilt dome and walls, lightly peppered with the dark stones that formerly lay on the scaffold tables. He filmed the People's Palace, stripped of its interiors, and he filmed attempts to reclaim it for public use as a gallery for experimental art. He met with the leaders of the movement to demolish the building and rebuild the Berlin Palace that had stood on the site prior to the bombings of the Second World War. The camera dwelt on the dark green wallpaper of a gentleman's study, the heavy mahogany furniture. The miasma of past glories filled the screen. He filmed protests against the demolition, against the obliteration of a recent past. He filmed the wrapping of the site with screen prints of the facades of the Berlin Palace. He filmed the demolished site.

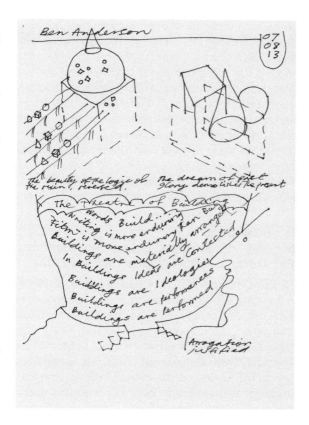

He asserted that the ideas behind the strangely symmetrical reconstruction and demolition were more permanent than the building masses that they animated. He suggested that the performances of these two events were the real substance of the architecture, the playing out of ideologies realist, idealist and populist at that moment at which the intellectual manifests in physical form. He argues that buildings are performed, are best understood as performances of contested ideas. That film is more enduring than buildings, words more enduring than film. That words build.

He documents how Ideas come racing out of the past to reassert their predominance over material form: that much is at stake when the history of Prussia since Frederick the Great is the ideal, and that when the real history of the recent past is supressed the present has its popular history squeezed out of it.

Suzie Attiwill
?interior practices of interiorization, interior designs, 2013

Suzie Attiwill conducts design research through exhibitions, curatorships and teaching Interior Design studios. Her practice questions dominant phenomenological models of interior and interiority. Suzie's fertile ground for creative production and connection with contemporary concerns comes through exploring ideas of interiority as a manifestation of inner lives; the substance of psychological existence individual and collective. These, once identified, are juxtaposed with the various manners and modes deployed by practitioners designing interior spatial qualities and characters. The means to this is her curatorial practice, one that transforms exhibition environments into sites of experimentation and engagement. As well as crafting it as a space of exposition she makes the gallery a working space; a space of investigation that displays and demonstrates manners and modes of designing.

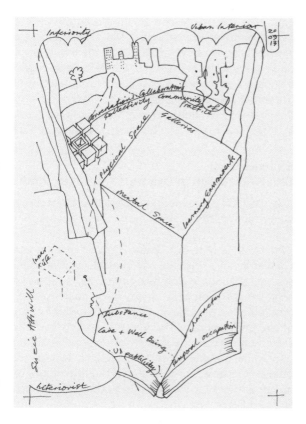

Suzie is a founding member of the Urban Interior (UI) multi-disciplinary research group. UI operates as a collective within which individual research trajectories cover a breadth of creative practices, scales and regimes of care. For the UI's 'Occupation of Craft Victoria' (2008) Suzie's inhabitation gathered, collected and considered a range of urban interiors demonstrating all the spheres of practice. Suzie's role, self-described

as an 'interiorist', is concerned with making the research manners and modes of designers manifest through occupations of spaces open to the public, and thus making this discourse part of the city life. During the ten day exhibition event UI publi(city) her curation brought the participants and the visitors together to produce a continuum of evolving communities of practice. Her more recent projects include further temporal occupations of sites in the urban environment and the design of supportive interior environments for young people placed in out-of-home care. Her designing approaches physical interiority through carefully articulated mental spaces. Thus she creates novel, poetic and acutely modulated spaces, events and conversations.
Her work helps us to reconsider the mental space of design.

Nigel Bertram
Making and Using the Urban Environment:
Furniture, Structure, Infrastructure, 2013

This PhD has been published in its entirety. Nigel Bertram, NMBW, *Furniture, Structure, Infrastructure: Making and Using the Urban Environment* (2013) Ashgate, London.

Nigel Bertram practices as architect in Melbourne with two partners. The firm, NMBW, is a small practice engaged in a plethora of project types. The scale and diversity of their commissions includes community buildings and the public landscapes associated with these facilities, commercial and office buildings, institutional renovations, houses and private residential additions. Nigel and NMBW approach design through close observations of existing spatial situations and patterns of occupation at urban, neighbourhood, street, and single building architectural scales. These locations are dissected precisely and surgically, taken apart and then re-constructed so expertly that their architectural propositions emerge as subtle and nuanced. The work is real, firm, robust in its regimes of care, and acute in its poetic. In *By-Product Tokyo*,[1] a book co-authored by Nigel, detailed spatial and temporal analysis of streetscapes and architectural thresholds of Tokyo reveal NMBW's observational stance as poetic, the expression arising from this way of looking, of really seeing things, as delayed and acute. The way NMBW transforms the art and rigour of this kind of noticing of things into design propositions in a range of other contexts is revealed. At the core of Nigel and NMBW's design manners and modes is an adherence to utility (commodity) and it's spatial opportunities and consequences. Nigel and his partners distinguish themselves from their peers in their ability to translate firmness across architectural scales and building programs into a pragmatics of delight.

Richard Black
Site Knowledge in Dynamic Contexts, 2009

This PhD, Site Knowledge in Dynamic Contexts, has been collected by the Centre for Art and Environment at the Nevada Museum of Art

With his wife Michelle Black, Richard Black practices as an architect in Castlemaine, a regional city near Melbourne. Times Two Architects is a small, practice which has completed a range of small scale realized projects and a number of very large scale rural and regional speculative projects. The practice culture tends to the 1:1 and full scale investigation of site and program. The realized works are crafted through carefully set up mimetic processes. The surrounding landscapes, underlying geological conditions and the specific surface topography define the domestic spatial envelopes and the regimes of care of the well-sited house and artists' studios that are the bread and butter of the practice. Richard Black approaches designing with a deep knowledge of Australian

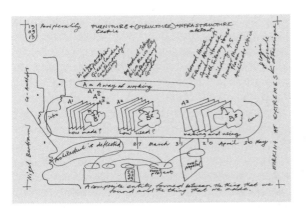

1 Bertram, Nigel, S. Murray, M. Neustupny (2003) *By-Product Tokyo*, RMIT University Press, Melbourne

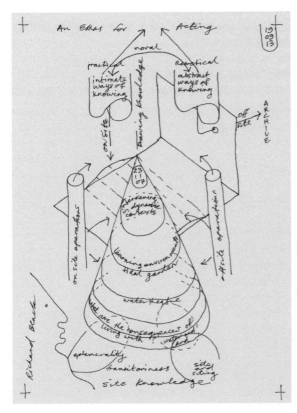

landscape conditions and its ephemeral processes. His maps and speculative propositions for the Murray River Basin go well beyond recording or problematizing the complexity of this hindered landscape: he draws out the subtle poetic systems of terrains that are richer than they at first appear to be. Richard's design manner and mode and his observational strategy and expression thereof depends on the seeking out a thickened poetic and acute/delayed ground to guide his interventions, and this produces architecture that draws the landscape into his architecture, registering it acutely and not simply siting the building within its happenstance setting. Richard's unique approach embeds a longer duration or a slow regime of care. This architecture comes into being through the means of landscape and thus creates a profound encounter between time, place, process, and site.

Stephen Collier
Paradigms of Observation, Azul Oscuro Casi Negro, a blue that is almost black, 2009

Few architects have a structured understanding of the mental space that frames their designing as does Stephen Collier. He has written: "a work of architecture holds the observations of the architect, an accumulation of images, feelings and sensations. These remain largely … invisible to the casual observer … becoming apparent as an idea glimpsed through an external point of observation." He continues: "… in its finished form (a work of architecture) is both the space of the architect and of the client." And he further argues, the creature of the city in which it is made[2].

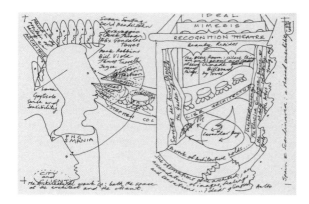

The conversion of the old boatsheds at Lavender Bay demonstrates Collier's meticulously conscious spatial history approach. The topography has been lovingly analysed, and the design cannot be appreciated without understanding that for Collier the building sits in the folds of the crust of the earth, it does not float above it. The drive to Lavender Bay is a curving descent down a wooded hillside towards a concealed destination, revealed at the last moment as the edge of a bay – the bay of all bays, captured by the Sydney Harbour Bridge that looms up as you arrive on the waterfront. So steep is the hillside that the rear of the boatsheds has been cut into it. Collier takes advantage of this to provide access to the new dwelling within at three levels: along the waterfront to the lower level, at the rear to each of the upper two levels. This appreciation of the uses of steep landscape is hard wired into Collier who grew up in the precipitate geographies of Papua New Guinea and of Tasmania. Stephen's site conscious designing is well served by the sophisticated use of oblique projection, a characteristic tool in his practice.

Imbued with the poetics of inclined planes, Collier brings an acute sensibility to work the expression of his architecture. He has honed this through his preference for works of occluded observation in the arts and in literature: Lorca, Torres, Jarman, Robbins, Turrell amongst others.

In Collier's work, the thickened section plays a role similar to that which the crust of the earth affords to his precise understanding and linking of levels. This gives to his architecture a sense of seamless connection, an ideal naturalness and a therefore easeful completeness, a slow regime of care, something quite rare in the post-colonial world.

While these moves suggest a minimalist if lyrical hand, the bathroom tiling reveals the architect's love of Spanish, especially Catalan, architecture, and his long fascination with its links with Scandinavian modernism. Aalto used to holiday in the Hotel Colon in Barcelona, and Collier has made a study of the ideas, ideals and mimeses of fringe modernism that stemmed from the historical removals of these countries from the behemoth of metropolitan modern architectural theory. Collier's architecture is thus an architecture of many layers, idea, ideal, abstraction, mimesis and delight.

2 Stephen Collier (2009) *Paradigms of Observation: A Blue That is Almost Black*, PhD School of Architecture and Design, RMIT University, p7

Graham Crist
Sheds for Antarctica: the Environment for Architectural Design and Practice, 2010

Graham Crist is a practitioner academic in Melbourne. He grew up in Perth. His grandmother had some very clear ideas about what constituted a house. He found these alien to what he observed. He studied architecture, began a small practice and a family, and joined the 1970s and 1980s migration of young professionals to South East Australia. His earliest work was a shed for a family that could afford no more than an off the peg shed. This shed was minimally modified to make it inhabitable as a dwelling. This beginning point was not merely a realist 'needs-must' event. It was the seed of Graham's more idealist approach to architecture. He persisted in finding sheds for his projects. The simplest envelope housed the fluctuating interactions of programs that he declined to fix or settle, firm in his understanding that relationships shift and move in orbits that are only ever partially predictable.

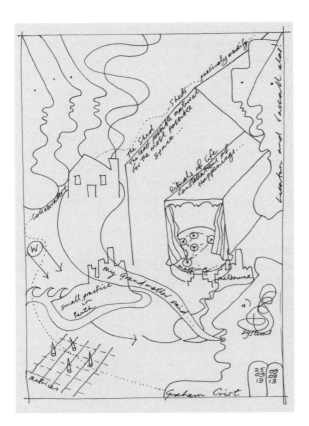

Graham thinks systems. He maps his position relative to those of his collaborators. He seeks out organisational modes that support partnerships that are equal, preferring a matrix to a hierarchy. Sheds are envelopes that need to be large enough to encompass the matrices. In urban situations sheds encompass that which is inside them, but they also create an outside shed, roofed by the sky. He designs these sheds too, foregrounding outside—as inside—the constellations of happenings that are the living part of architecture. A swimming pool is a shed that gets figured where it closely encounters the rituals of swimming and sun-baking.

The shed is a firmly parsimonious structure: the least possible material for the most possible space. There is always enough budget to passively modify the micro-climates inside and outside, creating sustainable regimes of care. Graham instils sustainability thinking into his students.

He found his sheds before Lacatan and Vassall found theirs. But he found his voice and his critics after they found theirs…

Lucas Devriendt
Paint it Black: My Research into the Black Plastic as a (self-) portrait in the Cabinet Devriendt, 2015

Welling up through Lucas Devriendt's research into his practice as a painter are a series of continuums. One runs through the continuities in the generations of his own family, through times of war and peace in a country that has been swept this way and that by violent conflict for many hundreds of years. Another continuum is found by revealing the family's constant concern with ways and means of seeing, and the meaning of seeing - through art; through X rays; through medical equipment and through medical procedures such as placing a square white handkerchief on the naked back of the patient whose lungs will be listened to through a cold stethoscope. Science and art interweave. The rays of Lucas's grandfather's radiology equipment reveal much but do not manifest themselves. In the "Cabinet Devriendt", Lucas's scientist forbear drew a refracting pattern onto walls to represent the bouncing light. Another continuum lies in the centuries of art practice in the lowlands and in the wider world. An artist does not paint a picture 'ab novo' but sees through the seeing of generations of artists. Lucas's research revealed this phenomenon through portraits and landscapes; and brought into being an imaginary held constant by a red studio table. A square of black plastic on a stored picture started a reverie about the painting of drapery, of which there is a long history, but also sparked references to every black square ever painted. Black squares turned out to have been bothering artists since the mid 17th Century.

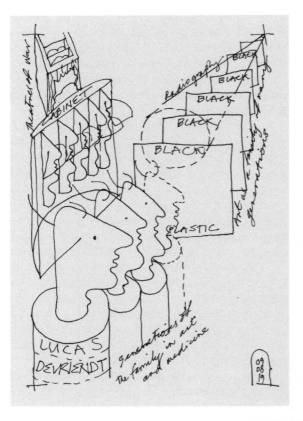

Harold Fallon
Metarbitrariness? An Architecture of Practice, 2013

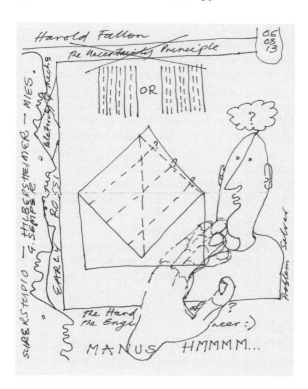

Continental Europe has a tradition of Engineer-Architects unparalleled elsewhere. The designing of architects in this hybrid tradition is distinctively different to that of architects or engineers. The doyen of the tradition, Gottfried Semper, 1803–1879, used classicism as a logical system of hierarchical spatial ordering and proposed an ontology of architecture that gave every component of a building a distinct role (column, beam and screen). The classicism of neo-Palladianism in the Anglophone world (but also that of Friedrich Schinkel, 1781–1841, in Prussia) was more about creating the effect of ordered harmony. Hilbersheimer 1885–1967, Mies Van Der Rohe 1886–1969 and O.M. Ungers 1926–2007 worked in this tradition. For them designing centred on finding a grid that had a grain of intervals suited to the needs of the program and the simultaneous construction logic. Harold engages with the manners and modes of this tradition mimetically.

Unlike many of his peers, Harold eschews effect (delight) as a goal, but allows it as a result. Front of mind is Vitruvian Firmness. Next comes Commodity or social utility. Delight is a possible resultant that is not striven for. There is an obdurate idealism in this approach. Even in the most compromised of site situations, an abstraction will be found that allows the deployment of the simplest possible combined spatial program and construction method. Paradoxically the resultant Delight often arises because the effect of the rigour of the logic is to understate the role of structure. This recedes to the point that a "Look Ma! No hands!" response wells up in the observer. Where peers look to expressing the craft of building, in Harold's work all trace of handiwork is completely removed. It is as if the ideal world that he creates has had an immaculate conception.

This contrasts with the idealising Rationalism of Aldo Rossi 1931–1997. That was based on the notion of a universally shared internalised architectural language of classical components derived from Platonic solids manifest in superstructures like viaducts and stadiums. Rossi argued for the insertion of new giant forms that could guide the future structuring of a city.

Modestly, and with an intense abstraction in manner and mode of designing, Fallon's work is, ironically, more in tune with Colin Rowe's realist Anglo-American Contextualism because Harold's work avoids making large claims, and tells only the story of its own logic and its own making.

Arnaud Hendrickx
Substantiating Displacement, 2013

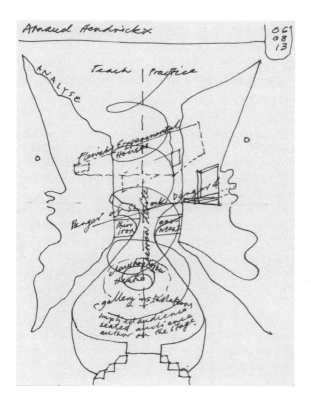

Arnaud Hendrickx has segued from being a practitioner designing and procuring daring houses in a recognisably Flemish figuration manner to being a practitioner academic who is tailoring his designing to the idea generated research collaborations that arise within academic institutions. This reorientation has been accomplished but not without some regret for the challenges of procuring architecture as such.

More than in most places exceptionally creative architects operate in a narrow defile in Belgium. There are twice as many architects per head of population as in the neighbouring Netherlands, and much work in Brussels is bundled up in the practice of a few major corporate practices. Another pincer is encroaching on small practitioners, as part time teachers are progressively required to get PhDs and become, in the jargon of university administrators 'research active', a process in wilful ignorance of the integrated scholarship that actually constitutes productive work practice. Where others have found a path to practicing and teaching, Arnaud has chosen a path that aligns with his love of the unusual, the ideal and the dangerous. His practice has become one that is situated in galleries, and one in which the clients are artists and curators.

Danger? One breakaway design projected live wires along a plank into space. Another created the illusion of an upper level walkway between gallery spaces, passage being impossible except in the mind. Spatial reconfigurations of galleries to suit specific exhibits followed, though the insertion itself became a figure on exhibition in the space. Another project recreated the spatial form of a Greek amphitheatre, but in a gallery and with a manner of access that closed after the audience entered, locking them in hermetically to the amphitheatre fragment.

In the demonstration project that concluded his reflective practice research with us Arnaud presented his various, meticulously charted, ideal authorial personae to an audience seated on a raking set of polystyrene plinths, set in a gallery containing representations of his key works. His audience became an object in the gallery, as curated as any of the set designs, taking their seats on white polystyrene plinths set on a white base of the same material. These plinths then slowly deformed under the varying weights of the people; the ideal succumbing to the realities of the event. The work arcs between several opposing positions, bridging from the abstract to the figured, from the naïve to the phatic, from the delayed to the poetic.

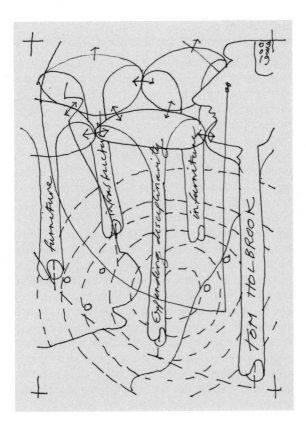

Tom Holbrook
Between Furniture & Infrastructure: Expanding Disciplinarity, 2014

Tom Holbrook's research into his practice drew his studio's collaborative processes into focus and gave them a conscious focus. Examining the 'ways of doing' what they do, and plan to do, revealed a very deliberate process of decentring attention from what at first eems to be the nature of any given project. Sometimes a client brief is couched in a logic so linear that opportunities for addressing higher order issues are precluded. For the studio this means that when for example, urban furniture is requested, widening the horizons of everyone's thinking reveals solutions that are infrastructural. Widening horizons means also that the architects have to think beyond the norms of their own discipline and consider projects through the lenses of other sometimes adjacent disciplines. Books have to be produced to document the wider thinking, and these have to be put in the mind's eye of decision makers. Geographical constraints of a political construct need to be dissolved in order to release fuller potentials than stakeholders have initially posited… This expanded thinking not only transforms project potentials, it gives rise to future opportunities.

CJ Lim
From Smartcity to the Food Parliament, 2014

CJ Lim investigated his extensive practice in visualising possible worlds created between the poles of science and literary culture. Growing up in Malaysia and then going to school in England with the metropolis of London on his mind, imbued there through childhood reading, he was also aware of the historic Chinese contributions to science and technology. CJ devises imagined worlds that address issues of governance and human need through the lens of an even-handedness that emerged from these childhood ideals. In his research he studied the relationships between his many published books, the worlds that they suggest and the designs that emerge from the imagining. His trajectory could be described as: "If you read, you write. If you write a thing, you have imagined it. To imagine you research cognate fields. If imagined, a system can be drawn. If you draw it, it can be…" His research took him from designs for smart cities that respond to needs as they are expressed to a re-imagining of the governance of a city as a place where every stage of food production and consumption is made explicit in a utopia of decency, of visibly met needs. The drawings are so fully imagined that they seem to be representations of new actualities, not simply designs.

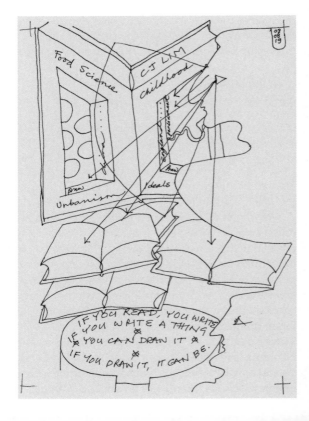

Paul Minifie
Design Domains: Their Relations and Transformations as Revealed Through the Practice of Paul Minifie, 2010

Whatever his personal history in space (it is to do with Melbourne's inner city and its more salubrious peninsula), Paul Mifinie, who is one of those relatively rare creatures: a mathematician-architect, is at home in abstraction. His often charismatically engaging projects are all mathematical concepts struggling into built form. His Major Project at RMIT used a Kline Bottle—the three dimensional offspring of the Moebius Strip—to create a new library complex with interlocking public and private space. His pioneering designs have an impact on his peers. Much later the Melbourne firm MCR built a much awarded Kline Bottle House. Paul was the key player in the redesign of RMIT Storey Hall, re-skinning it mimetically with mathematician Roland Penrose's non periodic tiling system that can cover any surface convex or concave with a combination of two tiles: a fat lozenge and a thin lozenge. ARM, the practice he was working for, continued with the mathematical seed he planted, hooked onto a Boolean figure derived from the work of the great mathematician who established set theory. Paul started a partnership with Fiona Nixon and they completed the Centre for Ideas at the Victorian College for the Arts, skinning that with a façade based on Voronoi cells, another mimetic process. The partnership segued to one with Jan van Schaik, and they completed the Healsville Sanctuary animal hospital, using as an imported figure, a Costa surface as the dome to an internal public ambulatory, and an automata to design the contrasting brick exterior. At Archilab in 2001 and 2003 Paul launched his thinking onto the international stage with a housing complex based on a mimetically repeating topological figure.

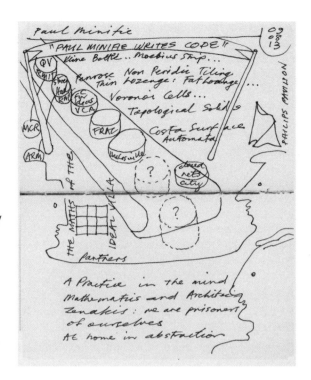

How do we understand architecture of this nature? In his essay on the Mathematics of the Ideal Villa, Colin Rowe discussed an ancient preoccupation with the nine square ideal – a precursor of the Rubic Cube. Such abstract ideals can result in powerfully figurative designs. Le Corbusier's collaborator, musician and mathematician Xenakis, designed the Philips Pavilion at the Brussels Expo, and was sacked when its hyperbolic form was so evidently more his work than that of his boss. Automata are used by Japanese architects to design immensely dense housing complexes with abstract forms. These are manners and modes in the mind, rather than practices on the ground. Paul's recent research, Cloudnets, uses set theory to create predictive models of urban growth, challenging many common sense beliefs. Like his predecessor in mathematical thinking at RMIT, physics professor Hein Wagenfeld, who would often be found doodling formulae for calculating fractally from a single sample the holes in a seam of brown coal, Paul will be found musing about some hitherto unexplored relationship between factors of urban development. Being at home in abstraction, Paul's practice is a practice in the mind. It invariably delights when it emerges on the ground.

Vivian Mitsogianni
white noise PANORAMA: Process Based Architectural Design, 2009

M@ STUDIO Architects, founded in 1999 by Vivian Mitsogianni and Dean Boothroyd, is a small Melbourne practice duo, which has produced a series of speculative and built projects. Vivian's manner and mode approaches design through an abstract, mimetic process, producing architecture by setting rigorous and highly orchestrated parameters that open up possibilities for designing. Her focus is rule-based, step-by-step, digital and iterative. She aims at generating architectural envelopes and surfaces from qualities intrinsic to program and site. She seeks to avoid the figuration which has become, as her research reveals, the internationally normative outcome for such process based designing. She also uses

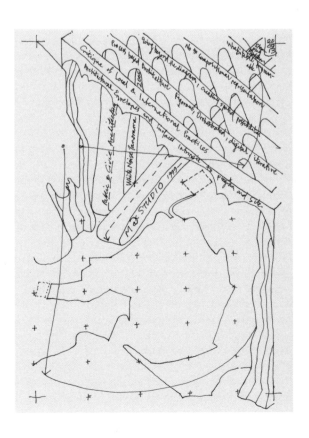

digital design techniques to create architectural facades and ornament. Her speculative works in the white noise PANORAMA series (2005–2009) critically reconsidered public and civic architecture, deeply situated within specific Melbourne architectural influences and the Australian context. Her works test the potential and scope of mimetic process-based architectural design, going beyond building the diagram and avoiding the common trap of developing endless figurations. Vivian's design mode is distinctly abstract while her manner is overtly process driven, and her distinctive contribution has been to create pathways that avoid 'stopping point' problem that bedevils rule based designing with the hitherto unavoidable collapse into figuration as the process is halted. Her manner allows for a transition from the abstract to the mimetic in designing, informing the architecture through her spatial and surface inquiries, and avoiding the tyranny of unconscious aesthetic preference. Her process produces spatial possibilities not compositional representation, the volumes are inhabitable and programmable not as an aside to but as a consequence of the initial rule set.

Stephen Neille
SPEED_SPACE: Architecture, Landscape and Perceptual Horizons, 2007

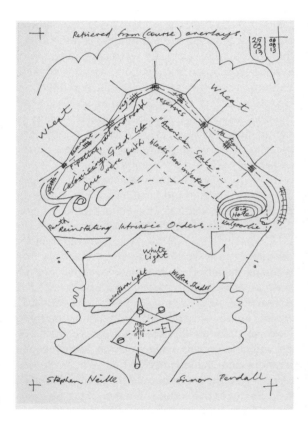

Stephen Neille is an architect with a spatial history that spans the continent. Working in Perth on the edge of vast Western Australia, he teaches, researches through design and, with Simon Pendal, designs houses, small buildings and monuments. And on the fringe of the island continent, he surfs. Surfing is a good analogy for Stephen's observational strategy. In surfing you develop an understanding of wave behaviour, an intuitive grasp of wave patterns. Stephen studies the landscape patterns of the continent, microscopically understanding its workings, place by place.

Poetically and acutely Stephen studies the force fields on sites, fields that are invisible, not discernible to those who do not 'surf'. Designing a visitor centre at the monastery of New Norcia, he combs the site for every inflection of its topography, every pulse of historical intent, every view line across and out of the site. Documenting these, he criss-crosses them as he designs, as if surfing repeatedly across the terrain and on each passage, adding definition to the enclosures that he is inserting into the field. The walls, floors, ceilings, cupboards and openings in the houses that he and Simon design have this quality – they are deliberately placed where a standing wave of concerns can support them in space. These are not imposed rooms carved into compliance with site needs; the rooms emerge from the desire to create atmospheres, so that light sometimes bounces in under a wall or over a cupboard, or beams softly along a wall that slowly becomes the side of a passage to darkness, or to light. In these houses the walls seem not to have material thickness, they are light-moderating planes floated into place and held there by deep site logic: spatial history.

Western Australia is mined for its mineral resources. Alien orders at a vast scale have been applied to its surface: the Super Pit at Kalgoorlie is an emblem of this process. But the surface of what was a Mallee forest has been cleared and is now a vast prairie Wheat Belt, modelled on North American precedents. This mimetic overlay has proved to be naïve as the removal of the trees has brought salt to the surface, and the entire region needs to be re-engineered. Stephen's large scale research traced the water pipe line from Perth to Kalgoorlie, running in a rail corridor, and punctuated by townships thirty miles apart, laid out in grids. He recorded each of the townships, and noted how in an ironic inversion the limited remaining forest was often found in the townships. The pipeline and the townships were rolled out to Kalgoorlie like a strip of carpet. Stephen abstracted a model that rolled the townships back out of Kalgoorlie to the coast, where the entire engineering idea could be held in two hands, and marvelled upon again, the current invisibility of its processes wondrously figured in a topological abstraction that suggest the reinstating of an intrinsic order, retrieved from the crude mechanistic overlays of resource exploitation.

Stephen's practice combs over landscape and site to find and express intrinsic orders masked by the processes of colonising capital.

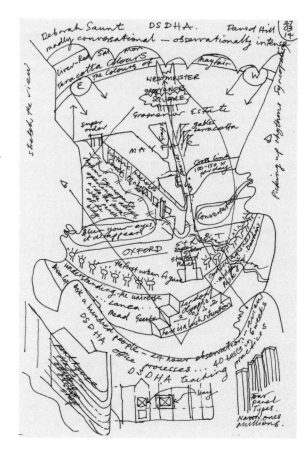

Deborah Saunt
Orbits and Trajectories: Why Architecture Must Never Stand Still, 2014

Deborah Saunt began her research journey holding the view that it was her energy and vision that propelled DSDHA, the practice she founded with her partner in life and architecture David Hills.

As her investigations proceeded, she came to understand that this propulsion was held within a productive field formed by conversations with her partner and their staff. Deborah discovered that the crucial role of high-quality conversations between program and site, between designers and clients and users and between studio collaborators. She began to map the ways in which these interactions worked, and as she did this, she formulated new engines of collaboration within the practice, some of them modelled on the biannual peer review process of the RMIT design practice research scaffold. A turning point occurred when the design for house for themselves that she and David were working on outside the office stalled, but re-ignited when brought back into the studio framework. Now, consciously using a people-centred approach DSDHA "deploys its spatial intelligence across a broad range of scales and urban contexts, always with the ethos that 'the city is our client'." (The Business of Research: Knowledge and Learning Redefined in Architectural Practice, AD 03/VOL 89/2019, p5)

Jon Tarry
Lines of Resistance, explorations of geopolitical space through art practice, 2012

Jon Tarry is an artist practicing in Perth, Western Australia. His early mentor Bill Busfield migrated to Perth from England, where he had been an Archigram cadet. Why Perth? Because it was like Los Angeles in the 1920s, wide open, seemingly malleable and responsive to new ideal futures. New ideas were in the air. Goonhilly Downs made the first satellite transmission to the South Western Hemisphere: 'What the world needs now is love sweet love' was the message. Soon after student work from the AA in London was beamed to Perth for the first ever long distance studio critique, Peter Cook chairing in London, Bill Busfield in Perth. Life as idea, as figure, as delight could, it seemed and still seems, be lived on a line.

Jon Tarry is the master of that line. Or rather, he is the master of the horizontal line. His early works obsessively document what happens to the flat coastal plane, the gentle incline of the inland escarpment, the endless flatness of the interior. Again and again he captures the line as it flares red with the setting of the sun. Flat canvass could not express the flatness, they depicted it, diagrammed it. Flat sculptures could describe it. Many ensued. What Jon wondered is vertical in this realm? He found footage of nuclear warhead tests filmed from farmsteads north of Geraldton, as a mushroom cloud rose over an offshore island, obliterating a test village. But even that vertical thrust was later found to have annealed the sea sand into a vast shallow crystal bowl. Human endeavour rises vertically. Rose Porteous married mining magnate John Hancock, rejuvenated him, and built Prix d'Amour – a massive villa modelled on Tara in the film *Gone with the Wind*. Jon filmed it being demolished, documenting the falling of the flimsy walls to make way for a subdivision. Flatness returns. Mistaken critics urge Jon to enter the third dimension. He is already in it. It is very flat.

Jon exhibits in Los Angeles, not the 1920s now, and site of many Prix d'Amour flattenings. He flies from airport to airport, living on a line.

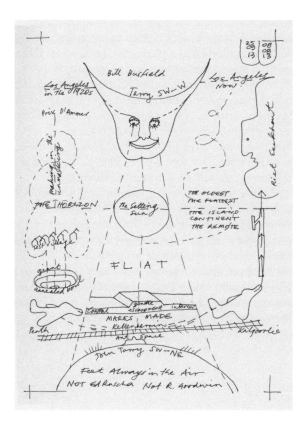

He sees the runways as they have not been seen before. He makes sculptures of them all from the single runway of Shark Bay, to the multiple runways of Chicago, choosing materials that relate to some prime poetic characteristic of the cities they serve. Ed Ruscha documented car parks, gasoline stations, amphitheatres, using photos. This is not what Jon does. Mimetically he goes through the surface to capture the gravity of landing on these strips. He notices the marks aeroplane tires make as they stop defying gravity and succumb to its pull. These marks he documents too.

Jon collaborates with architect Riet Eeckhout, whose designs are lives on lines. They exchange lines. Hers turn into cupboards in the long tradition of European Gemütlichkeit His return to the raw marks made on the earth by human endeavour.

Jo Van Den Berghe
Theatre of Operations, or: construction site as architectural design, 2013

When we first met Jo Van Den Berghe, a Flemish architect who teaches at St Lucas School of Architecture, he introduced us to an exquisite body of work created by practicing solo from his home office. He soon demonstrated how his office library constituted his world of mentors and peers, talking of books on Lewerentz and Asplund, and Flemish masters of their generation. He said that he admired the sparse but muscular intelligence of their works, their restrained palettes of natural materials. He organised the models of his projects in the office in clusters of like projects. His eloquent expositions of his work revealed his passion for the craft of architecture, a child-like wonder at how the making of works deepened the design of them, if you allowed yourself to ponder about the manner and mode and material of their bricoleur making.

His conversation was threaded through with references to the lacemaking that had preceded his wife's fashion practice in the house in which they lived with her mother. How a tramline to Brussels had once threaded its way through the fields and villages to their village, 'a kind of lace-making with rails'. The house, the front of which presents a Magritte-like bourgeois normalcy, he had remodelled into two apartments, forming a courtyard around a pool at the rear, framed by the lace workshop and storage sheds in black timber, and closing on a sliding wall that opens to reveal an orchard and paddocks beyond. Every part of the house demonstrated the intense, close up poetic of his craft.

When we toured a series of his projects we found the same qualities in different forms and materials—brick, curtain walling, concrete—but we also found an unusual use of scissor staircases set against the axial flow of the circulation. Such a stair integrated the levels of a three-storey house, and such a stair resolved the introduction of vertical circulation into a heritage-listed building. Where, we wondered, had this stair idea come from? The question puzzled Jo. It came to bother him.

At this time he read Spatial Intelligence, pondering its message about our spatial histories creating our mental space and influencing the spatial thinking used in designing. And it came to him that he had, as a child of four, momentously explored such a stair in his grandmother's house. From this realisation stemmed a long research into all that he could recall and reconstruct about this (now demolished) house, and in this research he accounted for much that 'he knew' as a designer, the source of much of his very particular design practice. Now he declares: 'You don't know what you know until you discover what you know!'

Gretchen Wilkins
Manufacturing Urbanism: An architectural practice for unfinished cities, 2012

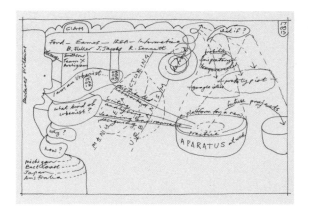

Gretchen Wilkins practices as an architect and urban designer in Melbourne with Anna Tweeddale. Studio Apparatus is a small, two-director design practice, bringing strategic, urban-based thinking to projects through multidisciplinary collaborations. Gretchen's practice is differentiated from her peers by her realist approach to mapping and engaging with systems of flow, capacity, and logistics in manufacturing to understand and to design complex urban morphologies. Her modes and manner of practice extend urban design and urbanism into abstract and mimetic operations where cities are reconfigured and transformed with a poetic rationalism and networked order. Her work explores how distributed architectural design, production, manufacturing, and realization can come together in contemporary contexts, where division of labour and offshore manufacturing is becoming outmoded. Gretchen's interests and pursuits are not unlike a contemporary version of Ray and Charles Eames. The Eames's careers in the 1950s mirrored America's post-war shift from an industrial economy of goods to a post-industrial society of information.[3] Gretchen's practice extends this somewhat further, by opening up possibilities for new forms of making architecture, returning the production of buildings to where they are consumed. Her examination and consideration for new materials and technologies, for example the cost effectiveness of 3D printers allowing for architectural plans to be quickly visualized and changeable, when considered at an urban scale is even more remarkable. Designing and building cities where design, manufacturing and installation are considered simultaneously and inform each other, allows us to reconfigure and question current separations of building and land use. Gretchen's networked cities and spaces become highly customizable for their inhabitants. These are not the spaces of hierarchical order and blandness but of ad hoc flow and flux, nimbleness and adaptivity, or accretion and connectivity. Her practice allows us to engage with Google Earth images and satellite imagery beyond their visually appealing compositions and patterns. Through her lenses she draws out interweaving relational orders. Manufacturing precincts and industrial production zones transcend transport and logistics, they evolve alongside residential enclaves into networked spaces of intertwined production and domestic life. Through Gretchen's projects we understand the new regimes of care that we are now seeing on the ground. She proposes ways of intervening in the new relationships and networks in the emerging global city of the mind.

3 The Eames' pioneering use of new materials and technologies, notably plywood and plastics, transformed the way many middle-class Americans furnished their homes. Thus introducing architecturally designed, functional, affordable, and often highly sculptural objects and furnishings into domestic and popular markets. In addition to furnishings and buildings, the Eames Office focused also its efforts on communication systems — exhibitions, publications, and films.

Benedict Anderson
The Architectural Flaw: Speculations on the Reconstructed City

My earlier research conducted between 1999–2005 on the practices of reconstructing the destroyed city focused on three sites in the German cities of Berlin and Dresden that expressed varying relationships connecting history and the rebuilding of their urban spaces. The study carried out 65 years after these sites destruction during the allied air war on Germany in WW2 (1943–45) detailed the complex issues surrounding destruction, reconstruction and history. The first site I investigated Berlin's *Karl Marx Allee*; a 2.5 kilometre long boulevard lined with apartment buildings designed in the architectural ideology of socialist classicism common in the Soviet Union during the 1950s and 60s was undergoing a facial change. At the time of my research the grandiose buildings lining the boulevard were undergoing the reconstruction of their façades that now, ten years later, have been completed.

The second site, the Socialist East German Government (DDR) political architectural symbol the *Palast der Republik* (palace of the people) built 40 years later (1972–74) than the *Karl Marx Allee* was being demolished (completed in 2007) to make way for the reconstruction of the *Schloss Berlin* (Royal Palace) now under reconstruction. The third site located in the city of Dresden focused on the massive shelving that stored the remnant stones of the baroque church the *Frauenkirche* (completed in 1743). Destroyed in the fire bombing of Dresden on the 13 and 14th of February 1945 the stones; numbered, tagged and interred in the shelves have since been reused in the *Frauenkirche's* reconstruction (completed in 2005). The research, writing and the accompanying three documentary films covering these sites, brought together my understanding of how reconstructing destroyed urban environments reform the history of the city. My belief at the time was that the practices of reconstructing destroyed sites, ensures the erasure of the destructive event to "make history go." This I still believe.

The Architectural Flaw

Foreword

The focus of my research is based on the practices of reconstructing destroyed buildings. However, to bring an understanding behind the spatial thinking that passes through my project is to offer two examples of reconstruction. One example is to recount my earlier profession in reconstructive surgery carried out on bodies not buildings. The other, a painting, examples the recording of medical knowledge through reenactment. Metaphorical in conception yet tangible, both examples gave me the insight to forward theoretical and philosophical positions and generate alternative spatial thinking to the practices of reconstructing the destroyed city.

Operations

Rembrandt's painting *The Anatomy of Dr. Nicolaas Tulp* (1632) is a pictorial reenactment of an event; a 'staged' anatomical lesson that shows a partial dissection of a dead man's arm[1]. The dead man is laid out on a wooden table that divides Dr. Tulp from a number of men who stand partially surrounding both him and the dead man. Dressed predominantly in black clothing, with their necks studded with pleated skirts of white-lace collars, these spectators form a mixture of medical practitioners and the plain curious. Central to the painting is the dead man and specifically his arm. The dead man's onlookers are being treated to a physiological lesson of the interior workings of the arm's vascular system. Cut to 470 years later and to the contemporary practice of medicine, modern warfare and my earlier profession as a surgical nurse attached to The Cranial Facial Unit located in a large general hospital in South Australia[2].

This unit conducted re-constructive surgery on young Vietnamese children marred with facial/cranium deformities. Many of the people who underwent these operations were the unborn children of women who came into contact with the chemical defoliant Agent Orange. Used extensively during the American War in Vietnam and Cambodia, this chemical was sprayed from low flying military aircraft over large areas of populated rain forests. In a matter of weeks the chemical denuded the trees and plants of their leaves, leaving the ground a deadened landscape of trunks and sticks. The effects of Agent Orange on pregnant women's unborn children were disastrous. After birth, the deformities caused by this chemical could be recognized in infants. Bone structures were either deformed or growth retarded, resulting in problems between bones and organs within the skull, endangering their life expectancy or, at the least, facially scarring them for life. In the surgical operation cartilage would be taken from the hip, thigh or rib areas from these victims to rebuild cranium cavity. By increasing organ space through reconstructing new bone mass, the framework was laid for these young lives to regain homogenized facial proportion.

The shift from Dr. Nicolaas Tulp's dead and opened body as the site of medical investigation to the sites of facial reconstructive surgery is crucial. Rembrandt's painting reenacts an event and pieces together actual historical truth and idealized visioning. The reconstructive surgical operation pieces together parts of a child's anatomy to give that child a 'normalized' aesthetic physical appearance and a better chance in life. One is recording an event in history the other; undoing history. Recording events collectively assemble histories. Histories are then constructed 'out of events', whereas visioning history informs the recording of histories 'as we know it'[3].

Top: *Flawed Thickness*, 16mm film still showing storage shelves housing the stones for the reconstruction of the *Frauenkirche* August 2003. Photograph courtesy of author.

1 The man known as Aris Kindt of Leyden, a thief, was caught and hanged for his crimes and his body given over for the advancement of medical knowledge; in this case to one of Dr. Tulp's anatomical lessons. For concise historical and critical readings refer to Hecksher, W. S., 1958, *Rembrandt's Anatomy of Dr. Nicolaas Tulp - An Iconological Study*, New York University Press and; Sawday, J., 1995, *The Body Emblazoned - Dissection and The Human Body in Renaissance Culture*, Routledge, London/New York.

2 The undertaking of facial reconstruction was carried out by the Cranial Facial Unit at The Royal Adelaide Hospital, Adelaide, South Australia. The chemical defoliant Agent Orange was used extensively in Vietnam and Cambodia between 1966—71. Containing dioxin, more than ten million gallons of Agent Orange were sprayed to clear foliage, which was used as cover for the Vietcong army for its supply lines. The estimated figure of Vietnamese suffering from deformities caused by Agent Orange range in the hundreds of thousands. American victims received a $190 million out-of-court settlement from the companies (→)

that produced the herbicide, but for the Vietnamese victims the US government, which has sovereign immunity, has dismissed compensation. With regard to the Vietnamese victims, there has recently been the attempt by more than 100 victims of Agent Orange to bring a court hearing against the 30 companies in the US who supplied the chemical — so far their attempts have remain blocked. Source — Guardian Weekly, 2005, issue May 6th—12th Vol. 172/No. 20, pg.3

3 Performance historian Della Pollack poses the question "...what happens when history seems to go away — when it seems to fade into its representations or fall into the fragments of time." Pollack, D., 1988 (edt.), *Exceptional Spaces*, The University of North Carolina Press, pg. 4.

Returning to this research necessitates a two-fold investigation. One focusing on the remaining site not yet completed (in fact just begun) – the reconstruction of the *Schloss Berlin* (Royal Palace) the other focuses on a hill formed out-of-destruction. Regarding the *Schloss Berlin,* the idea here is not to give a present account of the Royal Palace's rebuilding, absurd as it may be to rebuild monarchial architecture in the 21st century, but to retell the post-war history of the site; the construction and destruction of the *Palast der Republik* and the temporal appearances on the site that have advertised/advocated for the Royal Palace's return. Running counterpoint to this story is to highlight an altogether different yet connected narrative to the practices of reconstructing urban environments. *Teufelsberg* (Devil's Mountain) 'constructed' in the outer Berlin district of Wilmersdorf, tells a story of the rise of a hill and the burial of the 'lost city' of Berlin. Constructed between 1947–1968 from the rubble of Berlin's bombed-out buildings during the Allied air war on Germany (1942–1945), *Teufelsberg* forwards the practice of reconstruction as geography.

At their core, the two stories are bound by cartography. One, a hill, sited on the fringes of Berlin the other, a hole, located in the middle of Berlin. The sites account for their simultaneous bind on history and through their resurrection evokes the search for a lost urbanity. This chapter explores the practices of reconstruction as an archeological exploration; a digging through, peeling back and extraction of the physical stratum of remnant urban environments. The story of *Schlossplatz* and *Teufelsberg* and, my own history in reconstructive surgery, metaphorically connect, in my mind, to the city of Berlin's reconstruction: an imperfect ground—geography—*the architectural flaw.*

Façade – Stripped Down, Laid Bare

Sorting through my collection of archive pictures I came across a black and white photograph showing a parade of marching women and men holding banners. The year is 1952 and the GDR government is three years old. The marchers are marching to the anthem of a free German Democratic Republic. Freed that is, from the recent Nazi past and the 'corrupt capitalist ideals' of its neighbour, the Federal Democratic Republic (FDR) of West Germany. As I look further into the picture I notice there is no sign of the square's present name *Schlossplatz* (Palace Square). Instead, it is called *Marx-Engels Platz.* Name changes to places and streets in former East Berlin have marked the comings and goings of Germany's monarchical Prussians, Weimar republicans, Nazis and the socialist past[4]. Beside and around the marching people are more people unequally segregated; some standing on a *Tribüne* (grandstand) and some lining the parade way. I quickly surmise that the people in the grandstand wearing suits (mainly men) must be the authority, and that the marchers and the people lining the square must be under their authority.

The *Schlossplatz/Marx-Engels Platz/Schlossplatz* is one of those urban spaces where history collides. It is, I feel, one of the most important socio-political contests of urban space and architectural history in any place in the world I know. At the time of my research dominating the former parade ground stood the huge rectangular building the *Palast der Repbulik* (180 meters long, 90 meters wide and 8 storey's high). Buried beneath it laid the remnants of a building I couldn't see but whose footprint remains indelibly stamped. I was not interested at the time in something I couldn't see and instead gazed at the bronze and concrete building, struck by its ugliness. However, these thoughts change immensely over time. I am to become extremely interested in what is lying beneath the asphalt and I was to reposition my architectural aesthetics, as something not just based on materiality, form, context and 'looks' but also on ideas, ideology and building.

Top: Stalinallee 1954 Friedrichshain, courtesy of Landesarchiv Berlin/ Kruse, Wolfgang F Rep. 290; 33797. Middle: Marx-Engels Platz *Tribüne*, GDR National Day Celebration, Landesarchiv Berlin/ F Rep. 290; 64/876.

Bottom: GDR National Day Celebration 1952, courtesy of Landesarchiv Berlin/ F Rep. 290; 61/288.

4 In post 1989 unified Germany, street name changes were nothing new. In Berlin streets named after various socialist leaders of former East Germany have been replaced with the former names that existed before division. In my early Falk Plan of Berlin, streets named *Dimitroff Strasse* or *Otto-Braun Strasse*, have become *Danziger Strasse*, named after the city of Danzig, and *Otto-Braun Strasse* has been renamed *H. Beimer Strasse* etc. Source Berlin Falk Plan.

When the final destruction and removal of rubble from the Schloss Berlin was completed by the GDR[5] towards the end of 1950 at a cost of 32 million East German marks[6], the remnants of what was left (the foundations) were tarred over. In the absence of the Schloss Berlin a new square was created, and within a year a viewing apparatus, a Tribüne (grandstand) was built at a cost of 8 million DM. This transformation, from a former public embroiled in monarchical heraldry to a public now commemorating socialist representations, ensured the site's continuity as a space for dominance over the public and their public-ness. Forming its ideological center, this site became imbued with GDR propaganda, which was built around an orchestrated spectacle for the people. The square was performed through a combination of people, anthem and marching that would annually mark the socialist cause in the years to come. From its inception in 1951, until its demise in the early 1970s, the Tribüne was a prototype for what was to follow in the form of the Palast der Republik. The Tribüne served as the pivotal place for viewing the yearly marches, and for those in power it was the reflective space in which to see and be seen. The building of the Palast der Republik continued and developed this reflective space, going one step further than the Tribüne by incorporating the people within the spaces of the building[7].

The architect of the Palast der Republik, Professor Heinz Graffunder[8] conceived the building, in a design breaking from previous GDR institutional architecture, to reflect a functioning political system rather than to ideologically monumentalize the system. Graffunder's functioning plan covered the same area as the Tribüne and roughly one third of the original Schloss Berlin lying underneath the asphalt. The design and programming of the building had to fulfill many functions, from day-to-day political functions to social/cultural events. Building a 'palace for the people' was achieved inwardly through its lavish and functional interiors[9] and outwardly through the building's reflective golden exterior[10]. The building's many amenities included: a bowling alley, various restaurants, a 5000 seat concert hall, state theatre, a newspaper shop, an espresso bar, a mocha bar, a milk-bar, a post office, a souvenir shop, medical consulting rooms, conference rooms, planning rooms and, finally, the people's assembly chamber.

Graffunder's architectural aesthetic ran counterpoint to the surrounding assembly of buildings that frame the adjoining Lust Garten and Unter den Linden. The calls for rebuilding the Schloss Berlin, designed by the Prussian court architect Andreas Schlüter[11] are intricately wrapped-up with re-dreaming Schinkels Hauptstadt Traum[12] (Schinkels Capital City Dream). To accommodate this dream, a massive photo-realist depiction of the Schloss Berlin was erected on the Schlossplatz site in 1993[13]. Painted on plastic mesh (not unlike a film projection screen) and supported by a massive array of scaffolding, this depiction of the palace building retraced its outer boundary and blocked the Palast der Republik from view by covering most of its western facade. The photo-realist image duplicating the exterior of the former Hohenzollern Palace was a visual re-occupation of the site and the visualization of a hidden scene. The temporary reappearance of the Schloss Berlin gave an impression of what its proposed reconstruction would be like through a sort of test Marquette. The aim of the installation was to convey to the public that the proposal for the Schloss Berlin's reconstruction was dependent on demolishing the Palast der Republik. This idea was manifested through the construction of a large mirror (measuring approx.15x25 meters) attached onto the remaining visible western facade of the Palast der Republik. Visible from Berlin's grand boulevard Unter den Linden, the mirror reflected in perspective the painted picture of the Schloss, rendering the Palast der Republik invisible.

Destruction of Schloss Berlin 1950, courtesy of Landesarchiv Berlin/ F Rep. 290; 64/322.

5 The Schloss Berlin was heavily destroyed (but not beyond some say reconstruction) during WW2. Ideologically opposed to monarchy, the GDR decided that the palace be destroyed and the foundations covered with tar.

6 Documented in the papers detailing the quantity (in cubic meters) of rubble removed, and costs charged from both truck and barge carters. Source Landesarchive Berlin.

7 This inclusion could be read in two ways: as a demonstration of the developing socialist ideology of the GDR system, or as a massive propaganda stunt, the most successful in GDR's 50 year history.

8 Professor Heinz Graffunder (1923–1994), chief architect of the Palast der Republik, also built the Cottbus and Neukoelln Universities, GDR Embassy in Budapest, Stelzenhaus (Alexanderplatz) and apartment buildings in Marzahn.

9 The Palast der Republik's interiors were a mixture of ornamental and decorative treatments composed in the flair of the period. With strong accents on colour, fabric textures and furniture that visually encapsulated its visitors.

10 Seen as outwardly opposing its surroundings, the Palast der Republik's reflective glass exterior manages to capture the surrounding buildings. In that way it claws back the argument of Graffunder's brutal design aesthetic.

11 Andreas Schlüter (1659–1714) was born in Danzig and took his apprenticeship under the sculptor Saponius. In 1694 he moved to Berlin to became court sculptor. Returning from a study trip in Italy he was appointed construction supervisor of Berlin's Arsenal and Palace. 1702–04 saw Schlüter director of the Arts Academy. 1699–1708 Schlüter concentrated on the design and construction of the Schloss Berlin. In 1713 he left Berlin for St. Petersburg working for Czar Peter 1st. He died one year later in 1714.

12 This refers to Karl-Friedrich Schinkel's dream for a resolutely German architectural style, an interpretation of the neoclassical style of the late 17th and early 18th centuries. The embodiment of this style lies in the cultural institutions surrounding the Schlossplatz site. To complete this urban picture, the reconstruction of the Schloss Berlin (Schinkel designed the dome) is also dependent on the complete rebuilding of the Friedrich 1st Denkmal (memorial) and Schinkels Bauakadamie (architecture academy).

13 Led by Herr von Boddien, the Förderverein Berliner StadtSchloss (Palace Foundation) has been financially responsible, together with its sponsors for producing three temporary constructions of the Schloss Berlin.

The mirrored simulation of the *Schloss Berlin* acts as a testament to the power of its creators. The French philosopher Jean-Francois Lyotard establishes a concept for reflective power as "evincing its status as reflective judgment." Lyotard would have us know that such constructions create a position of visual submission for their spectatorship. In the *Analytical of the Sublime* he posits a visual context for the nature of reflection by declaring, "The 'weakness' of reflection is what also constitutes its 'strength'" (Lyotard 1994:2). Martin Heidegger in his essay *The Age of the World Picture* remarks that "Initially the word "picture" makes one think of a copy of something. To be 'in the picture' resonates with: being well informed, being equipped and prepared. Where the world becomes picture, beings as a whole are set in places as that for which man is prepared; that which, therefore, he correspondingly intends to bring before him, have before him, and, thereby, in a decisive sense, place before him" (Heidegger 2002:67). Heidegger's concept of "world becomes picture" sheds light on Lyotard's concept for reflective strength, in which the image created overpowers the real: 'to be' "in the picture...does not mean 'picture of the world' but, rather, the world grasped as picture" (Heidegger 2002:67). By simulating and mirroring the *Schloss*, its image is passed from maker to spectator, a consequence that connects with Guy Debord's seminal societal critique *The Spectacle in Society* in which the "...spectacle, as the perfect image of the ruling economic order, ends are nothing and development is all..." (Debord 1994:15).

When it stood, the *Schloss Berlin* was not a building that denoted public space for it was not a space for the public to inhabit. Even so, the public could traverse the *Schloss* via its second courtyard saving the time of having to go all the way around the building. The illusionary 1:1 depiction of the *Schloss Berlin* inadvertently re-activates the return of the gaze onto the public and its domination by the nobility. This re-activated *Schloss* returns the image of the building to the contemporary urban environment as a phantom apparition seeking the return of gazes long since forgotten. Lyotard tells us, "It's a strange ostentation of destination, to maintain and entertain posed paint. It has a relationship to time. The posed paint will not 'pass', it will always be now. That's the principle" (Lyotard 1991:144). The phantom apparition of the painted and reflected palace is now becoming reality. In his book *The Production of Space* the French theorist Henri Lefebvre suggests that space is in a constant state of flux and in an on-going process of invention and innovation: 'To speak of 'producing space' sounds bizarre, so great is the sway still held by the idea that empty space is prior to whatever ends up filling it' (Lefebvre 1991:15). One might ask what would it mean to reconstruct the palace without building? The opportunity to reconstruct without building has now passed, for *Schlossplatz* site is now being resealed back into history. Constructing without building introduces the second site to the project, this is a story of reconstruction as geography.

Geography – new forms for reconstruction

There is something profound about walking up *Teufelsberg* in Berlin's outer western district of Wilmersdorf. Firstly, it's a big hill in fact it comprises three hills. Secondly, it is man made; the highest point rising 115 metres and third, it is entirely constructed from the rubble of bombed-out buildings as a result of the Allied air war on Berlin in WW2. Given its association to death and destruction it is used as a veritable playground. In summer you can run and fly a kite there, stroll through the forest, picnic and swim in the *Teufelssee* (Devil's lake). In winter you can go tobogganing in the snow (I have done the latter two).

I have a collection of archive pictures taken during the construction of *Teufelsberg*. They show lots of dirt, rubble, bricks and other building materials along with trucks, truck drivers, hand-shakes and beer.

Top: Installation of scaffold construction, *Marx-Engels-Platz* 03.06.1993, courtesy of Landesarchiv Berlin/ Platow, Thomas F Rep. 290; 349670.

Middle: *Stadtschloss Attrappe, Marx-Engles-Platz Blick von Schlossbrücke*, 16.08.1993, courtesy of Landesarchiv Berlin/ Kasperski, Edmund F Rep. 290; 352809.

Above: *Stadtschloss Attrappe*, (detail of painting) *Marx-Engles-Platz, Blick von Schlossbrücke*, 16.08.1993, courtesy of Landesarchiv Berlin/ Kasperski, Edmund F Rep. 290; 352809

Top: *Palast der Republik* August 2003. Partial
demolition of facade. Photograph courtesy of author.

Above: *Teufelsberg* Radar station der US Streitkrafte,
(US radar Station) Sommer 1976, courtesy Landesarchiv
Berlin/ Siegmann, Horst F Rep. 290; C8795.

One picture shows a female driver sitting on the bonnet of a truck with a wide smile, a man in a long coat shaking her hand. Below, and attached to the truck's grill, is a sign containing a single digit followed by a number of 0's then M3 at the end. The figure stands for the amount of rubble in millions of cubic meters that had been carted from the streets of Berlin. This sign has 10,000,000 M3 written on it and the year is 1952[14]. Starting from the early 1950s to the mid 1960s and moving from black and white to those very typical brownish tones of the 1970s, the photographs I have accumulated are my ready made archive that charts the history of *Teufelsberg* from its planning in 1947 to its completion in 1968.

Accompanying *Teufelsberg* is seven *Trümmerberge* (rubble hills) located in Berlin's metropolitan regions that are also constructed from the rubble of bombed-out buildings post WW2. Collectively *Teufelsberg* and the *Trümmerberge* perform 'annihilation geography' out of and within the city of Berlin. Experiencing *Teufelsberg* and Berlin's *Trümmerberge* is to be part of the city's continuity with history and through the physical engagement with the invisible city under one's feet and vistas of the visible city falling away below. Theirs is a movement with history, in-and-out of history. Therefore, the construction of *Teufelsberg* and the *Trümmerberge* account for a visual yet invisible remembrance of Berlin pre and post war. Simultaneously, they also account for historical forgetfulness; anaesthetized by their performative geographies of high-rise walk-up public parks.

Berlin's movements within remembrance are formed in-and-out of its history of destruction and reconstruction. Yet Berlin's destruction had already been sought before the Allied bombing campaign by recalling Nazi Germany's master architect Albert Speer and Adolf Hitler's plans for a grand boulevard symbolizing the architectural aesthetics of *Das Dritte Reich* (The Third Empire). Speer developed this vast urban plan hand in hand with his famous treatise titled *Theory of Ruin Value*. Speer and Hitler's building schemes for Berlin, constructed in the lasting material of stone, were conceived to pass into ruins during the thousand years *Reich*. This passage from grandeur to ruin was supposed to produce a simulation that would simultaneously include Berlin as the third cornerstone after Athens and Rome in the classical ordering of modern civilization.

By the end of the war, Speer's 1000-year theory of ruins had reached its zenith in Berlin within three years (1943–45) through the Allied bombing campaign. In the manner of the sublime, Berlin's post war reconstruction saw Speer's plan realised not through grand architectural schemes to rival Athens and Rome but as new urban geographies. Berlin's entry into the triangle of classicalism with Athens and Rome and their seven hills, came in the form of their now shared geography in the construction of Berlin's seven hills – the *Trümmerberge* and the additive *Teufelsberg*. This sublime reordering of Speer's scheme supplants the poetics of nature that has inserted itself into Berlin. No longer a flat city, it is now a walk-up city, a city of views, topographies and geographical links[15].

My attention to *Teufelsberg* accounts for the opportunity to mount an archaeological excavation, something that is both seductive and repulsive to me. But I can't hide my attraction to the 'dig's' connection to the 'unearthing' of history and to the appearances and disappearances of urban environments through the practices of reconstruction.

On Disappearance – the anesthesia of space

Returning to my photographic archive, images of women, men, boys and girls, vast holes, trucks and rubble is to peer into the physical labour of *Teufelsberg*'s construction. The emptying of Berlin's mounds of rubble via a system of small trains and rail tracks that traversed the city's temporal topographies would reappear in the rise of *Teufelsberg*. Where there were no trains, women and men would push the carriages of rubble to awaiting trucks to be carted away. Besides the trucks, and rail carriages,

Top: *Teufelsberg* Frau Anatoniazzi and Bausenator Rolf Schwedler, 14.11.1957, courtesy of Landesarchiv Berlin/ Schütz, Gert F Rep. 290; 56575.Schwedler56575_14.11.1957

Bottom: *Teufelsberg rümmerschutt*, 1952, courtesy of Landesarchiv Berlin/ Schwab, E., F Rep. 290 F Rep. 290; 264853.

14 Other pictures show 21 million and 25 million. These achievements, accompanied by smiles are a cause for celebration in ridding rubble from Berlin's chocked streets – a vast undertaking given the city's complete annihilation.

15 The Speer/Hitler plan for Berlin came to emulate in a sublime way the city of Rome and Athens by recreating topographically their seven hills in the seven *Trümmerberge* (rubble hills) built from bombed-out buildings.

the clearing of rubble was a task carried out by hand and by tools of the hand. This hard labour of the hand singularly changed the geography of Berlin making possible the disappearance of the destroyed city to its reappearance as a hill.

Yet within this labour, on closer inspection of the images, the clearing away of rubble and the building of *Teufelsberg* repositioned Speer's *Theory of Ruin Value* to a new plan – a plan of physical emancipation. This psychological transference from the horrors of destruction to the hand of labour and the exhaustion of the work in shifting the ground of the city, established new associations to devastation and ruin. In his book *On The Natural History of Destruction*, W.G. Sebald charts the collective impartiality permeating every level of German civilian life and literature that awoke in the aftermath of WW2. He attributed a collective German forgetfulness to a "self anesthesia" "...shown by a community that seemed to have emerged from a war of annihilation without any signs of psychological impairment" (Sebald 2005:30). This, Sebald informs us, accounts for the lack of any substantial historical documentation, from a German perspective, of their horror and loss in the war. Sebald tells us that where there were accounts, they "...did not alter the fact that the images of this horrifying chapter of our history have never really crossed the threshold of the national consciousness"[16]. Sebald's "self anesthesia" finds its place in the spatial anesthesia contained in *Teufelsberg*. Like the forgetfulness in remembering names or places, the forest of tress, shrubs and flowers now covering the rubble of former homes and lives of Berlin pre 1945 is also the forgetting of that city post 1945. Out of *Teufelsberg* rises the self-portrait of forgetting, an image of looking away rather than a looking in[17].

In *Memoirs of the Blind – The self-Portrait and Other Ruins* Jacques Derrida conceives the self-portrait as self-ruining: "In the beginning there is ruin. Ruin is that which happens to the image from the moment of the first gaze. Ruin is the self-portrait, this face looked at in the face of memory of itself, what remain or returns as a specter from the moment one first looks at oneself and figuration is eclipsed." (Derrida, 1993:68) Derrida's articulation of the capturing of oneself in the act of self-portraiture is important for it somehow explains the self-ruining captured in the images of *Teufelsberg*. The subjects in my photographs can be defined by their ruining in the site in which they appear: "...for one can just as well read the pictures of ruins as the figures of a portrait, indeed, of a self-portrait" (Derrida, 1993:68).

Spatially thinking through my project *Teufelsberg* serves two purposes. The first allows for a constant change in the reading of the site. The second allows *Teufelsberg* to remain indifferent to the sediment of Berlin's lost urbanity. Through its disappearance and sublime reappearance as a hill, the everyday hard-labour of *Teufelsberg's* construction; the digging, carting and off-loading of millions of tons of rubble that 'shifted' the city of Berlin to its new resting place. This new geography of the phantom city buried, created the opportunity to recast the history of Berlin as a self-portrait of destruction and ruining. Through the constant reviewing of my archive of photographs the spatial performance of reconstruction is revealed in the portraits of the women, girls, boys and men. Their collective labour to the work at hand; hour by hour, day by day, year by year in the construction of *Teufelsberg* tells the story of people within ruins; physically and immemorially.

Top: *Teufelsberg* Women and men planting saplings (date not given), courtesy of Landesarchiv Berlin/ Sass, Bert F Rep. 290; 53748,

Bottom: *Feldbahnloren Konigsplatz, Platz der Republik*, Berlin, 17.06.1948, courtesy of Landesarchiv Berlin/ Gnilka, Ewald F Rep. 290; 172325.

16 The "images" Sebald has in mind is the annihilation of German towns and cities during WW2. "...the question of whether and how it could be justified was never the subject of open debate in Germany after 1945, no doubt mainly because a nation which had murdered and worked to death millions of people in its camps could hardly call on the victorious powers to explain the military and political logic that dictated the destruction of German cities". Sebald, W.G.,2004, *On The Natural History of Destruction*, Penguin, London, pp.11–13.

17 Sebald references the Danish reporter Stig Dagerman who on a train in Hamburg distinguished himself as a foreigner for "...no one looked out of the windows, and he was identified as a foreigner "because he looked out." pg.30

Future Practice – figuring spatial thinking

The future of my project has been spatially thought but not yet spatially conceived. Since revisiting this research and thinking where to turn, it became apparent what the future practice of this project could be. The peering into my archive of images, the acknowledgment to the labour of the hand that cleared the millions of tons of rubble from the streets of Berlin to build *Teufelsberg* and likewise the *Trümmerberge* has revealed a disappearance of another sort. Born out of a lack of acknowledgment (will?) in present day Germany to the thousands *Trümmerfrauen* (Rubble Women), boys, girls and men who laboured in the rubble of the 131 German cities and towns destroyed during WW2, I have encountered little for the remembrance of their part in the reconstruction of their country. I do know of a small statue of a woman; a standing figure representing a *Trümmerfrauen* not far from the Marx/Engels statue in central Berlin and one in Volkspark (People's Park) Hasenheide. Both statues, in the worthy material of bronze are hard to find; 'lost' as they are in the park also makes it at odds to the many visible statues and memorials to heroes (male and often war) throughout the world. Given that men make war and women clean it up, the project for *Teufelsberg* is to depict the realities of the *Trümmerfrauen*; the labour of their hands and the hardships endured in clearing away the rubble from Berlin's streets and further, to the building of *Teufelsberg* and the *Trümmerberge*. This future depiction, a memorial to their labour, comes not through the figurative form but through a figurative-ground archeology of extracted cores of rubble. Through 'unearthing' the surface of *Teufelsberg,* by drilling and extracting its rubble more than sixty years after it's building is to reform Sebald's concept of "self anesthesia" toward a series of self-portraits; standing monograms of core rubble to the *Trümmerfrauen* of Berlin.

References

→ Anderson, B., 2005, *The Architectural Flaw* – PhD (research by practice), RMIT University, Melbourne.

→ Debord, G., 1994, *The Society of the Spectacle*, translated by Nicholson-Smith, D., Zone Books.

→ Derrida, J., 1993, *Memoirs of the Blind - The self-Portrait and Other Ruins*, translated by Pascale-Ann Brault and Michael Naas, University of Chicago Press.

→ Hecksher, W. S., 1958, *The Anatomy of Dr. Nicolaas Tulp - An Iconological Study*, New York University Press.

→ Heidegger, M., 2002, *Off The Beaten Track*, edited and translated by Young, J., & Haynes, K., Cambridge University Press.

→ Lyotard, J-F., 1991, *The Inhuman*, translated by Geoffrey Bennington & Rachel Bowlby, Polity Press.

→ Ladd, B., 1997, *The Ghosts of Berlin; Confronting German History in the Urban Landscape*, University of Chicago Press.

→ Lefebvre, H., 1991, *The Production of Space*, translated by Donald Nicholson Smith, Blackwell Press.

→ Pollack, D., 1988 (edt.), *Exceptional Spaces*, The University of North Carolina Press.

→ Sawday, J., 1995, *The Body Emblazoned - Dissection and The Human Body in Renaissance Culture*, Routledge, London/New York.

→ Sebald, W.G., 2004, *On The Natural History of Destruction*, translated by Anthea Bell, Penguin Books, London.

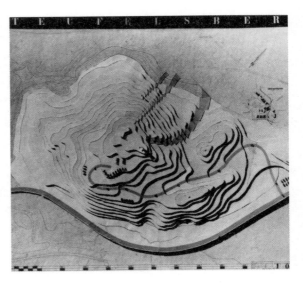

Top: *Teufelsberg Modell für die Aufschüttung* (Model for the Landfill), 24.06.1959, courtesy of Landesarchiv Berlin/ Zocher, Christian F Rep. 290; 65117.

Middle: *Teufelsberg Ruine der Wehrtechnischen Fakultat,* (Ruins of the Army Technical Faculty), 11.12.1951, courtesy of Landesarchiv Berlin/ Zocher, Willy F Rep. 290; 16083.

Above: *Teufelsberg* view to Charlottenburg (detail). In the background is Le Corbusier *Hochhaus* (Highrise), 11.08.1976, courtesy of Landesarchiv Berlin/ Ehlers, Ludwig F Rep. 290; 192987.

Suzie Attiwill
?interior, practices of interiorization, interior designs

?interior, practices of interiorization, interior designs contributes to the discipline of interior design by opening up and inviting new ways of thinking and practising interior. The motivation for this research was the prevalence of assumptions in relation to 'interior' and how—even though it is designed—the term 'interior' is rarely posed as a creative problematic.

Two questions have moved with the research. A formal PhD research question posed at the beginning: 'if one shifts from Cartesian and phenomenological concepts of object/subject relations, then what kind of interior(s) become actualised?' And a question connected with 'interior' – more of a tacit question engaged with by the practice and one which surfaced through the research with the question shifting from what? to when? where?, how? and which? – from interior? to ?interior.

These questions were posed through projects and practices of exhibition, curating, writing, craft, design and teaching. Here, exhibitions and other projects were experiments. Experiments not in a deductive way where a set of parameters were established beforehand and then tested. Instead they were experiments as a process of production engaged with the experiential world—materials, forces, chance, constraints—to see what can happen, what can be done, said and seen.

The PhD has enabled a way of positioning research through practice that values experimentation, experience and expression.

?interior is more of a proposition than an answer to a question, a posing of interior where the invitation is to attend to it as a design, as a question in relation to practise which as a creative problematic needs to be addressed each time anew; to place the question of ?interior in the world.

The following piece of writing rearranges the text produced for this PhD.[1]

1 Visit http://researchbank.rmit.edu.au/view/rmit:160402 for full text; http://vimeo.com/user3911530/videos and search 'Attiwill' for video of examination presentation and http://flic.kr/s/aHsjCAJCYD for still photographs of the examination taken by Ramesh Ayyar.

why?

This PhD was undertaken as an opportunity to address a practice situated in exhibitions and writing through an engagement with the discipline of interior design. Prior to undertaking this body of research, I had produced a series of exhibitions – each an experiment with the making of an exhibition. I was particularly interested in the material, spatial, temporal dimensions of exhibitions. I called myself an 'interior designer' rather than a 'curator' or 'exhibition designer'. Like interior designs, exhibitions involve the arrangement of things and engage with the production of spatial and temporal conditions to mediate between people and their surroundings. Exhibition objects and subjects also implicate ideas of interior and interiority.

Projects by artist Fred Wilson were, and continue to be, an important reference for this practice. In particular his curatorial projects where he re-arranges objects, labels, lighting and other design elements to produce different meanings. His project, *Mining the Museum* (1992–3) rearranged collections of the Baltimore Historical Society. For example, Wilson selected various objects made from metal and placed them in a showcase with the label 'metalware' and dated eighteenth century. The arrangement, which included ornate silver tableware such as candelabras as well as slave shackles, produced a potent encounter. Another rearrangement was titled *Frederick Serves Fruit* – an eighteenth century painting by Ernst G Fisher (1815–94) dated c1850 that depicted a wealthy Deep South American plantation family having a picnic lunch. Selected from the museum's collection, Wilson hung the work and changed the title on the label from *Country Life of a Baltimore Family* to *Frederick Serves Fruit*. He also changed the lighting from a flood which focused on the central party to a spot light which illuminated an otherwise unnoticed figure in the background – a young black boy serving fruit to the leisurely party. The renaming and focusing of the light illuminated another aspect of the surface and through the process of selection changed the meaning produced in the encounter from a celebration of the wealthy to a moving portrayal of slavery. These rearrangements manifest the potency of curatorial and design practices in the production of meaning, objects and subjects; the objects are the same objects, but rearranged. Different meanings are produced. As noted in the catalogue for this exhibition, Wilson explores 'not what objects mean but how they mean'.[2]

My practice in exhibitions highlighted certain assumptions in ways of thinking about objects, subjects and space that underpinned both exhibitions and interior design. Within the discipline of interior design, 'interior' is expressed as an entity—as 'the interior'—and interior is equated with space, usually described as 'void' or 'negative', and as enclosed space. The subject/viewer is another assumed given as a conscious self and one inflected by phenomenology.

An aspiration of the PhD was to engage with the thinking of the philosopher Gilles Deleuze. I have been reading Deleuze's writing since 1984. Then, and since, I have found reading Deleuze inspires a different way of thinking about a project, a proposition, a problem – life. Engaging with his ideas produces a sense of lightness and ability to move. Deleuze's dismissal of both phenomenology and the concept of interior as an already constituted and independent entity are challenging in relation to the discourse, practice and theories of interior design. Yet words such as 'in', 'internal' and 'inside' inflect through his thinking to position interior and interiority as productions rather than givens. The potential here in relation to a practice of interior design as one of designing interiors—as a production of space and subject—was and continues to be exciting.

The sky in the early evening of 22 November 2006 in Wagga Wagga while walking with Linda Lou during the installation period of *a matter of time*. Photograph: Linda Lou Murphy.

2 See Lisa Corrin, ed., *Mining the Museum. An Installation by Fred Wilson* (Baltimore, Maryland: New Press, 1994). 14.

what? how? which? where? when?

'What' is usually the key interrogative word used with research – 'What are you researching?' In one sense the response here is straightforward – the question of interior. However the question 'What is an interior?' has not been a useful one to pose and yet it keeps coming back, highlighting the challenges in moving from an understanding of interior as an entity. 'What' also produces a direction towards developing concepts – a new concept of interior. Led down this path several times during this PhD, one gets caught up in a process of defining and positioning interior beforehand – before doing; before practice.

A second research question located the question of interior in relation to the specific interests of my practice: 'if one shifts from Cartesian and phenomenological concepts of object/subject relations, then what kind of interior(s) become actualised?' The research involved a move from thinking and addressing interior, space, objects and subjects as things to thinking about the production of objects and subjects, processes of interiorization, objectification, subjectification and spatialization.

Exhibitions and other projects were approached as experiments: as a process of production engaged in the world—materials, forces, chance, constraints—to see what happened, what could be said and seen. Each project produced different momentums, directions, orientations and opportunities to experiment with interior designing. Questions of how, which, when and where became more useful to pose than 'what?'

This shift is expressed through a rearrangement of interior? to ?interior. Rather than focus on defining an interior through posing 'what is an interior?', moving ? before interior produces a pause, even a stumbling, before responding, before answering. ? before interior opens interior to the outside; to the current; to movement; and invites a response. Posing ?interior with each project creates 'a new problem … new orientations'.[3]

Three exhibitions compose the first half of the PhD: *SPACECRAFT 0701* (2001), *a matter of time* (2003–06) and *making relations* (2006). Each was a significant project in my practice and presented unforeseen opportunities to engage with the question of interior.[4] There were also two major writing projects *Between Representation and the Mirror. Tactics for interiorization* (2008) and *interiorizt* (written in 2011, published in 2013).[5]

SPACECRAFT 0701

My practice in exhibitions leading up to this PhD addressed spatial issues. I positioned this practice as interior design/exhibition design to make a deliberate distinction from curatorial practice. As a designer and curator of exhibitions I highlighted spatial design and spatial encounters between people, objects and space. The kinds of curatorial practices I challenged included the way objects were located in space that fixed them within an existing schema – the curatorial framework. An a priori approach where meaning pre-exists the encounter and the exhibition becomes a form of representation and the work becomes reduced to an illustration of the idea. Fellow curators referred to my practice as a spatial curatorial practice and me as a spatial curator.

SPACECRAFT 0701 was the first project of the PhD.[6] It was an exhibition that foregrounded an 'exploration of encounters'[7]; encounters with things not already fixed in advance of the encounter to be discovered or recognised. The viewer was invited to spend time with the surface effects of objects affected by lighting and spatial qualities without the implication of something to be recognised and identified in the process. Close encounters were encouraged through the selection and arrangement of the objects where spatial proximities produced different views, information and ideas. Here the practice of placing worked spatial

A photograph taken in a museological collection near the British Museum, 2005. Photograph: Suzie Attiwill.

3 Claire Colebrook, "The Joy of Philosophy," in *Deleuze and the Contemporary World*, ed. Ian Buchanan and Adrian Parr (Edinburgh: Edinburgh University Press, 2006), 214–227. This use of the question mark is another idea picked up from Deleuze and his posing of ?being 'to create a new problem … new orientations'. 225.

4 The projects composing the PhD have been actual events and as creative projects have been assessed as research outcomes. The exhibitions have been held in public galleries with public programs involving forums, talks and educational activities. With the three major exhibitions of the PhD, I have been invited and commissioned as a guest 'curator' to produce an exhibition for the gallery. The exhibitions have also been large in the sense of exhibiting the work of a number of participants — usually more than twenty. The exhibitions have been reviewed in newspapers and journals, and engaged with diverse and large audiences (a matter of time was viewed by 61,627 people according to the acquittal report prepared by the Tamworth Regional Gallery). Each exhibition has been accompanied by a catalogue and curatorial essay. There have also been a number of published essays, invited book chapters and peer-reviewed conference papers.

5 Suzie Attiwill, 'Between Representation and the Mirror. Tactics for Interiorization.' In *Interior Tools. Interior Tactics. Debates in Interior Theory and Practice*, edited by in Joyce Fleming et al, UK: Libri Publishing, 2011; and re-printed in *Interior Design and Architecture: Critical and Primary Sources*, edited by Mark Taylor, UK: Berg Publishers, 2013. Suzie Attiwill, "interiorizt." In *The Handbook of Interior Architecture and Design*, edited by Graeme Brooker and Lois Weinthal, UK: Bloomsbury Publishing, 2013.

6 Invitation to curate exhibition of craft and design for the Monash University Art Gallery (at that time located at the Monash University Clayton Campus). 17 July to 25 August 2001. Collected together within the three spaces of the gallery were objects by designers, craft practitioners, jewellers, interior designers, architects and visual artists.

7 Gilles Deleuze, *Proust & Signs*, Theory Out of Bounds (Minneapolis: University of Minnesota Press, 2000). 27.

and material conditions, as distinct from a curatorial approach that places objects in relation to a curatorial theme or narrative.

As one moved between the three galleries, sightlines were worked to destabilise the idea of a centrally-placed object – a key technique used in exhibition hangings where objects are placed centrally and in particular when viewed from one gallery into another, usually signalling a key work in the exhibition. Things were sited/sighted off-centre, sometimes with the back of the object facing the main approach – so people had to walk around to view the front or face of the object. Some invited/required people to walk up close to inspect; surfaces of some things became animated through movement producing moiré patterns, slipping from view, reflecting not only the viewer but surroundings. Like UFOs, each thing before it became object produced multiple encounters and invited viewers to suspend the imperative to find meaning – even if only momentarily. As singular sightings, UFOs land and make site specific – as distinct from being site specific. In this way, the exhibition was composed of singular sightings where meaning is not produced in relation to an existing context but emerges through encounters over the duration of the exhibition – becoming singular, one-off.

There was an on-going attempt in my practice at this time to shift the privileging of the object—to open up 'the "empire of the object" beyond its immediate boundaries'[8]—through an emphasis on the spatial aspect of interior design rather than thinking of space as a void where objects are placed in empty space and displayed in an autonomous kind of way. The concept of 'spacecraft' as a verb highlighted the activity of crafting space. This was a tactic to shift from the design of space as one which might concentrate on the container and architectural features to one which engaged with and explored space as a medium, as matter, in the manner of craft as a practice concerned with materials, making and techniques. The homogeneous space of the white cube was a medium to be worked.

As both an exhibition and a concept, 'spacecraft' engaged with the space of the white cube. The conjunction of 'craft' with space made space feel tangible and emphasised an idea of spatial production and space crafting in relation to interior design. Techniques included ways of working to activate the space. As a way of determining the arrangement of the exhibition, I continuously walked the gallery to actualise forces and think through potential encounters and connections: along walls, across spaces, around corners, in and out of spaces, in and out of the gallery building. Spatial choreography was a term I used to describe my approach to making/designing exhibitions – a choreography involving things, people and objects working spatial encounters to shift from the expected engagement with an object.

In SPACECRAFT 0701, the dominant relationship of subject and object as knower and known was not privileged.[9] The interior of the object as an embodiment of meaning and the interior of the subject as an autonomous independent sovereign entity (like the Cartesian subject of perspectival viewing) were side-lined even if temporality – to see what else might happen. Different forces were worked through the selection and valuing of craft – as object, as a mode of making, as UFO. Materiality, haptic encounters, phenomena, lighting, sightings, citings, sitings rendered experience 'meaningful not by grounding empirical particulars in abstract universals but by experimentation'.[10] Curiosity was encouraged.

SPACECRAFT 0701, Monash University Museum of Art, 2001: Danielle Thompson White Good One 2000; Gregory Bonsasera Super Uber Vase designed in 1999, this one made 2001; Susan Cohn See-through Doughnut designed in 1995, in production since 1996. Photograph: John Brash.

Still taken from video of curatorial floor talk, August 2001: Gregory Bonasera Super Uber Vase.

8 Bart De Baere and Irit Rogoff, "A Linking Text," in Stopping the Process? Contemporary Views on Art and Exhibitions, ed. Mika Hannula (Helsinki, Finland: NIFCA – The Nordic Institute for Contemporary Art, 1998), 129.

9 Alfred North Whitehead, Adventures of Ideas (Great Britain: Penguin Books, 1933). 204.

10 Inna Semetsky, "Experience," ed. Adrian Parr, The Deleuze Dictionary (Edinburgh: Edinburgh University Press, 2005). 89.

a matter of time

'It is useful to think of craft in terms of multiple temporalities'.[11] This quote from an introductory essay by Sue Rowley in *Reinventing Textiles* was a proposition I directed to myself while curating the 16th Tamworth Fibre Textile Biennial.[12] I carried it with me to different hotel rooms and studios, driving through rural landscapes, visiting townhouses in Australia Street, flying to Ramingining and Elcho Island in Arnhem Land while looking at work, meeting people and discussing their practice. The quote also made connections with interior and interior design for me, in particular through the reading of Elizabeth Grosz's *Architecture from the Outside* where she proposes the question of time in relation to inhabitation and a different way of thinking space: 'How can we understand space differently, in order to organise, inhabit, and structure our living arrangements differently? … It is central to the future of architecture that the question of time, change and emergence become more integral to the process of design and construction.'[13]

Grosz's focus on the question of inhabitation and living arrangements made connections for me to the practice of interior design and the fact that then, and still now, interior design is referred to a spatial design discipline and the temporal, while acknowledged in terms of the performative and programming, is understood in relation to space as an existing condition rather than as Grosz suggests in the production of space.

So while the connection between textiles, craft and temporality was the main focus of the exhibition, *a matter of time* became a vehicle for engaging with ideas addressing time and thinking in relation to interior and interior designing.

The *SPACECRAFT* exhibitions had hovered around a question of the movement of an exhibition – with the movement of objects from one space to another and the effects and affects produced through this process of movement and landings in different contexts.[14] The potential to experiment with this further was presented with the invitation to curate a touring exhibition. *a matter of time* toured to nine metropolitan and regional public galleries from December 2004 to September 2006.[15]

For each installation, I arrived three to four days before the opening to work/walk out an arrangement for the exhibition. This process evaluated not only the particular spatial aspects of the gallery but also involved an experience with movements and sightlines through the galleries, the dynamics between the works in relation to the situation and how I was affected by the work over the duration of the tour as different works became amplified and different ideas surfaced through the conjunction with other works. There was a sense of making the exhibition each time anew and of working spatial and temporal conditions of the situation in relation to dynamics and forces inclusive of works, people, spaces and circumstances.

Each installation was a singular installation of the exhibition – an arrangement responding to spatial and temporal dynamics, external and internal forces, the works themselves as well as between them. This shifted the emphasis from the spatial medium of white cube. There was a sense of crafting and an actualization of time where each exhibition was like an arrested moment where movement was temporarily slowed down through the process of arranging into a temporary consistency. There was a sense of being 'in' as distinct from an encounter with an object. There was a different kind of closeness/proximity from close encounters with *SPACECRAFT*.

The works in *a matter of time* changed over the duration of the exhibition. I became aware of how all things are in continual movement, how change is not reversible and how the idea of sameness is usually privileged over difference. Here, flux and change were foregrounded rather than things as stable entities. In a short piece titled 'Time & Space', the writer Michel Tournier says time 'is the very fabric of life' and notes time 'is distinguishable from space by its irreversibility alone'. *a matter of time* made palpable time

a matter of time installation, Bunbury Regional Art Gallery, May 2006: Meredith Hughes *Silence* 2002 and Sharon Peoples *Tracings* 2001. Photograph: Suzie Attiwill.

a matter of time installation, RMIT Gallery, July 2005: Sue Blanchfield *Made in Australia* 2002 and Andrew Nicholls *(Untitled) Time After Time* 2004-2006, Photograph: Suzie Attiwill.

11 Sue Rowley, "Craft, Creativity and Critical Practice," in *Reinventing Textiles*. Vol 1: Tradition and Innovation, ed. Sue Rowley (England: Telos Art Publishing, 1999), 1–20. 13.

12 The invitation from the director of the Tamworth Regional Gallery, Brian Langer, to curate the national touring exhibition came in 2002. The exhibition opened late 2003 and toured until 2006.

13 Elizabeth Grosz, *Architecture from the Outside. Essays on Virtual and Real Space*, Writing Architecture Series (Massachusetts: MIT, 2001). xix.

14 *SPACECRAFT 0701* — Monash University Museum of Art, Clayton from 17 July to 25 August 2001. Six objects from this exhibition were moved to another space and became *SPACECRAFT 1001*, in the gallery-foyer space of Level 11, Design Park, 522 Flinders Lane from 22 October to 21 December, 2001.

15 Tamworth Regional Gallery, RMIT Gallery, Gosford Regional Gallery, Jam Factory Craft and Design Gallery, Wagga Wagga Regional Gallery, Cairns Regional Gallery, Bunbury Regional Gallery, Object Gallery — Australian Centre for Design and Craft, Ballarat Art Gallery.

as this 'very fabric life' and drew my attention to the powerful potential of posing ?interior as a practice open to movement and in time.[16]

The experience in *a matter of time* produced a significant shift in my thinking from a practice of interior design as one addressing organized space and spatial relations to one which opened interior to movement and time – where movement is privileged and not subordinated to space as something that happens between established points in space; a shift from thinking interior in relation to objects in space to thinking interior designing in relation to time and how time affects and determines things, subjects and objects in an ongoing process of change.

making relations

making relations is the title of an exhibition I curated and designed for Contemporary Art Services of Tasmania (CAST). Invited as 'an outsider'—outside the state and the island—the brief was to curate an exhibition of Tasmanian craft and design for CAST's 2006 gallery program.

The role of outsider made the brief compelling as a project to take on as part of the PhD. By extending an invitation to me, the CAST brief had created a curious subject—an outsider interior designer—and I was keen to be cast in this role. Coming from an outside, the established view of interior design as a practice of designing from the inside out comes into question. So was the reverse then implied – a designing from the outside in?

I had been thinking about outsides and insides when I received CAST's invitation to become an outsider. In April 2005, Gini Lee and I convened a symposium on behalf of the *Interior Design/Interior Architecture Educators Association*. Titled *INSIDEOUT*, the symposium brought interior design and landscape architecture together with the aim of encouraging 'new thinking, research and teaching between interior and landscape discourse and practice'.[17] In convening the symposium *INSIDEOUT*, I was keen to bring inside and outside, interior and exterior together without a determining structure between them as a way of opening the given interiors of enclosed space and buildings that underpin the discipline of interior design. However, rather than a discussion about insides and outsides side by side, the focus and emphasis was on processes of production – framing, selecting, arranging to produce interiors and exteriors within an immanent world of relations.

Grosz, invited as the keynote speaker, presented a paper titled *Chaos, Territory, Art. Deleuze and the Framing of the Earth*. Her reference to the activity of the *Scenopetes dentirostris*, a bird of the Australian rainforest, made a strong connection for me to curatorial practice and interior design. Sometimes referred to as the *Brown Stagemaker*, this bird cuts—separates—leaves from a branch, which fall to the forest floor where it then turns each over 'so that the paler internal side contrasts with the earth'. After completing the arrangement, the bird returns to an overhead branch, fluffs out its neck feathers—which are pale gold at the roots—to sing 'a complex song'.[18] Working in an outside, the bird selects, highlights and rearranges to produce an interior through composing forces – a stage, a performance, a songster, a territory.

In relation to my PhD research, *INSIDEOUT* posed the question of interior and inside to exterior and outside as a production of composing forces. At the beginning, I posed interior? in relation to landscape; after, I was left thinking about ?interior and the potential of interiorizing as a process of separation and arrangement in a generalised exterior.

This thinking continued with CAST's invitation to be an outsider and through this – to become an outsider interior designer. Located outside required thinking about interior design practice differently from the established interior design approach of working from the inside out. The activities of the rainforest bird highlighted the potential of a curatorial

a matter of time installation, Object. Australian Centre for Design & Craft, 15 July 2006: Monique van Nieuwland looking at Louiseann Zahra's *my own time I spent sleeping* 2002, Photograph: Linda Lou Murphy.

a matter of time installation, Tamworth Regional Art Gallery, 10 December 2004: Linda Lou Murphy *drawing threads* 2004 to 2006. Photograph: Linda Lou Murphy.

16 Michel Tournier, *The Mirror of Ideas*, trans. Jonathan F. Krell (USA: University of Nebraska Press, 1998). 100.

17 Melbourne Australia, 22 to 24 April 2005. Visit http://idea-edu.com/symposiums/2005-insideout/ for lists of participants, symposium papers and details.

18 Grosz, "Chaos, Territory, Art. Deleuze and the Framing of the Earth." *IDEA Journal* (2005): 15–28. See footnote 8, 27. Here Grosz is referencing Gilles Deleuze and Félix Guattari, *What Is Philosophy?*, trans. Graham Burcell and Hugh Tomlinson (London: Verso, 1994). 184.

practice, as an act of selection and arrangement, in the production of a composition, a territory, a system.

The work I selected for the exhibition made relations which actualised exterior forces. I responded to works which made relations in a way that was not about control but invited forces of contingency, chance and energies. These works were then brought into an arrangement where the relations between them were worked and made; things that had not been brought together before, came together and produced something new. As an outsider interior designer, making relations as relations of making effected a shift from relations of 'is', which focus on what already exists and work from the inside out of intention and meaning embodied in the object, to relations of 'and' and this and ...

During this time—which included the experience of *INSIDEOUT* and *making relations* as well as the touring of *a matter of time*—my practice moved from an attention to working with objects in space and spatial encounters, as a spatial designer, where interior design practice was engaged through the design of exhibitions to one where curatorial practice became a way of thinking and practising interior design. Making relations became a focus of attention and experimentation.

making relations installation, CAST Gallery, April 2006: Pippa Dickson *Variable Coupling* 2006. Photograph: Suzie Attiwill.

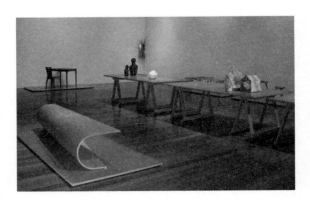

making relations installation, CAST Gallery, April 2006. Photograph: Suzie Attiwill.

urban interiorist

In 2008, I started using the word 'interiorist'. This naming was as much a provocation to my practice as it was a description of what I did: an interiorist interiorizes! This happened at a time when there was a change in my practice from one involving curatorial roles in exhibitions and the selection of objects to one of interiorizing, attentive to interiorization as a practice of arrangement. Becoming apparent during *making relations* and the tour of *a matter of time*, this shift became more pronounced through my involvement with the research group Urban Interior.[19]

In September 2008, Urban Interior held a two-week program in the galleries of Craft Victoria called *Urban Interior Occupation*. We played the word 'occupation' as both inhabitation and also work/occupation/practice. A set of business cards was produced for each Urban Interior member. This is when I came up with the term 'interiorist' for my 'occupation'. To be working in a space dedicated to craft was an interesting shift from the previous exhibition projects where I was invited to present craft in contemporary art spaces. This had the effect of making me aware of and sensitive to the value of craft in my practice as an interiorist. By this I am not referring necessarily to an idea of craft as skill so much as a kind of attention and care; an attention to making and a level of care and the potential this has then to unfold in encounters.

This awareness and sensitivity came to the fore when it was proposed that the gallery space remain empty of artefacts for the opening and also in between the different occupations. The emptiness had a sense of neglect and lack of attention; the architectural space was too strong. The forces and energies were stale and dormant. I felt the need for an interiorization that could activate the gallery and in a way that gave people a sense of expectation and stirred interest to return. I painted the words URBAN INTERIOR floor to ceiling height on a long wall that ran the length of the gallery using a low sheen white paint on a matt white wall. As people walked into the gallery, light coming in through the windows and from the lighting track was reflected differently on the painted wall. From different angles and at different times of the day, the words URBAN INTERIOR appeared and disappeared. The scale and softness of the letters made a tactile, haptic relation with people as they walked along and beside the wall. Qualities of light and movement were crafted and actualised; the vacant emptiness of the gallery was transformed into an interior of expectation.

19 Urban Interior was formed in 2007. RMIT academics from the disciplines of interior design, architecture, landscape architecture, industrial design, fashion, sound and performance-based practices were curated/ brought together by Professor Leon van Schaik, leader of the then Customising Space stream in the Design Research Institute at RMIT University. He called this group, Urban Interior. Coming from the interior design program with a strong trajectory of using the city of Melbourne as a laboratory for interior design projects, I was excited about this conjunction between urban and interior and the potential this invoked for further research.

'I am interested in the conjunction "urban and interior" in relation to the design of interiors and what a practice of interior design has to contribute to the contemporary city. ... The idea of urban interior challenges an assumption that interior design necessarily has to take place inside a building and shifts the focus to a relational condition – here the "and" between urban and interior as a question of designing and making the relation. This invites other possibilities for thinking and designing interiors—and the practice of interior design—as well as brings the sensibility and techniques of interior design to the urban environment. The character of the urban interiorist is introduced as a propositional figure to focus on questions of practice, techniques and constraints.'[20]

The idea of an urban room was the focus of a design studio offered to second and third year undergraduate interior design students in 2009. The studio brief asked students to design interiors within the urban environment of Melbourne.[21] Different practices of interiorization were presented including the concept of site specificity and working with built environment of cities. The *1748 Map of Rome* by Giambattista Nolli and Camillo Sitte's theories in the *City Planning According to Artistic Principles* (1889)[22] were references in how a city's built fabric can be reframed as a spatial assemblage of enclosures and openings. Another practice posed working with conditions rather than a site – rather than site specific, this practice makes site specific.

Beginning with movement rather than structure, conditions rather than the built environment, situations rather than sites, students were asked to document lighting and light, shadows; materials and immateriality; movements and flows, densities of circulation and stillness; behaviour; sound; historical layering; urban/city character; programs and activities such as eating, sleeping, meeting, selling, performing, shopping, public intimacies; seasons and weather; 24 hours and 7 days.

They were then asked to produce interior plans that did not rely on the built fabric to define the condition of interior in relation to interior/exterior boundaries. A student, Alice Kohler, observed a street vendor selling photographs who drew chalk lines to organise movement – an interior plan. She mapped movement where confluences of speeds and slowness produce densities and intensifications; interiorizations – like eddies in a stream.

Student projects addressed the flow/stream of people, goods, capital; a perceived anonymity of the city; the seeming disengagement of people in their habitual occupation of the city. Interior-making came between these flows and forces to produce interiors through processes of intensification. A proposition by another student, Sarah Jamieson, for an intersection made use of existing infrastructure such as public seating and trams and rearranged thermal forces to produce a warm interior: passing trams provided energy to heat water running through existing pipes and infrastructure; stopping trams become walls which periodically contain the heat.

The subject of an interiorist enabled a different way of thinking about my practice and the role of an interior designer as well as the potential of an interior-making within the urban environment: working within movement as an arrangement of forces, flows and energies to produce a temporary consistency which enables a different inhabitation.

In 2011, 'interiorist' became 'interiorizt' with a 'z'. This happened during the writing of an essay commissioned for *The Handbook of Interior Architecture and Design*. The essay became a concluding project of my PhD and one which makes a contribution to the discipline through posing ?interior.

urban interior occupation installation, Craft Victoria Gallery, September 2008. Photograph: Jacob Walker.

Situation analysis: street vendor, Swanston St, Melbourne, 2009. Photograph: Alice Kohler.

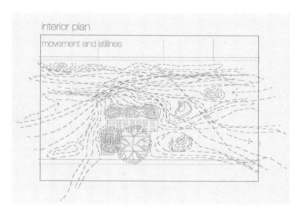

Alice Kohler *Interior Plan. Movement and Stillness* 2009. Drawing in response to the *Urban Room* design studio brief.

20 Suzie Attiwill, "Urban and Interior: Techniques for an Urban Interiorist," in *Urban Interior. Informal Explorations, Interventions and Occupations*, ed. Rochus Urban Hinkel (Germany: Spurbuchverlag, 2011), 11–24. 13. "A temporal consistency" in Davide Fassi (ed) *Temporary Urban Solutions* Rimini: Maggioli Editore, 2012 (published in English pp.147–155 and Italian pp. 179–185).

21 With RMIT Interior Design colleague Roger Kemp. Part of the 2009 State of Design Festival project – *2040 City*.

22 Camillo Sitte, *City Planning According to Artistic Principles*, trans. George R. Collins and Christiane Crasemann Collins (London: Phaidon Press, 1965).

inFLECTION

Posing ? beforehand is to pause and appreciate there are things we don't know; to open interior to movement and time. This is not a question mark in search of an answer or a set of principles which would preclude posing ?interior again and again, rather it is a question mark that invites practise. This is celebrated in interiorizt practice where interior becomes a singular unique production in time and space—a temporal consistency—each time anew, producing a multiplicity.

The research questioned the idea of pre-existing context and the value of establishing a structure beforehand in relation to interior designing, and also in relation to the production of knowledge. Deleuze is useful here as he encourages a move from knowledge to thinking. He is critical of knowledge as a knowing that comes beforehand as it produces an object of recognition—a reflection—and method as a process that 'protects thought from error'.[23]

For Deleuze, thinking happens through a shock that comes from the outside that causes one to think – to open up. This also involves a different idea of truth from ones based on coherence between propositions or correspondence to objective facts. Deleuze uses the word 'vivify' in discussing truth. 'Thus, to say something is true is not to say something verifiable in some way, but to say something that vivifies and alters a situation.'[24] This thinking has produced a way of engaging thought in practice; '… to think while making or rather while doing: to think as doing.'[25] The research has produced a capability to think – to pause and open up to the outside. This has enabled a way of positioning creative research that values experimentation, experience and expression.

Posing ?interior is the significant contribution of this PhD – to my practice and the discipline of interior design. It is a simple yet powerful gesture that poses the question of interior—opens it up to an outside of contingency, chance and variation—and invites an interior designing each time anew.

This research places the question of ?interior in the world.

PhD examination — exhibition and presentation, *?interior, practices of interiorization, interior designs*, RMIT Design Hub, Project Space 1, 17 October 2012. Photograph: Ramesh Ayyar.

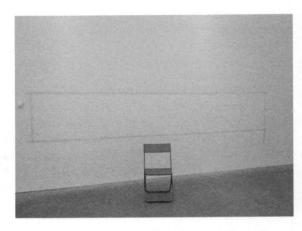

Installation in process — *?interior, practices of interiorization, interior designs*. RMIT Design Hub, Project Space 1, 12 October 2012. Photograph: Suzie Attiwill.

I would like to thank the following for their valuable contribution and support: Peter Downton as primary supervisor; Leon van Schaik; Norman Davis; Mick Douglas; Laurene Vaughan; Gini Lee; Susan Cohn; Linda Lou Murphy; Ramesh Ayyar; SueAnne Ware; Paul Johnston; Peter & Judy Attiwill; students and postgraduate candidates I have worked with and supervised — whose practices and thinking have informed, challenged and inspired me; everyone involved with the projects — participants, gallery staff, colleagues; and RMIT Interior Design colleagues.

23 Ronald Bogue, *Deleuze and Guattari* (London, New York: Routledge, 1989). 18.

24 James Williams, "Truth," *The Deleuze Dictionary*, 289.

25 Grosz, *Architecture from the Outside*, 59.

Nigel Bertram
Making and Using the Urban Environment:
Furniture, Structure, Infrastructure

The collection and arrangement of previously published and built works, interspersed with reflections on topics which have arisen through the doing of those works, is done with the aim of putting forward an idea about urban architecture. It attempts to make clear a line of thinking which has been implicit in the individual works produced over the past ten years, but perhaps not fully articulated. This argument is to be understood, however, not as a historical account, but in the present: as the current iteration of a cumulative position, developing continuously through the repeated act of doing projects and working with others.

A strategy of concentrating on the very large (urban) scale and very small (material/experiential) scale is used as a method of avoiding or bypassing the middle scale which is the usual scale and preoccupation of architecture. This middle scale is that of the 'object', the whole thing, in isolation and complete. It is the scale on which form is often studied, modelled, considered and communicated.
By comparison, the very large is the scale of infrastructure, or shared metropolitan systems, and the very small is the scale of furniture, or personalised and highly-responsive micro-environments.materials, fittings (how the urban environment is made).

(In certain cases it could be argued that the architecture has itself become furniture; or acts like furniture in relation to its environment.)

The first question is how to think about the making (or fixing) of such pieces in relation to thoughts on the making of the primary spatial enclosure. In the Somers House this issue came into focus, as the fittings required for domestic life were one of the key differences between occupying this structure as a dwelling and occupying it as an agricultural building or shed. In a house more furniture is required. The fittings came into two categories; off-the-shelf proprietary items, and purpose-made items. We treated each as clearly distinct from the primary enclosure though essential to the composition as a whole. The effect is that items such as the outdoor shower, light fittings, or custom-made hanging rails are deliberately 'placed-on', rather than integrated-into or concealed-within the building. That is, their role as 'fixtures' is explicitly maintained. There is an implication that these items could simply be removed, pulled off, and the building could revert back to another type of use. This effect heightens an understanding of the current occupation as provisional or contingent, and the non-seamless, non-integrated quality in relation to the architecture points to these furnishings as moments of customisation.

How to structure the material is really the subject of this PhD (how to find order in a field of inter-related and complex things). The structure of what is presented defines what is important at this point, and like the work itself, aims to clarify a found and evident condition through revealing the forces which produced it and the way it appears in the world.

The text in the project folios is taken from presentation of the works at the time of their completion, and is a direct explanation of the components of each project from the designers' point of view. The booklet texts are new, and cumulatively form the framing essay or exegesis for the works and the process of making them. Each starts with a reflection on a particular topic, which is an attempt at a conclusion or summary set of principles. This is generally written in the third person, but the examples or evidence is always specific, written from a particular instance of my/our experience. This type of creative enterprise is inherently collaborative, and hence there is an interchangeability or equivalence between "I" and "we" in the first-person texts and accounts of projects.

The booklets each finish with a section "Discussion" in which selected works of others which have been important or influential in the process of designing are noted. Taken together, these sections form a literature review and project review for the document as a whole. Each work is discussed as part of a living field or community of works which inform and relate to our own works, and I have chosen to discuss quite specific aspects of each example to explain their relationship to the topic of the particular booklet, even though each work referred to has multiple layers of relevance. I hope that taken as a whole, read perhaps both backwards and forwards, these layers and the matrix of connections between them are made evident.

PhD folder, contents page.

Thoughts about order and openness

The final PhD document is arranged into a series of booklets and folios. Each is intended to be able to be read independently, and to stand on its own either as the description of a single work, or as a summation of thoughts on a certain topic as developed and demonstrated over a series of works. Taken as a whole, the collection of booklets adds up to a cumulative argument. As a group they describe a reflective practice through documenting what has been done in a systematic and structured way.

The booklets and folios as individual entities should be able to be read in any order, but for the purposes of structuring this presentation they have been given numbers and placed in sequence. The matrix, however, is multi-directional. Each discussion is not intended in any way to be comprehensive on the topic, but to demonstrate through comparative examples how a specific addressing of each topic has arisen through a series of completed, concrete works. The topics are intentionally broad. Each could be the beginning of another investigation, the start for a new project, a future design studio brief or just a reflection on a fragment of architecture.

Given this structure and the need for each booklet to be able to stand independently, some repetition of material is inevitable. This serves to reinforce certain points, and to show how a particular approach or solution can be understood both in relation to other decisions made within the same work, or by comparison to similar investigations and decisions made across a series of different works over time.

How to structure the material is really the subject of this PhD (how to find order in a field of inter-related and complex things). The structure of what is presented defines what is important at this point, and like the work itself, aims to clarify a found and evident condition through revealing the forces which produced it and the way it appears in the world.

The text in the project folios is taken from presentation of the works at the time of their completion, and is a direct explanation of the components of each project from the designers' point of view.

The booklet texts are new, and cumulatively form the framing essay or exegesis for the works and the process of making them. Each starts with a reflection on a particular topic, which is an attempt at a conclusion or summary set of principles. This is generally written in the third person, but the examples or evidence is always specific, written from a particular instance of my/our experience. This type of creative enterprise is inherently collaborative, and hence there is an interchangeability or equivalence between "I" and "we" in the first-person texts and accounts of projects.

The booklets each finish with a section "Discussion" in which selected works of others which have been important or influential in the process of designing are noted. Taken together, these sections form a literature review and project review for the document as a whole. Each work is discussed as part of a living field or community of works which inform and relate to our own works, and I have chosen to discuss quite specific aspects of each example to explain their relationship to the topic of the particular booklet, even though each work referred to has multiple layers of relevance. I hope that taken as a whole, read perhaps both backwards and forwards, these layers and the matrix of connections between them are made evident.

The final booklet is a transcript of an extended converstion (with Kim Halik) in which we discuss some of the external relationships generated by the NMBW works included in the PhD. A number of key influences and associations arise naturally, in the same mode and as an extension of many similar conversations which took place during the design process itself.

This discussion captures the spirit and thinking behind the works very naturally, while also introducing new questions, and areas for further inquiry.

PhD folder: Nigel Bertram 2010. Lever-arch file containing 18 individual booklets, each stapled and punched.

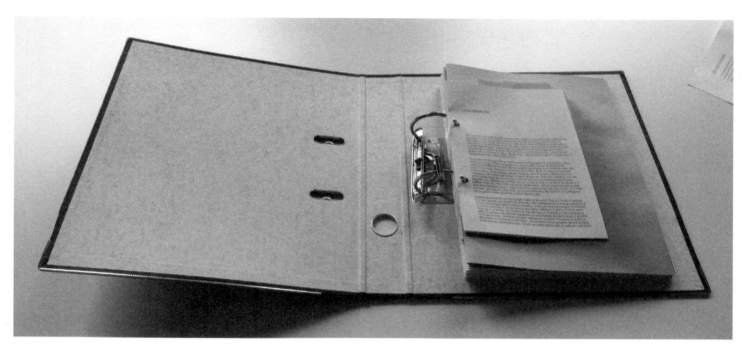

Top: PhD folder and loose booklets.

Bottom: Lyons Office, NMBW Architecture Studio 2009.
Image from 'project folio' 2010. Original photo by
Peter Bennetts

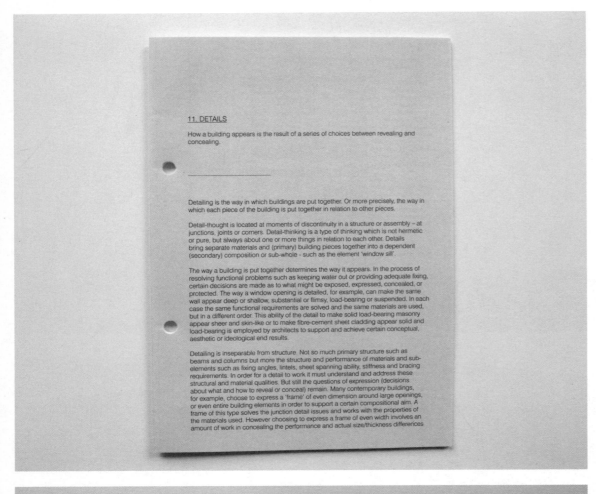

11. DETAILS

How a building appears is the result of a series of choices between revealing and concealing.

_____

Detailing is the way in which buildings are put together. Or more precisely, the way in which each piece of the building is put together in relation to other pieces.

Detail-thought is located at moments of discontinuity in a structure or assembly – at junctions, joints or corners. Detail-thinking is a type of thinking which is not hermetic or pure, but always about one or more things in relation to each other. Details bring separate materials and (primary) building pieces together into a dependent (secondary) composition or sub-whole - such as the element 'window sill'.

The way a building is put together determines the way it appears. In the process of resolving functional problems such as keeping water out or providing adequate fixing, certain decisions are made as to what might be exposed, expressed, concealed, or protected. The way a window opening is detailed, for example, can make the same wall appear deep or shallow, substantial or flimsy, load-bearing or suspended. In each case the same functional requirements are solved and the same materials are used, but in a different order. This ability of the detail to make solid load-bearing masonry appear sheer and skin-like or to make fibre-cement sheet cladding appear solid and load-bearing is employed by architects to support and achieve certain conceptual, aesthetic or ideological end results.

Detailing is inseparable from structure. Not so much primary structure such as beams and columns but more the structure and performance of materials and sub-elements such as fixing angles, lintels, sheet spanning ability, stiffness and bracing requirements. In order for a detail to work it must understand and address these structural and material qualities. But still the questions of expression (decisions about what and how to reveal or conceal) remain. Many contemporary buildings, for example, choose to express a 'frame' of even dimension around large openings, or even entire building elements in order to support a certain compositional aim. A frame of this type solves the junction detail issues and works with the properties of the materials used. However choosing to express a frame of even width involves an amount of work in concealing the performance and actual size/thickness differences

Selection from
Chapter 11, *Details*.

aware of their particular qualities: qualities in the material's own right, in comparative relation to other adjacent materials, and in relation to the construction ensemble as a whole.

C-D face plywood
Even though it is sometimes associated with cheapness, plywood is not the cheapest of available surface lining materials. It is, however, one of the most efficient, in that it performs on many levels at once. Plywood has a set of definite, discernible properties which can contribute to the construction process and also, importantly, have a type of resistance, meaning that these properties can still be understood in the final finished work:

1) It has equal bracing strength equally in all directions, and hence provides a structural membrane if fixed correctly. 2) It has a relatively strong, self-supporting edge – there is no need to trim or cover with architraves, skirtings, or other products used to cover less durable sheet linings. 3) It has a definite grain and figure which exerts a presence on the space and has a strong ornamental effect. This grain shows through any applied protective surface finish, such as oil, stain or paint. 4) It is able to withstand the weather, and can be used both internally and externally.

In all of these attributes plywood is the opposite of plasterboard. Plasterboard is homogenous, neutral, weak on its edge, requires paint, and cannot be used externally without protection. Its material properties are generally neutralized or obscured through the building process of stopping up, trowelling and painting. With the use of plywood, by comparison, it is possible to construct in a way where one is more conscious of the surface cladding, and hence also more aware of the act of cladding which has occurred.

The resistance/ presence of plywood, both physically and aesthetically, within a space means that the surface lining is not a neutral background or describer of form, but becomes active – operating more in an (ambiguous) middle-ground position within the overall architectural composition. Staining of the surface, which we generally have used in linseed oil, white or black semi-transparent coatings, transforms the material but also retains an understanding of its grain (its material presence). You are always aware of its underlying properties, and hence the structural similarity that

13.2

13.3

Sorrento House under
construction, NMBW
Architecture Studio 2009.

between top, sides and base of any penetration or structural unit.

It is important to acknowledge that every detail does this to a certain degree. However in certain junctions or assemblies the way in which this revealing and concealing has been done, and the reasons for it are more apparent than others. The way a building junction is assembled, if done logically and judiciously, can describe both the nature of the problem being solved and the qualities of the materials and elements which form the solution. We have observed that it is often in situations of very tight economy or pragmatic necessity where this occurs: where the nature of the question is evident in the answer provided.

By studying examples where cost and efficiency have driven the solution, rather than aesthetic goals or beliefs, the nature of material structure and performance can be more finely learnt. There is a raw expediency in such examples as agricultural or industrial details, where nothing superfluous is included; in fact elements of conventional details are left out if at all possible, to reduce constructional complexity and cost. This leaving-out of superfluous elements, together with a straightforward and direct approach to the problem at hand, underlines the clarity and self-evidently didactic nature of these 'primitive' solutions.

The question of detailing is also related to the question of size. Many everyday decisions an architect has to make are decisions of dimension; how thick a tabletop is, how wide or tall an opening, how deep a fascia, how low a ceiling, what diameter a column... These decisions are usually arrived at by balancing the operational requirement with the overall impression or aesthetic effect desired, or by considering notions such as proportion or a module or datum across the building as a whole. In a purely pragmatic environment, by contrast, the answer will always be "as little as possible", combined with "whatever is easiest". These two parameters are often at odds with each other, as the relative value of materials versus labour changes over time, as does the notion of what is standard practice. (For example, web-truss beams common in the 1950s are a highly efficient use of steel, but are rarely used today due to the high labour content in comparison to hot-rolled sections. The ongoing cost of maintenance is also a factor due to their comparatively large surface area)

11.2

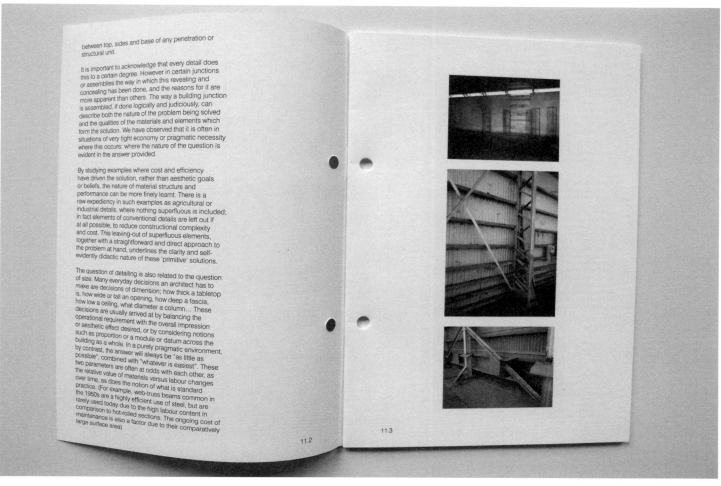

11.3

Grain storage shed, Nhill railway station.

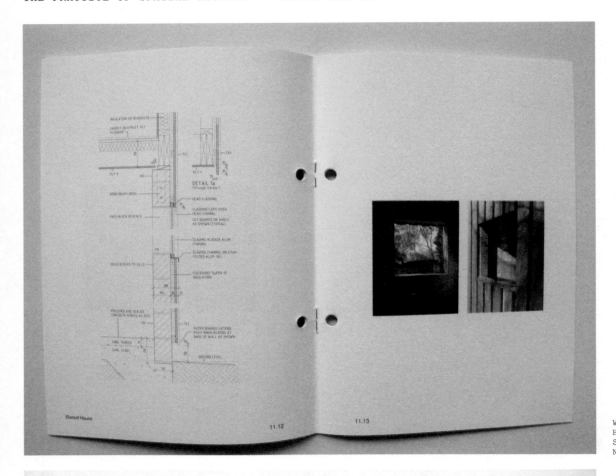

Window details, Elwood
House, NMBW Architecture
Studio 2007. All photos
Nigel Bertram

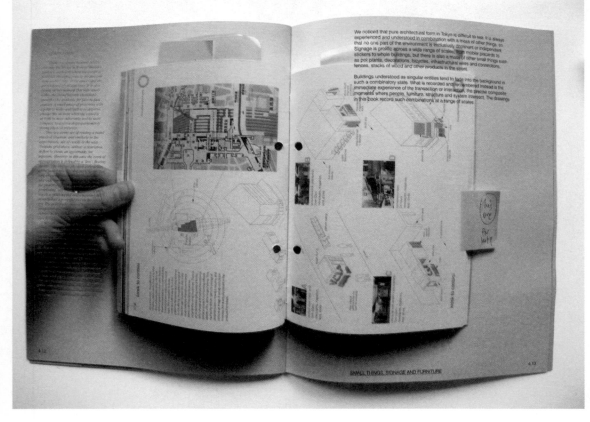

Pages from folio:
By-Product-Tokyo,
2010, showing original
publication from 2003
with annotations. A book
within a book.

An exhibition was designed as a performance space for the adjacent examinations of both Paul Minifie and I. Tables and chairs were arranged so that examiners and audience were seated within the exhibition — as participants rather than spectators.

Models from the office show a literal working process, and provide a three-dimensional experience not possible in the booklets or oral presentation.

Models by NMBW Architecture Studio, produced over the period 2000-2010. Tables designed by NMBW Architecture Studio for RMIT Building 45 (2008) with glass tops added for exhibition. Exhibition design by Nigel Bertram and Paul Minifie, Guildford Lane Gallery. Melbourne, 2010. Photos by Peter Bennetts.

What the suggestion here is that you put a boundary around a plot of land and then you have that building along the edge of it. Which is a bit like the Smithsons...

NB: ...the Smithsons' Upper Lawn Pavilion, which is an example that keeps on coming back. [Alison and Peter Smithson, *Solar Pavilion*, Upper Lawn, Fonthill Estate, Wiltshire, 1959-1962 (9,10)]

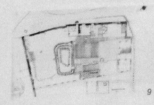

ON THE SUBURB...

NB: In Elwood, in order to get the car in you couldn't really have a post on the corner, and there's an easement beside the site which really isn't a road, it's just a gravely bit that belongs to Melbourne Water. The building literally follows and describes the boundary but the use doesn't. So the use of the car has to cut through the site, and then the use of the kids who walk to school sometimes cut the corner and sit on this rock, and also the use of this porch; looking out the other way (towards the canal). The ground surface is literally the same. So we in a way erased the plot boundary, but also reinforced it (11).

KH: It strikes me; it's a very courageous act, both on the client's part and yours. Because a lot of clients would just freak out at the idea that the internal space of their property is just so literally open. You know kids could just come in there and spray can and do whatever they like... and the interesting thing is they probably wouldn't...

16.8

NB: ... they don't: When they put up their previous fence, a paling fence, it was graffitied in about three minutes, but this one – touch wood – has not been graffitied yet. We have a few sensor lights around, which are lighting entry gates and things.

KH: But what is also interesting about this is the sense of the informality in the way the ground plane is used, this is really to me, this is like Jeparit, this is almost like a little fragment of what you did in Jeparit. Its interesting this sense of finding - in the middle of the city, I mean it really is in the middle of the city - almost a fragment of some kind of rural condition...

This is a clear connection but one that I had not fully realised before. In 2004 NMBW had studied the soft edges of roads and paths and the rich potential of undefined and loose spaces found in the small Victorian wheat belt towns of Rainbow and Jeparit, with a broad team of collaborators including Kim Halik and one of the clients for the Elwood House, Carey Lyon (Rainbow + Jeparit Urban Design Plan, 2004).

NB: That's literally the gravel or 'soft edges' as we called them in Jeparit, where the road just merged with the verge (12)... there are lots of empty sites with no fences in the country. And we discussed it with the clients; you know you couldn't do that with any normal client, we didn't really have a normal client. This idea that you give something away in order to gain something; by giving that piece of land a porosity, by giving something up, you also then gain the 'borrowing' of this whole space out here [beyond the boundary] as an extension of the site. It works in two directions; by removing the fence and making the boundary informal.

KH: In this sense I think you've reconnected with the suburban utopian tradition (NB: laughs) in Australian culture. No seriously, like with [Walter Burley] Griffin, what he did with the backs of the properties in Eaglemont where he had that communal area and there were no fences... [Walter Burley Griffin, *Mount Eagle Estate*, Heidelberg, 1914; and *Glenard Estate*

An edited collection of these projects and writings has been published in full by Ashgate Publishing (London) in their new series 'Design Research in Architecture':

Nigel Bertram, *Furniture, Structure, Infrastructure: making and using the urban environment*

ISBN 978 1 4094 4927 0
268pp, paperback
November 2013

Richard Black
Site Knowledge in Dynamic Contexts

The PhD commenced with the question: what are the consequences for a range of architectures of living with the River Murray — rather than living against the River Murray?

The PhD is concerned with the construction of site knowledge and how this is transformed into knowing where and how to intervene in a river system close to ecological collapse. It involves three overlapping topics:

→ **Site knowledge and its impact upon the design process**

→ **Development of tools and techniques appropriate for working on a particular type of site condition: the threshold between land and water**

→ **Transitory: the impact of dynamic processes and events on inhabitation**

Site knowledge emerges from a process of investigating a location. It is generated by on-site and off-site operations. This involves the architect in a dynamic set of relationships — between encounters on the ground in the here and now, with more remote encounters with the site from the studio and archive. This mode of site study amplifies the impact of scale shift and it exposes the variable and provisional status of a location, while also providing a way of operating in environments that can be considered dynamic. The PhD is premised upon the need for a work to relate to its surrounding environment.

Introduction

Dynamic contexts occur at the convergence of land and water. As water recedes and advances along a shoreline it creates a landscape of change. The River Murray is Australia's second longest river and has been likened to a long inland shoreline. When settler Australians first encountered the Murray, they found an unpredictable river governed by cycles of flood and drought. Big floods would spill out across the land for up to 20 kilometres from the main channel, whilst drought periods saw the water recede exposing the river bed. During the early part of the twentieth century, dams, weirs and barrages were constructed along the length of the river transforming it from a wild river into an irrigation canal. Now, too much water is extracted from the river and its natural flow regime has been inverted, bringing the Murray close to ecological collapse. Ecologists realise that the cycles of flood and drought, that regulation had minimised, are part of a river's ecological life. Current thinking argues for a return to a variable flow pattern, and it is this point of view that is embraced by the project work of the PhD. But while the ecological benefit of a variable river has been well documented, there has been little discussion of its impact upon the river towns or the land-uses that presently occupy the floodplain. Living with the River Murray is a proposition to embrace a future where land-use and ways of inhabiting a floodplain do not compete with its ecological processes. The project work of the PhD sets out to examine the floodplain and its river, as a means to develop a range of amphibious architectures that are mapped closely to its terrain, derived from, and working with, the process of the river's rehabilitation.

Top: Murray River Flood, Renmark, South Australia, 1956. (Image SLSA: B23213)

Bottom: Co-existence of everyday life around inundation. Murray River, Mannum, South Australia, 1956. (Image SLSA: B23201).

Structure of the PhD

The PhD is structured into four parts. These are: Site, Mapping the River Murray, Living with the River Murray, and then finally Conclusion: Designing the Site. Chapter summaries are outlined below. The first chapter situates the research and how it addresses perceived gaps in the field. The subsequent chapters then proceed to map out the various directions of the design research. Finally, in the conclusion I reveal a way of generating site knowledge that can have a significant impact upon the design process.

1. Site

The research is located within the field of site study and its influence upon the design process. A site is seen as dynamic place possessing shifting spatial and conceptual relations with its surrounding context. The research is positioned to straddle a perceived gap that exists between site analysis and design. This is clearly evidenced by the lack of architectural literature that adequately accounts for the transition between site processes and design. Project work of the PhD straddles this space, making a more coherent transition between how a site is approached, invented, and then how these operations motivate knowing how and where to intervene in a location. The hinged meaning between the terms a site and to site have relevance to the design process. A site, as a noun, suggests a specific place, such as a plot of land, whereas the verb, to site, suggests that a work will be placed in relation to other things. Site knowledge is thus generated through the act of describing a place, through the act of making drawings and other descriptions of that place. It generates ways of conceptualising a site and leads to action: knowing how and where to intervene in a location. Through the hinged relationship of a site and to site I proceed to build an argument for a site specific design practice. At the heart of my argument is the proposition that site can exert a formative influence upon the design process. But, this requires a more creative exploration of a sites full potential in the formative stages of a project; only then can it motivate where and how to intervene in a location.

Below: Landscapes of the Murray River, distance 2500kms, 1999–2008.

Above: Interrelationship of the existing river channel, the shoreline of the 1956 flood, the river towns

2. Mapping the River Murray

This marks the commencement of the project work of the PhD and is structured into three chapters. Mapping the Murray charts the techniques used to construct an understanding of a river system.

2.1 Inventing a site: the River Murray.

This is the beginning of transforming a river into a site. It examines three different ways in which the river was approached: from the archive, from the ground, and from above. These are strategic techniques used to examine a location implicating scale change and time as integral for engaging place. Material from the archival work generated a new drawing of the River Murray that explored three relationships: the flood river, the existing river channel and the survey grid of each town. Another sequence of encounters with the river, this time from the ground, generated an intimate understanding of the spaces depicted in the line drawing. I travelled thousands of kilometres, driving to and along the river, walking it, canoeing along part of it, crossing it and living temporarily by it. Over this period I progressively worked my way along its length, from its upper reaches at the Hume Reservoir, to its estuary in South Australia. Photographic documentation assembled these journeys as a sequence to be read in relation to the drawn line. And in the process, the River Murray began to be defined through the presence and absence of water; a flood river (floodplain), a drought river, and the river of the present. While this phase of the study revealed the immensity of the Murray it also formed an overview of the river towns and their precarious siting on its floodplain.

Right:
Shoreline to Shoreline. July 2001, 24 Kilometres. A walk across the Murray River floodplain. Calperum Station, South Australia.

2.2 Transitory.

Water Theatre was a commissioned work for the visual arts program of the Melbourne Festival. It required the making of an installation for a laneway on the city campus of RMIT University. While it was physically distant from the river, it became a project where I could develop a way of working with water on an intimate scale. For me it provided an opportunity to shift scale to work at one-to-one on a project that would be constructed. From the distance of Melbourne, the river provided a conceptual context for the work: firstly, to make a transitory work informed by the dynamic flood events being discovered along the river; and secondly, to explore the potential of water as material. The installation grew out of a close understanding of the physical context as a site already filled with a presence of activity. The installation explored what a transitory occupation of the lane might be. Water was pulsed into its spaces to resonate with the memories of flood events along the Murray. As a transitory event, the interaction between the planned and the unexpected was seen as a significant outcome. Additionally this project introduced the political implications of water use, which took me into further reading that would contribute to the next chapter.

2.3 Mobile Landscapes.

This chapter articulates a proposition for living on the floodplain and consolidates a broad range of subject material. It summarises my understanding of the river threading a path through the archival material and journeys, and then relates these to other disciplinary areas of knowledge on the river, particularly its ecology, management and politics. The key issue to emerge was that the flood was seen as a normal event for the river. Its floodplain was understood as a mobile landscape defined by the absence and presence of water. This created a set of specific conditions that could be directed back onto each town to challenge their future. How might the towns begin to live with the river? This text was a significant turning point for the project work of the PhD where the various topics began to converge and the study of site informed possible projects. But what was not yet clear was how these descriptions of the River Murray could impact upon the verb understanding of site: that is to know how and where to intervene in a location.

> "Billie and Les Mitchell grew up during the 1930s in Echuca's regularly flooded Shinbone Alley, an area inhabited by itinerant workers, timber cutters and other trades people. During the 1930s, as flood waters rose each year, Billie's father hung their furniture on hooks attached to the ceiling. A dining table and chairs made of water-loving red gum were left where they stood. The doors and windows were left open so water could flow freely through the house, and the family would move into a rented home in town. When the flood waters receded, their house would be freshly painted and they'd move back in." [1]

Above: Watertheatre installation, October 2002

1 P Sinclair, The Murray: a river and its people, Melbourne University Press, Melbourne, 2001, p 213

3. Living with the River Murray

3.1 Amphibious Architectures.

The text Mobile Landscapes summarised key issues from which I framed five teaching programs for the design subject stream at RMIT University. Moving the research into a teaching environment offered a way of exploring several locations along the river in further detail. Interventions were revelatory, marking the territory of the floodplain with building and landscape elements. More importantly, the design studio offered me an opportunity to spend time in communities along the river to gain an intimate understanding of the issues raised in the previous section – but this time from the perspective of being on the ground. Towns identified as sites for a studio program were selected for their relationship to the floodplain and inundation. Site visits proved to be invaluable, and the significance of off-site and on-site operations became apparent. This shift into a teaching environment, also suggested a way into an architectural scale of engaging the Murray, which thus far had been hindered by the immensity of scale encountered in the mapping phase of the study. While the studio phase of the study solved the scalar problems and established rules for selecting particular sites, they did not sufficiently engage with the range of site material now accumulated between the scale of the town and the scale of the river.

Left: Amphibious Architectures: Murray River design studio featured in the Australian exhibit, 2nd Rotterdam Architecture Biennale, 2005.

Below: A Mobile town: buildings being moved from Tallangatta to the new town site on higher ground, to avoid flooding, 1954.

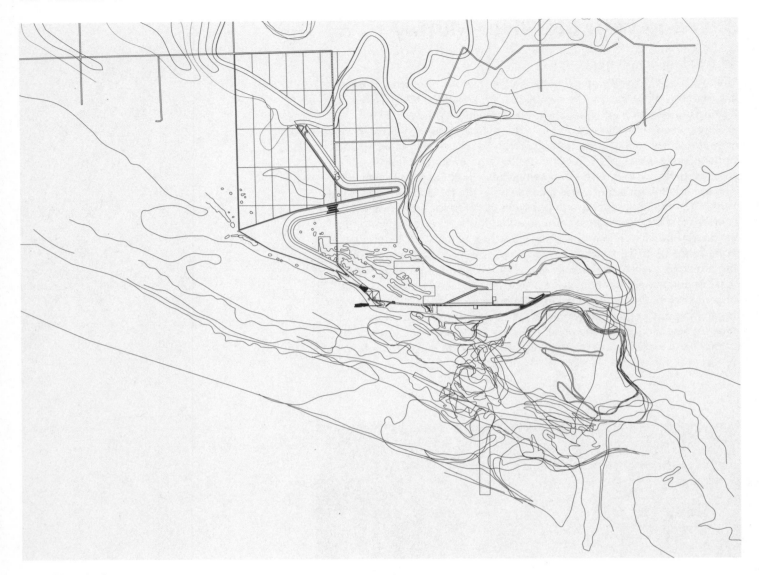

Plan, Tidal Garden.
This drawing shows how the landscape and
infrastructure scale interventions, and more intimate
scaled buildings, have been sited within the dynamic
estuary landscape. The red line indicates the 1:100
year flood level, while the many overlayed lines
trace the movement of the estuary shoreline over the
last 100 years.

3.2 Tidal Garden.

Tidal Garden is a speculative design project for a location on the floodplain within the river estuary. Site process used to engage the whole river were re-visited, but here applied at a different scale – to an Island in the rivers estuary. This instigated another series of off-site and on-site operations that constructed (what I had begun to refer to as) site knowledge. The process of constructing site knowledge became instrumental in the development of the project. I demonstrated how a study of site can have a significant impact upon various aspects of the design process: from site selection, to the development of programs and land-use; to knowing how and where to intervene; and how formal, spatial and material characteristics are derived from this understanding. Tidal Garden explored the potential of living with the river by transforming a disused grazing property (purchased by the State and Federal Governments) into a meaningful visitor destination. While providing opportunities for eco-tourism, a range of new land-uses were also proposed that would bring various river communities and government organisations into relationship. Tidal Garden is a mix of landscape and infrastructure scale interventions into which small scale buildings are nested. It is a place constantly evolving; its spaces being constantly altered by the transitory action of the estuary landscape.

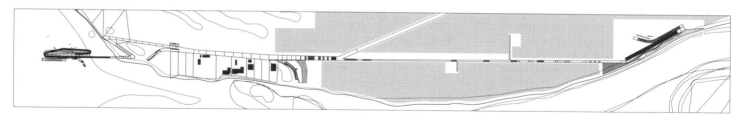

Plan Detail, Urban Walk, Tidal Garden

Research Assistant: Nicholas Strathopoulos

Bottom of page:Urban Walk sequence, shoreline to shoreline, Tidal Garden.

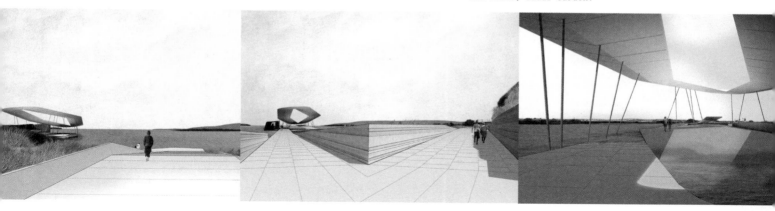

4. Conclusion – Designing the Site

The PhD demonstrates the need to commit time to understand the particularities of a river before knowing how to act. The consequence then, for living with the Murray River, is to derive new approaches that do not separate the study of site from the act of designing. It is a way of operating that is neither bottom-up or top-down, but takes aspects of both of these approaches to create a dynamic set of relationships that allow a more imaginative way of living with a river. The construction of site knowledge and its application into the design process is seen as the significant contribution to the study of site. On-site and off-site are key operations shifting the focus of the site from a static entity into a provisional state where site is constantly constructed through its relationships with the natural and inhabited landscape. This approach implicates a wider range of scalar investigations with a specificity of time as a way of investigating a location. This allows me to design the site.

Afterword

Insights gained from the PhD are impacting upon commissioned architectural works from my architectural practice, Times Two Architects (with Michelle Black).

These insights are continuing the scholarship of site study in the landscapes of central Victoria, still within the Murray catchment. A considered series of architectural responses are emerging, on an intimate scale, often with small budgets, that continue the explorations of an architecture sited with care. These built works are displaying a way of living lightly on the land.

Siting strategy, designing for light and shadow. Ceramic studio, Newstead, Times Two Architects, 2008.

Residence and studio, Castlemaine, Times Two Architects, 2011.

Residence and studio, Castlemaine, Times Two Architects, 2011.

Siting strategy, preparing the ground: a designed interaction between ground and building, inside and outside. Residence and studio, Castlemaine, Times Two Architects, 2011.

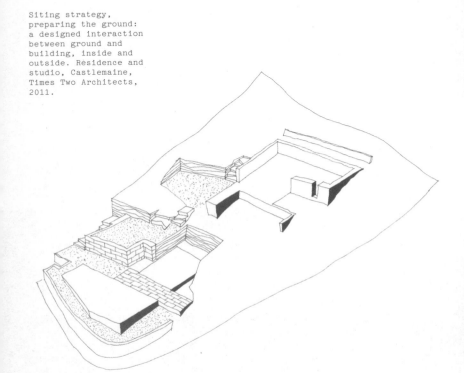

Stephen Collier
Paradigms of Observation:
Azul Oscuro Casi Negro:
A Blue that is Almost Black

"A blue that is almost black", signifies a state of ambiguous being. It refers to something (which in this case is a colour or a mood of such deep blue) that is so close to being something else (black), it is neither one nor the another but *both* one *and* the same. This sense of seeing through a veil, of one thing shadowing another, is an essential part of how I conceive and imagine space.

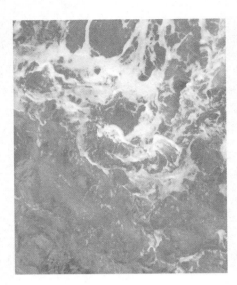 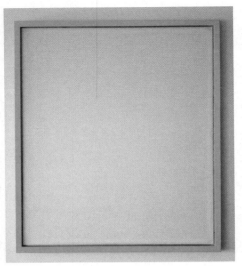

I ask you to imagine…
A vast tableau of light
Looking up with wonder
Falling down into blue water, burst of bubbles
Surrounded by the form of a plush blue-purple room: Purple
A fire in a grate
A cast iron bath at sundown, fire burning slow and red underneath,
leaves and branches of eucalypt trees rustling above
A naked, silent, warm body in bed in the morning
Light through trees
Light through clouds
Pale light
Deep glowing light
Yellow
The nape of a neck
A smiling glance
The smooth surface of half resting hands
A full-blown laugh
Light cast through coloured glass
Smell of leather
Smell of a book
Darkness that you can see
Darkness that you can't see
Painted traffic arrows
Stillness…of trees, sky and ocean
The stillness of solitude
Music reverberating through rooms and corridors
Clouds as seen from the window of a plane
An empty room
An unmade bed
A room with just a few objects
A room that is also not a room
A room that appears to have no boundaries
A look that consoles
Eyes that see
Empathy expressed
Joy revealed
The smell of a rubber plantation
New-ness
Sweet joy of wonder
Joy of silent recognition

A work of architecture holds the observations of the architect, an accumulation of images, feelings and sensations. These remain largely detached and invisible to the casual observer. Every project is a balance between the personal and the impersonal; of things that are internalised and externalised. The memories and observations that I collect and translate are legible to me but someone else will experience them in a completely different way. (I hope that) people will experience my buildings as I conceive them. But in their own way, they will affect a transition between the personal realm of my imagination into the physical space of (their) occupation. This constitutes the movement between client and architect. In the finished work, everyone will develop their own narrative. These are the parallel stories. A building has to account for this ambiguity; the possibility that it can be many things.

In his novel, *Portrait of the Artist as a Young Man,* James Joyce has his narrator Stephen Daedalus, take the position of the observer, observing the observer observing. As an autobiographical device of observation it relays both the detail and the context. In my mind, I observe myself observing. I think of space, by observing myself in space. I am able to step in and out of myself (Stephen). Sometimes I am the person observing (and feeling) and sometimes I am observing an(other) observer observing. By stepping in and out of myself and of others, I am able to ground my thoughts in the personal but I can do it in a way that bestows a measure of creative doubt and uncertainty on the process. The restlessness of this doubt pushes ideas into new territories of thought.

Opposite page:
Left: Mediterranean sea near Marseille, northern winter 2011

Right: Tomislav Nikolic #6, 2012, Acrylic, Marble Dust and Gold Leaf on Canvas, and Timber 116 x 99.5 cm, at home, Sydney. Purchased in memory of someone special, December 2012

THE
BLUE
ROOM

A room appears, a place in the mind, from which all other expressions of personality and space emerge over time. This is the physical time of my being and placement in the world. It is blue. The colour forms a metaphysical and psychological representation of the room, from which all other subsequent variations unfold. The *blue room* becomes the space of the subconscious, forming itself around the preoccupations of that subconscious at a given time, opening and closing like a kind of diaphanous membrane to embrace its yearnings. Everyone frames and expresses their differences through the personal rendering of this room. Mine is blue, a subjective component, coloured and manufactured from experience and desire. It holds the invisible 'outside' of experience that is then translated through a distortion or transmogrification of that experience. Projected into this context, the sensuality of the *blue room* is founded on the toughness of observation and experience as well as its sweetness. The room is both a signal and representation of my understanding of modernity. It is modern in that it is a *both / and* space, allowing people to inhabit the opposite emotions and experiences of existence; to mix them into one form, whilst at the same time allowing them to retain their uniqueness and individuality. It encloses and darkens in times of suffering, sadness, trauma and; lightens to the point of iridescence and an almost luminous half-present point of disappearance, when these shadowy emotions dissipate.

The *blue room* is the inner voice. It is also a temporal space, without permanence. It operates as a kind of theoretical 'opening' between states of thinking or being. A place of private thinking as well as public description (interrogation) and it's the temporal place that allows translation to occur between these two things. So whilst it is imagined as a room, there is a point of transition where the boundaries of it disappear to encompass the infinite zone of contact between me and others. It is my 'room' but other people can be a part of it (even though they may not be aware of it). It is in this way that the notion of private and public intersect. For example, you (the reader) or a client move into the *blue room* each time I (try to) describe the work and the idea is apprehended. Other parallel notions of ambiguity, the sense of being an outsider, and connections between cities where I have lived (in both Spain and Australia), form the fabric of the room, below, above and at the sides. Translations occur through this fabric as the encounter with and filtering of the self. It is a space that reflects sexuality but in this sense and at its core, sexuality is expressed though its sensuality and intimacy. There is an element of extroversion in the way this sensuality is projected to a public audience; it defines the forms of closeness, boundaries (and the lack thereof) of the spaces that I choose to create. This extroversion also finds its opposite form, of introversion, in the way the architecture makes itself. The *blue room* provides an essential form of retreat, a place to dwell in the shadows of thought, to translate the visual essence of the un-translatable (the things which remain silent). There is also something unexplained about areas within the *blue room*: as a place within the psyche where corners disappear into shadowy depths; relating to the darkness of experience. So as something contained within the fabric of this room, hidden and blurred as though it were viewed through water, but ultimately never 'placed on the table', this becomes part of the miasma, of colour, darkness and stillness that seeks an outlet in creativity.

In a spatial sense, the *blue room* makes its appearance felt in different ways: In Project 01 and Project 04 (the bathroom-in-a-living room house, 2007), at inception, during the translation of ideas into material detail, at the rupture of its conclusion; in Project 02 (Madrid competition, 2006) at

Left, top: Felix González Torres close-up image of *"Untitled" (Portrait of Marcel Brient)* 1992

Left, below: Felix González Torres *"Untitled" (revenge)* 1991 and *"Untitled" (loverboy)* 1989

The quantity of sweets is determined by the weight of his lover when he died of AIDS. Visitors are invited to eat the sweets.

In the politicised process of making architecture, ideas are laid out like these sweets, to tantalise. Each one has a message of a form or a feeling embedded within it, written or visualised in a private language of my own, which if chosen has the capacity to become something. The client takes from this, and in a gradual process of accretion creates the work in its own image. With each step I move further inside the idea. Through these projects, I entice clients to feel and visualize a nuanced way of thinking about site, program, Australian-ness, Spanish-ness, history, water, as well as the beautiful degradation and discolouration that can take place in architecture over time.

Project 01
St Helens, Australia (top)
The *blue room* as framework of spatial understanding in my work and the pitfalls inherent in the process of making architecture, first makes its presence felt

Project 10
Canberra, Australia (bottom)
Most recent project representation of the *blue room*

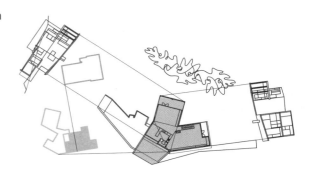

the moments of calibrated collaboration when an idea fit, the room within the scheme where my mind wanders and dwells whenever I think of it (a long, high, dusky darkish blue tinged space at the transition between the old and new parts looking out into a cloistered garden). In Project 05 (2006) it hovers within the mood and texture of a room in the original house, and suggested a transition between old and new that involved separating two adjacent rooms with a tiny rooftop patio (which the clients rejected). In project 07 (2010), the adjacency of extreme poverty and beauty, poetry and pragmattism. In project 09 (2012), the intimate and productive connection between client and architect. In project 10 (2013), the chance to reflect on what could have constituted a unique Australian form of modernity.

The transitory nature of the *blue room* is a mark of its beauty and intimacy, in that it can't be pinned down and held in space because it is based on different realities of observation. The *blue room* exists where there is a 'common' space; a kind of collective 'ambient' space of shared purpose and understanding.

TEN PROJECTS

Project 07 Urban, Fez

Five intersecting layers:
01. New tree lined river
promenade
02. Roof top rainwater
collection over new
artisan workshops,
restaurants, cafes and
hotel
03. Internal courtyards
inserted into new and old
buildings provide passive
cooling and natural light
04. Place Yalla Yeddouna
connects through to the
river promenade
05. New and old buildings
combine to create a
cohesive and understated
urbanity

Place Yalla Yeddouna:
An historic crossroad
between the east and
west Medina and a centre
for artisans, tanners
and blacksmiths since
the 6th century. The
city of Fez accommodates
163 times more people on
an area of land that is
596 times smaller than
Sydney. Fragments of
both cities are shown to
the left and far left,
at the same scale.

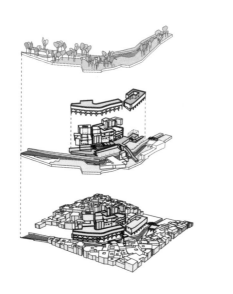

Project 09, House,
Lavender Bay

The Lavender Bay Boatshed
is a pair of attached
two storey boatsheds on
Sydney Harbour, and form
remnants of a typology
of buildings that once
lined the western
side of Lavender Bay.
The historic use as a
working boatshed was
rendered obsolete by
environmental controls
and the buildings
have been adapted for
new uses including
offices relating to
maritime industries and
residential apartments.

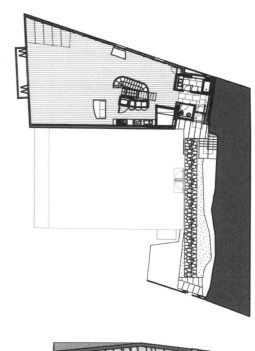

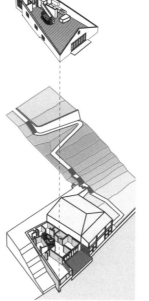

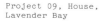

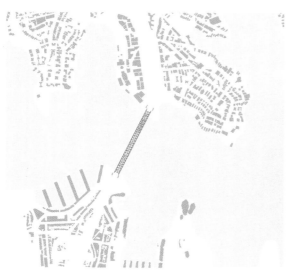

PARALLEL STORIES

Parallel stories shift in and out of focus. Between the present and the past, the touchable and the untouchable, there is a space, a thin gap. The gap is formed of two opposites; it is not static or closed but changing; the sides can be jagged, abrasive, brooding or light filled, bright, silky, watery; a membrane; a slither of space that connects one side from the other. The slices shape themselves to the form and moment of thought; brought about by the convergence of memory and desire on the one hand, and the cutting through (apprehending) of reality on the other. This forms a story. There is a story behind every work; but rarely is that the same story that the client sees. It is the presence of the idea in the physical work.

Perhaps what I find interesting, are the stories that I construct in my mind that lead to an idea, which will in all probability remain invisible to all but me. These are the things (feelings, emotions, textures, colours) that I use to make it real. I search for ways to make these things visible. But I also look for ways to turn down and conceal the degree of visibility of an idea so that it is only implied, for example, a pattern of movement, the changing colour and shape giving potential of cast light, the mood and substance of something old, against the crispness of something new. It describes a movement between the visible and the invisible.

I carry ideas in my head of the kind of spaces that I would like to be given the chance to create: for example, I have often thought that I would like to make a luxurious room of the deepest blue, with the faint glow of light, a muted and subdued space and yet rich with colour and woven texture: a kind of space that absorbs: a silent place from which to retreat and observe. González Torres' work inspires a similar desire to enter the frame, turn it into a room, a space, to capture the emotion. Where do these come from? I imagine people experiencing my buildings as I conceive them in my mind: silently moving through the space marked by voids, being drawn towards light, seeking refuge in shadow and corner, simple pleasure from alternately being able to feel cold and warmth and to see colour. There is a transition between the personal realm of imagination into the physical space of occupation. But at some level there is an absurdity to the impossibility of this notion. The things that I collect and translate are legible to me in a very specific way: but someone else will experience them in a completely different way. A building has to account for the ambiguity that this process of conception and realisation entails: the possibility that it can be many things.

With Felix González Torres, a deeply personal idea is being conveyed behind something that is so very public and the idea has been positioned in such a way as to be receptive to an audience; an audience that probably has no interest in discovering or knowing what the real story is about (gay love, exile, death, grief) but is still quite happy to engage with it at another quite superficial level. At some level this surface level of engagement becomes the work and is a source of its beauty and its ordinariness (the photo of a recently inhabited and unmade bed). González Torres makes no judgement about this. The viewer experiences something intimate and yet remains a stranger to the work (and from one another). Commonality is based not on identification with the art object but from the distance at which it is viewed and from which the real meaning is concealed (the sweet work). In fact he purposefully uses it to literally disassemble the work (the pile of sweets which he invites people to take, thereby slowly eroding the work). This removes the element of fear: will anyone understand what I am trying to do, will it be valued? For the architect these fears have the potential to cripple the creative process.

So in the politicised process of assembly, I lay ideas out like sweets. Each one has a message of a form or a feeling embedded within it, written or visualised in a private language of my own, which if chosen

Loose associations, unrehearsed connections and bindings; from the ordinary to the sublime. Not one Spain, but many, and not one Australia either.

Folkloric
Courtyard
Garden
Intimacy
Freinds
Love
Colour
Shadow
Light
Material
Home

= Modernity

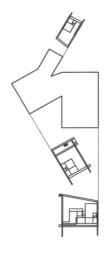

Project 08

Felix González Torres
"Untitled" (Blood) 1992

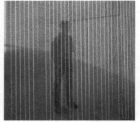

Project 09

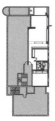

Project 06

Project 09

Project 09

Project 09

Project 05

Project 02

Project 09

Project 03

The curiosity and wonder
of imagining another
place on the other side
of the world.

Project 06

Project 03

Home, Barcelona

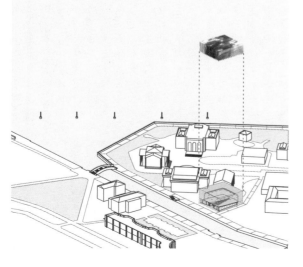

Project
05

has the capacity to become something. The client takes from this, and in a gradual process of accretion creates the work in its own image. With each step in the process of evolution, I move further inside the idea. And so, in wondering, I often think of the past and that which lies behind the evocation and embrace of beauty; about the sweet smell of perfume on pale golden, lightly tanned skin, its smoothness, faintly tinged by the odour of personality, an essence, the look in the eyes, knowing, understanding, wishing, reciprocating, hoping, desiring, mirroring (him / you), a neck, the line of hair at the nape, the smile, dark eyes, compassionate (which he believes he sees), the ego (which I am blind to at first but progressively discover), the laughter, the flirting. Boy after boy, similar features, similar characteristics, always seeking to sink into his beauty (or is it yours?), to be a part of him, inside him, to feel the touch of the hair on his chest, the smoothness of his skin, the shiver of delight, a response to you and as you hope (vainly) only you, the search for a kind of immersion in the myriad forms of beauty and sensuality and an irritability when it is denied. Each of these stories holds the presence of another story within it.

It is through the creative act that I reach a state of pure, incomparable consciousness, of myself in the world and of the world in relation to me. This consciousness is made heavy and light with sensations imprinted on the mind through observation. Without which it would not be possible to create. Each manifestation of the room holds out the hope that another room will be revealed that facilitates a new path of memory connected to a new path of thinking about the same thing in a new way. The neuronal pathway between this act of consciousness and the psychological process that constitutes the room, turning it into something real that is then articulated in a project, sitting silently behind it, is the signature of creativity.

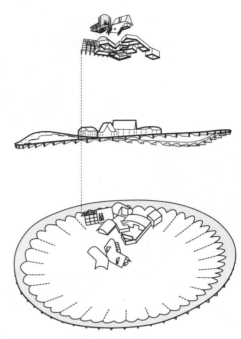

3 key ideas

1. A permanent and protective structure of roof forms (reflecting our democracy) with a flexible interior (representing our culture)

2. An undulating visually porous boundary defined on the outside edge by a ring of deciduous trees and vaulted cave-like spaces of art underneath.

3. A private stroll garden, of amplified native landscape, gently sloping up around the outside edge

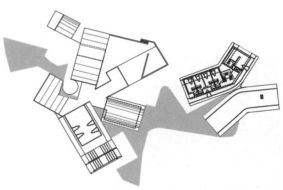

Project 10
Lodge on the Lake

A competition to design a new residence for Australia's Prime Minister in Canberra. The image (right), by artist Michael Cook, encapsulated our motivations for the project. What if the British had embraced aboriginal culture in 1788? What if there had been less insistence on property boundaries? What if the lodge was a place where both an indigenous and non-indigenous prime minister could feel equally at home?

Michael Cook
"Broken Dreams" 2010

Graham Crist
Sheds for Antarctica: The Environment for Architectural Design and Practice

Graham Crist is a practitioner academic in Melbourne. He grew up in Perth. His grandmother had some very clear views about what constituted a house. He found these alien. He studied architecture, joined the 1990s migration of young professionals to South East Australia, and began a small practice and a family. His earliest work was a shed for a family that could afford no more than an off the peg shed. This shed was minimally modified to make it inhabitable as a dwelling. This beginning point was not merely a 'needs-must' event. It was the seed of Graham's approach to architecture. He persisted in finding sheds for his projects. The simplest envelope housed the fluctuating interactions of programs that he declined to fix or settle, firm in his understanding that relationships shift, move in orbits that are only ever partially predictable.

Graham thinks systems. He maps his position relative to those of his collaborators. He seeks out organisational modes that support partnerships that are equal, preferring a matrix to a hierarchy. Sheds are envelopes that need to be large enough to encompass the matrices. In urban situations sheds encompass that which is inside them, but they also create an outside shed, roofed by the sky. He designs these sheds too, foregrounding outside—as inside—the constellations of happenings that are the living part of architecture. A swimming pool is a shed that gets decorated where it comes closely encounters the rituals of swimming and sunbaking.

The shed is a parsimonious structure: the least possible material for the most possible space. There is always enough budget to passively modify the micro-climates inside and outside.

Graham instils sustainability thinking into his students. He found his sheds before Lacatan and Vassall found theirs. But he found his voice and his critics after they found theirs...

THE AFRICA CENTRE

The Shed Position

Camels, Noise, Sheds and the Space for the Contingent

A camel is a horse designed by committee. Despite this being a description of derision, I prefer the camel to the horse. I like its form despite its odd proportion, and I prefer the committee to the solo voice, despite its messy inefficiency. A camel is a robust survivor in a hostile environment, unlike a thoroughbred horse which is precious and delicate in its high performance. What does a camel look like? The camel is an analogy to the impure and contingent design object, and it demands a description of its form. Even when it is not the result of formalism or a formal process.

The committee which made the camel requires description too. The position toward architecture described here was formed in a newly created, ad hoc committee of an architectural practice called antarctica. That practice is the context for this work, and the body of work described here is the work of that practice. Even though a committee sometimes wastes time and dithers; it also debates as it accounts for social complexity. It struggles with uncertainty. This committee is a term I use loosely to also describe the environments we juggle; a wide physical context, a mental space, a table full of random players, and unpredictable forces like finance.

Another way to describe this position is through noise. The gap between the way architectural design is often described and the experience of architectural practice has to do with the environmental noise that surrounds the design process. I like the noise of the environment around me because I want to be fully in the world and open to that environment's noise. I have a responsibility to listen and to respond, and not silence that noise. This makes the task of architectural design, one of tuning in to our environment, and yet it is common to pretend that our work occurs in a controlled acoustic chamber.

Yet another way to describe this position is via the poles of activity either side of it, and which we see in our colleagues. On one hand, too much typology or sociology brings with it a taste for the austere and a suspicion of excess. On the other, too many process experiments tend to decouple us from the found world and the richness of everyday life. Hovering as a third trajectory is the desire to remain rooted in the environment as we find it, precisely in order to embrace its unpredictable delights and chance, both modest and enormous, banal and excessive.

The shed is a spatial model which aims to describe and embody a position embracing the contingent environment, and to give it a robust form. It is a well worn and restrictive term, yet it has the capacity to radically expand. These projects are each an attempt to test an expanded notion of the shed, to place it in a larger context, and to see it as spatially analogous to the camel.

The projects here describe a long arc of reflection, The first 2J house was revisited and reconsidered years after its completion. The Africa Centre and Greenhouse were made right in the petri dish of the newly formed practice and of thinking through the threads of a postion. Most were made under the extreme pressures of constrained money and lack of time. Projects such as the Flowerdale Community House and Gondwana were made possible through the reflective process of the PhD project, and are the first steps of builidng upon that.

Previous page: Africa Centre, model.
The Africa Centre museum is part of a design competition for a South African new town; its key public building. It was designed at a moment in my PhD reflection where I was considering the place of time in the design process. I identified the polarised but simultaneous need for the permanent/ inert (characterised by Aldo Rossi) and the agile/ ephemeral (characterised by Cedric Price). This converged with the curators' brief for open-ended flexible spaces. The composition of abstracted plan drawings was the means to test these possibilities.

Its image did not easily infer a function; might not give up its secrets of how to use the space. It appeared more as an abstract tableau, and less as a diagram of spatial function. Eager to simultaneously avoid a spatially inert or neutral hangar and highly programmed or figured spaces, flexibility was interpreted as a functionally ambiguous arena, where possible uses were negotiated within a charged space. The curators' rich descriptions suggested that the institutions' negotiations with the space would be lively.

A series of points punctuated the plan, making a paper constellation which inferred a floor plate. These points formed into a catalogue of elements serving the space. They became columns, shafts of services (water/air/power); pods of program ranging from rooms to cabinets, holes of light above, floor lights below, and furniture. Each was treated as similarly as possible; droplets of varying size scattered on the floor.

In a flat drawing it is easy to disperse pattern, to camouflage the functional and spatial divisions, to lose a sense of recognition in a forest of dots. The test for effect on experienced space added inflection of the dominant roof canopy by an imagined context; to test how little distortion from a default plane was needed to avoid a seemingly inevitable pure form which might result from orthogonality. The aim was to be neither rational nor organic, neither natural nor universal. Similarly, the floor resisted being either a separate plane above the ground; or a seamless part of the ground. Neither natural nor artificial; a gradation of both.

Perhaps more than any piece in our body of work this tests the expanded notion of the shed; something that bridges the gap between Rossi's city and Price's terrain. It also reflects the link between the modest poor architecture, and of the major public institution. The techniques of the shed are common to both.

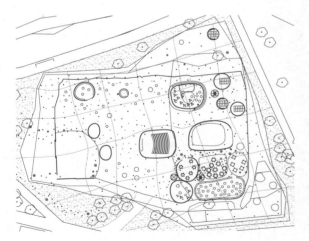

Ground floor plan of the Africa Centre, South Africa

The credits for each of the six projects and their images (2J House, Greenhouse, Africa Centre, Knox Warm Water, Flowerdale and Gondwana) are ANTARCTICA, with the exception of 2J House which is Graham Crist with Kate Hislop and Hannah Lewi. The photographs of each project are by Graham Crist, with the exception of Flowerdale which are by Dana Beligan.

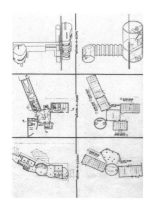

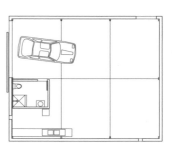

2J House

2J coincided with the House with No Style — a Japanese competition project. Here the canon of modern villas was stripped bare and recast as assemblies of common prefab sheds and other ordinary infrastructure. The famous plans were tested for their resilience as a diagram; Wright's Fallingwater was tested for recognition in altered and compromised circumstances.

The 2J house was designed in 1991 for a valley an hour east of Perth. Intend as the minimum budget, temporary house, it remained in place of a permanent building. It is barely a house, built from a rectified off the shelf shed. It was chosen from a limited pre-designed range, with conventional steel elements assembled on site. We selected the smallest footprint available, the largest height (4.8 metres), and the largest door available. We ordered two windows (the maximum number in the package). We got a hundred square metres of double height space for just twelve thousand dollars. One extra window was added; the largest off the shelf slider available, and cut this into the steel wall. Similarly, translucent corrugated sheet made a strip window. Two red steel packing sheets had been discarded as rubbish after construction.
We cut these and composed them into ornamental façade panels, placed around the openings. The interior was lined in fibreglass, and left as open as possible. Its space was big, open, barely defined and at the ambient outdoor temperature. It was barely an interior — the car drove directly inside, and the sparse furniture was moved about to wherever it was needed. On a small bathroom box inside was a crude facsimile of the mural from the canonic Rose Seidler House.

GREENHOUSE

The Greenhouse began as a prototype for a lightweight and recyclable flat pack construction system, and a promotion for urban food production. Being wedged into a vacant space of Federation Square triggered a specific study in contrast with the buildings pressing either side. Exposed steel stud, straw bale, rough ply and vertical planting are exposed in a blunt fashion. Where Federation Square is complex, precious and permanent, the Greenhouse's gestures are formally dumb and materially rugged, reading more like a remainder of the modest sheds used while constructing the larger project. The project is between a slow event (operating as a bar over summer) and a short lived building, put together in extreme time pressure, by a committee of architect, engineer, operator and builder, each doing their part simultaneously.

KNOX WARM WATER

The Knox Warm Water pool was the latest addition to an accretion of buildings in an outer suburban pool complex. It grafts on to the main gabled hall and takes that hall for its geometric cues. The techniques to do this are a combination of splicing, pulling and stretching; and subsequently of saturating. So the section creates some precarious structure as its portal is stretched over the new pool and spliced back on to the older section. All the skins were treated as higher saturation versions of those existing, and unsealed to open to their environment.

We would say, during the process of making this project, that we are starting with nothing, and starting with everything. We meant, there was no design aspiration attached to project, to the point that design of building was not even part of the briefed commission. It was something entirely brought to the project. At the same time, everything, all the ingredients for the design were there on site, the only addition to pour on was the tiled language of the RMIT Building 8 we visited every day. The tension at play is to make sense of a public space, by bring to it a level of intensity, and without leaving all the accreted parts wasted in its wake.

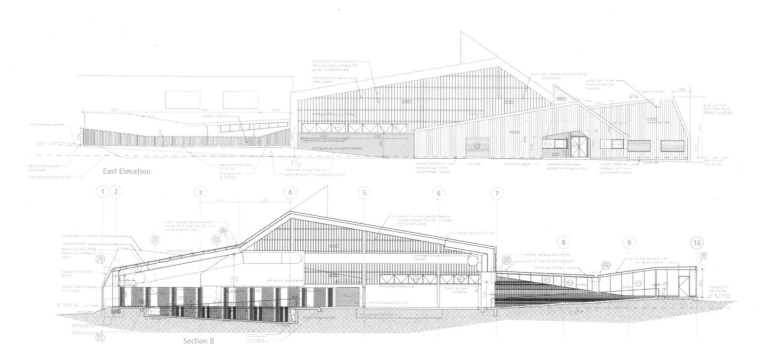

East Elevation

Section B

FLOWERDALE

Flowerdale Community House is a structure built directly off the back of the PhD work; and in response to the Victorian bushfires of Black Saturday. The large loose shed roof facilitated a huge range of the town programs in a series of adaptable rooms expressed as independent boxes of varied size and material. These range from medical consultation in the small rooms to belly dancing in the large hall. They are distributed beneath large span open wooden trusses which hold the rooms together under the volume they create, and open to reconfiguration over time. The large bent gable inflects and distorts just as it needs to; kicking up to an open undercroft space facing playgrounds and exposing the trusses as deep beams, and folding down over walls. It is penetrated at particular moments under strict bushfire regulations, to open a view of the treescape. The boxes are tucked under or hang out of the roof as needed. The roof surface is tattooed with the tree symbol of Flowerdale that came to be associated with its regeneration after the fires. It mirrors the local pub which is decorated with the town's name on its red tin roof.

GONDWANA

The Capithetical design competition, reflecting on the creation of Canberra as Australia's national capital one hundred years ago, sought propositions for a re-thinking of the Australian capital for the next century. Ours was a proposition to distribute most administrative functions to the current large urban centres, and locate a symbolic and transient city on the north coast near Darwin, and closer to its Asian region. Conceived as a structure smaller than a city and larger than a building, it inscribes a line perpendicular to the coast, heading inland. That vast line intersects with varied landscapes, and marks itself on the ground with varied thinness. At its sea entry a grid of buoys mark the line, and at the other end a grid of flag poles and windsocks disappear into the desert. When the strip occasionally perforates it forms civic space, at other times the roof forms a double skin for the harsh sun above. It is a structure only partly filled by the transient public structures and places for visitors; waiting to be filled or re-thought. It is a structure where the conception of the capital, its framework, would be permanent; yet its shed qualities would make it able to survive complete transformation. Its name Gondwana, imagines the tiime when Australia is no longer a disconnected and isolated island.

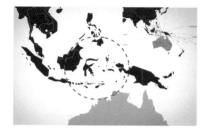

The Contribution of the Shed

The terms junk, and longevity and accretion have become useful for me in elaborating this spatial position. Junk is a word that signals a desire to broaden and expand the field of engagement for architectural design with the built environment, including the most abject. It infers the rejuvenation of the discarded. Longevity points to thinking of the design process as a long engagement with the designed object rather than as an inspired moment which is complete when the Designer departs. It points also to thinking of the designed object as a commodity placed in the hands of many generations to follow. Accretion follows from this point, and demands that we accept the condition of the built environment as we find it, and accept that our design work is simply part of a sequence which includes subsequent alteration, erasure and distortion.

Sheds have been identified as a spatial model which captures these demands. The shed is characterised by a loose relationship between program and form and between its interior and its external envelope. That envelope is characterised as simple without being minimal, and as materially raw enough to accept accretion. That is, it contains enough qualities of the incomplete, impure or imperfect to provoke or allow the possibility of future operations on it.

The architectural practice of Antarctica was identified as an environment corresponding to this model. It is a loose collaborative venue defined by a group and a place rather than by an individual personality. It has a conventionalised exterior capable of engaging with the `normal' constraints of practice. Participation is a central notion to this model, equally within the group and beyond in the wider context of the projects. It remains critical of some versions of participatory design, and which differentiates front-ending from backfilling. That is, our contribution is best made by recognising our own particular spatial intelligence, provoking a process at the front end, and passing this on to others. This is instead of, managing the participatory input of others, then backfilling that input with our own design cleanup.

The implications of this position are ethical. It might fall under the term sustainability, or more simply as environmental responsiveness.

Architectural design is called on upon to respond to very large questions related to transformation in the urban or social environment. It is best adapted to respond when its aesthetic concerns, and its design processes are robust and inclusive. An alternative view frames architectural design excised from its context and defined as a narrow and specialised section of the built environment. This is unsustainable.

The propositions of this work navigate a series of binaries. Formal complexity versus minimalism is sidestepped as irrelevant. The opposition of formalist or aesthetic positions versus ethical and anti-formal positions is rejected, with the aim of drawing compositional questions into all fields of the environment equally. The bifurcation of the built environment into the ordinary everyday versus the exceptional or signature building is another situation which limits the contribution of architecture.

All this might simply be summarised as carrying our spatial intelligence into fields where it doesn't belong, but where it is needed.

Greenhouse viewed from Flinders Street

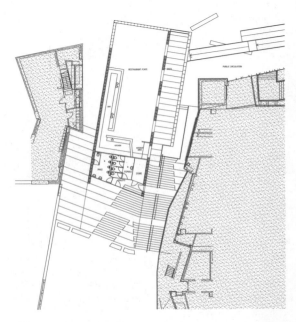

Greenhouse ground floor plan

Lucas Devriendt
Paint It Black: My Research Into The Black Plastic As A (Self-) Portrait In The Cabinet Devriendt

The Cabinet Devriendt in the Museum Dr. Guislain in Ghent was the culmination of an investigation into the possible sources of the painting Black Plastic (2007), which I realised in 2008 on the occasion of an exhibition at the Galerie Tatjana Pieters in Ghent entitled *Mijn rechteroog ziet beter* (My right eye sees better). The study started at a time where I fully realised that the inspiration for a new work never just presents itself out of nowhere, but is rather a logical consequence of a series of decisions you make throughout the development of your work.

The research was limited only by the boundaries of my own existence, my work and the presently accessible data. Art, however, according to the Lebanese writer and filmmaker Jalal Toufic, moves like a non-linear continuum in all directions. As a result, he is convinced that Francis Bacon's oeuvre in painting was influenced by the book Gilles Deleuze later wrote about him. It sounds absurd, but from the point of view where art is seen as a time-space in multiple dimensions, this reversal is not implausible. Also in science, there is plenty of discussion about the reversal of cause and effect.

My former teacher and artist Dan van Severen was also very conscious of this reversal when he forbade us to look at Morandi because 'those who have done it, have not survived him as artists.' Of course, despite the warning, I did look at Morandi. One of the first impetuses that led to the writing of this thesis was a small book on this painter, which I bought in Paris at one time. The title of the book is 'Lumiére et mémoire' (Light and Memory) and written by Youssef Ishaghpour. The following quote got my absolute attention; it was as if I suddenly understood it after all those years what Van Severen had predicted. "Il a une profonde connaissance du passé. Mais sa relation au passé est de l'ordre de la réminiscence. Et la réminiscence est un pur mouvement du temps, non pas une mémoire submergée de souvenirs, de dépendances et de citations d'oeuvres d'art. C'est une vision qui se réalise dans l'acte de la peinture. (…) **Ainsi, pour Morandi, la vision du présent comme réminiscense, et du souvenir comme présent, s'épanouit en image et devient, en même temps qu'un état présent, quelque chose d'intemporel qui tranche sur le présent."** (Youssef 2001, 15–26)

Not only did I realise that my research was moving out of time as a linear continuum, but it slowly became clear that the quest for the Black Plastic would also inevitably spread to what my father had in mind during his life, or rather to what his motives were for choosing the profession of doctor, more specifically the specialization of Internal Medicine. And this following a consultation with my father, with me as a patient, of which I made a video entitled *het onderzoek* (The Examination). Because of this incident, there was a connection that transcended the physical DNA and translated our 'I' into a 'we'.

The roots of my being an artist reach beyond my own self, and have their origins in my, or rather our, common inquisitiveness and curiosity for anything happening under the skin. The world that is not visible to the 'naked' eye. The inquiring gaze—or the diagnostic gaze Luc Tuymans alludes to in his series of epony—mous paintings: Der diagnostische blik, trying to find its way in the universe of the body: through the skin of the painting, through the skin of a body, and outside of the spectrum of visible existence.

Two pictures, which my father was given by his father who was a radiologist and a dermatologist, form the capstone of my quest. These pictures of my grandfather's radiography cabinet proved to be the catalysts that gave shape to the research. The irresistible urge to look farther than the eye itself, and this regardless of our instruments, was the answer to my urge to connect with the visible world around me, to give it a skin that breathes and lives and feels and that appears to present the only possibility to exist.

Leon Devriendt, 1924.
Medical X-Ray Room Sacred
Heart Clinic Kortrijk
(photograph)

The idea of the cabinet

During a conversation I had with my father Herman Devriendt, who is a doctor, he mentioned two pictures he had recently found in an envelope, and which had belonged to his father Leon Devriendt, who was also a physician. He handed me the two black and white photographs from 1924. These were the only tangible remnants of the office of my grandfather and radiologist Leon Devriendt, who was also a gifted photographer and who had taken these pictures himself. The office was located in the former Sacred Heart Clinic on the Buda Island in Kortrijk, founded upon the initiative of the Sisters of Charity in 1888. During the Second World War the radiology clinic—one of the first in Belgium—was completely destroyed by fire.

Mirjam Devriendt, 2014. The Cabinet Devriendt (Lambada print)

Right away, the two pictures intrigue, surprise and amaze me. The office, after all, does not look at all like a clinical workroom replete with medical high-technologic devices and hazardous radiation where broken bones were being diagnosticated. The sleek doors rather refer to a living room in a townhouse. Someone, I guess my grandfather, had painted abstract shafts of colour, apparently depicting X-rays, onto the walls. It immediately reminded me of the film *Das Kabinett des Doktor Caligari* (1920), a feeling provoked by a rather uncanny reflex (sensation, reaction, connotation, atmosphere).

Upon reflection, my fascination with these photos seemed to be not only personal in nature, but was rather—and mainly—inspired by painterly interests. Was the abstract pattern of the mural painting meant to depict something? Was there an underlying mathematical system?
What did the whole drawing look like? What colours would my grandfather have used? What significance did these mural paintings / drawings have for him? Were they purely decorative, instructional / educational, or was it a statement? In short, a torrent of questions and thoughts.

Sometimes things fall into place at the right time. I was fully immersed in an investigation into the genesis of my own work, *Black Plastic* (2007). With the question: How does an idea for a work come into being? Assuming that an idea has a history, that it is the result of a thought process and that it occurs within the span of one life cycle.

I had, in this respect, already pondered the fact whether my ideas were actually really mine, or were rather notions that lay dormant over different generations. Much like the concept of original sin.

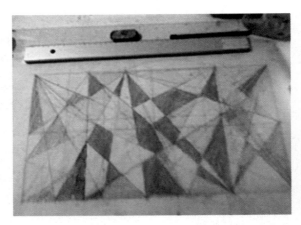

Lucas Devriendt, 2010-2014. X-ray: drawings, colour sketches and models with various dimensions.

"Ich suchte etwas und wusste nicht was; kein Schreibzimmer, kein Arbeits-, kein Wohnzimmer, ein Zimmer, so als ob es der Mensch vor mir bewohnt hatte, der ich gerne geworden ware. Es klingt so lacherlich,—aber es hat mich tagelang durch die strassen getrieben,—auch vergebens..." (Hayasaka 2012, 193).

Now imagine that I would reconstruct the office, and use it as a vehicle to interpret, understand, exhibit my own work in this new context. Use it as if it were a time machine. To go back in time so as to understand what I am doing now. It didn't sound all that crazy to me, since the working title for my research was 'the painting as time machine'.
In my quest for the origins of my work it actually seemed inevitable, at least in retrospect, that the creative and inquisitive ideas of my grandfather would embed themselves within my research.

The office could be a realisation in which the plastic image as a whole, complete with all its parts, evokes a longing to bring to the fore both the invisible and everything that lies under the skin in one fragmentary whole. In which my grandfather, my father and I are connected in this construction through this one quest and it becomes clear what drives us, a curiosity about that which, at first, is not visible. The professional know-how to make the invisible visible has turned out not to be an end in itself, but a means to reveal the knowledge acquired.

Lucas Devriendt, 2010-2014. X-ray: drawings, colour sketches and models with various dimensions.

I approached artist Hans De Meulenaere to work out some ideas on this, which soon turned into a project in which he himself went on to construct the platform for my—or rather our—Cabinet, which would bring together my work, my grandfather's cabinet and my father's practice.

The project

A painterly reconstruction

We were not merely interested in translating the images into a reconstruction, and certainly not into a literal reconstruction of this cabinet. As the term 'Cabinet' already suggests, it is a physical space, but also a mental space. We consciously chose not to place these two elements side-by-side, but rather aimed to interweave them.

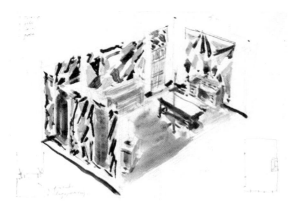

Lucas Devriendt, 2010-2014. X-ray: drawings, colour sketches and models with various dimensions.

1. Reconstruct the physical space of the cabinet with the mural paintings in a mental way.
2. Physically (re)present the mental world of the doctor / radiologist scientist / artist (i.e. grandfather Devriendt) vis-à-vis the spirit of his time within that very structure. The room in the photos was translated into a transparent wooden structure, whereby the edges of the picture are made to coincide with the edges of the (re) construction, allowing one to step into the reality of the picture. This wooden structure will also function as a physical base for the research itself.

I presented the mural painting of the photographs as a 'blueprint' in the exhibition space. It is not a direct translation of the mural painting, but a painterly translation and reconstruction realised on the basis of these two black and white photographs.

An exhibition in an exhibition in an exhibition

From our perspective, the cabinet became an investigation into the issue of 'exhibiting', whereby a number of different stories were brought together within the installation.

It was the intention to find both a purely artistic translation for this research and a workable equilibrium between Hans Demeulenaere and myself. It became a joint story, fashioned out of our individual practices. It also became a project that called into question our position as artists, not only in respect to each other within this collaboration, but also in respect to the way in which we position ourselves as artists in this context. This study (and doctorate) also allowed existing (older) work to be redefined.

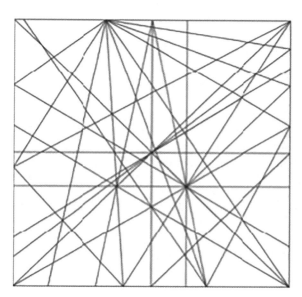

Lucas Devriendt, 2010-2014. X-ray: drawings, colour sketches and models with various dimensions.

The problems and questions that surrounded this were not easy: a presentation of and about the world of doctor Devriendt placed in a socio-historical/scientific/artistic framework. How do we approach this? How do we present an archive or a collection, and how de we translate this into the 'Cabinet'? Is personal memory ultimately assimilated into a collective memory of images? What is the meaning of the artist's studio as a reconstruction?

An important element in this project had to do with the way in which the artist's studio is used as a reconstruction in exhibitions. In museum M, the studio of Patrick Van Caeckenbergh was rebuilt in his exhibition. Does the studio add an extra perspective or access to the work, or does it function as an autonomous installation? If we go back further, we inevitably come to the Merzbau by Kurt Schwitters, an installation and yet simultaneously a reconstruction of a kind of studio space, which referred to, but conversely also inspired, the work of other artists. The reconstruction of the studio of Piet Mondrian also regularly pops up in several retrospectives. This studio is not just a means to transport us to another place and time in which Mondrian lived and worked. It is above all a place that shows how he approaches his own work, how he applies things (works) towards his thinking (and not vice versa). In this way, he creates a new reality, which, in turn, generates new works (like a machine). Is the idea of this cabinet of Dr. Devriendt not similar in this respect? Is it not the man's aim to make these invisible X-rays emitted from strange devices visible in an artistic manner? Does the doctor not create a new reality in this cabinet in which he tries to grasp this scientific phenomenon?

The Cabinet is a research space where results function like the legend of a map upon which are traced new contours that are placed within a rewritten history that spans several generations. It is a space whose inside wants to move outward and vice versa. A space where different boundaries evoke different realities.

Hans Demeulenaere,
Lucas Devriendt, 2014.
The Shelves
(Left Hand Room)

Hans Demeulenaere,
Lucas Devriendt, 2014.
The Shelves
(Right Hand Room)

Three generations
Leon, Herman,
Lucas, Devriendt

Make visible what is invisible
(My grandfather, my father, I)

Leon Devriendt, radiologist and dermatologist:
X-rays as wall painting

When I looked at both of my grandfather's black and white photos and began to imagine the space more clearly, I could also see the logic, or rather the functioning of the space my grandfather had in mind. There is the space, there are the two radiology units that form the centre of it all, and the peripheral devices that have to make them work. Also in the picture was an item that seems obvious because it simply belongs in a research space, a desk placed behind the radiology unit for lying patients against the mural painting on the only free wall of the 'living room'. The desk is an American oak model with a typical rolling shutter which was considered very modern at the time. This desk is in my possession, and I therefore know its exact dimensions, which are essential to determine the actual size of the mural painting. The pictures themselves are taken with a tripod, which makes that the lens was approximately at chest level, some 30cm below eye level. In hindsight this appears not to be an unimportant detail. What also visually affected the picture was the distortion caused by the lens of the camera. This made the room appear much larger, and gave the mural painting on the photo truly monumental proportions. The light in the room is artificial, for the simple reason that my grandfather covered both the windows located behind the unit for standing patients, since the cabinet was also used as a dark room. I could not determine what the colours of the mural painting were, yet I suspected that black and white were used; the other shades of grey could have been any other colour. When I asked my father who as a child would occasionally have lingered in those rooms, he couldn't remember anything. The desk is placed centrally against the wall in the room, like an altar; it is fronted by the central mural painting that presents itself as an altarpiece. All the other murals are a continuation, a derivative of that one work.

Lucas Devriendt, 2014. The mural painting (Leon)
positive (300x300cm)
Image: Richard DuyckHans

The central mural painting

Reconstructing this mural was a strange experience. You see a result, a creation, and then you have to go back in time to grasp the origin of the work. Step by step, you want to trace the evolution of the decisions made when the work was created; an investigation that did take quite some time. The first fact I could find out about the format was that it was a square. The second fact I figured out, using the desk as a parameter (87,5cm in width, 1m 48,5cm in length, rear height 1m 14cm and front height 79cm), were the dimensions of the mural painting, although I realise this will always be an approximation. There are plenty of reference points in the photo itself, such as the height of a chair, the height of a handle on the door, and so on. The dimensions, then, turned out to be approximately 3m x 3m.

Ine Meganck, 2014. Invitation
(Design postcard Format, recto verso)

Abstract selfie

You could best compare the picture to an abstract selfie, one of the viewer and the device, an image with two viewpoints or flight points. Two points combined with the Pythagorean theorem – became the matrix of the painting. Two points, one which refers to my grandfather's eye level, located in the middle of the square, and a second point on the right of the diagonal which passes through the centre point, and which refers to the height of the lens of the radiology device. Those two points also make that the painting is not symmetrically composed from one single point. The use of these two points puts the lines and surfaces in disarray, and gives the painted surface a very dynamic and powerful appearance.

Lucas Devriendt, 2014. Re-painting in studio. (Acryl on wall, 300 x 300 cm)

Lucas Devriendt, 2014. The mural painting (Leon)
positive (300x300cm) Image: Richard Duyck

My studio became his cabinet and vice versa

In my studio, I made a copy of the mural located behind the desk in the photo, using the same dimensions as the original, and placed it, as can be deduced from the picture, centrally on the wall at the same height from the floor. The mural is located in the most important place in my studio, the wall with the best natural light where I work on my paintings.

The cabinet has invaded my studio, and I now live, through this reconstruction, fictitiously in the research area of my grandfather. The result of this 'translation' (or reconstruction) is that the colours, scale, proportions and spatial positioning are wilfully distorted. The incomplete data, the lack of precise information and reliable accounts create a 'distortion' in the reconstruction; in this way, it becomes the basis of the painterly research I envisioned.

In hindsight it was a good decision to first try out the reconstruction in my own studio before transposing it to the cabinet in the museum. For the simple reason that I could take my own interpretation of the mural as a starting point and a basis from which to take the research a step further, becoming even more detached from the past... To make visible what is invisible.

Herman Devriendt, Internal Medicine: research as video

Aside from the artistic reconstruction of the mural painting of my grandfather, the Cabinet Devriendt also includes a video in which my father, holding a handkerchief on my back, is listening to my lungs. It is a reconstruction of an examination in which I figure as a patient and my father as a doctor, directed by my oldest son Alexander Devriendt. The whole scene took place in my studio.

The inspiration for this work was a visit from my father in 2010 because of a bad cold I had at the time. I realised that this event was an important experience for me. Which is why I wrote a text about it;

'One day in January 2010 I was ill. I called my father. He's an internalist and also my general practitioner. He told me he'd come by train. We had a conversation over coffee and I knew that during the talk, my father looked at me and observed my behaviour. He evaluated my speech, examined the brightness of my eyes, the sound of my voice, the colour of my skin… every detail, like a painter creating a portrait. At a certain moment, he asked me to undress my upper body, and he started looking for his stethoscope. While I was waiting, he realised that he had lost it, probably on the train.

He smiled, took a handkerchief out of his pocket and said: "let's do it the old way." With his two hands, he unfolded the freshly ironed handkerchief and put it on my back, gently, carefully. I was sitting on a chair. He put his ear on the handkerchief, on my back. At that moment, I connected with him on a different level.'

This event caused a redefinition of my 'I', and this on a much broader level than my then level of consciousness. Suddenly, there was more than just my history as a man and as an artist. A connection was brought to the foreground, one in which my father and grandfather became a very important part of my history. This was the reason why I decided to also literally involve my family in my work and research.

Lucas Devriendt, 2011. The Check-up (Stills from video) Video: Richard Duyck, Emile Duyck, Leon Duyck Regie: Alexander Devriendt

Lucas Devriendt, 2011. The Check-up (Stills from video)Video: Richard Duyck, Emile Duyck, Leon Duyck Regie: Alexander Devriendt

Lucas Devriendt, Artist: The Black Plastic Painting

How does a painting come into being? What is its prior history? What was its necessity? What is it that makes you paint it eventually? Is it a foundling, an orphan? Or does it have family, ancestors, parents, children? At a certain moment, it emerges. It suddenly appears. It can get in the way, it can be hung, it can hang around. It is present and sometimes not. Seen from the side it is not so thick—just a few centimetres—unlike the front side, which at best suggests an immensity.

The back is like a dress with a bare back. As an object, it is a lightweight. Something is suggested on the carrier, the canvas, the painted canvas, the painting. Or is it? Alberti writes: 'Since painting strives to represent things, let us examine how things are seen.' On it, I painted black plastic that reflects light. I wondered why on earth I had done that. Was there a reason, was it a coincidence? I had the impression that
I had mainly not painted something. And this because of… Of what? What did I not want to paint? The absence? Did I want to paint the invisible? Can you paint a thing that is not visible? In the painting, you can sometimes see its physically past, traces of actions and touches of the brush and the paint that—loosely and together—tell a story.

The painting is constructed on a base of colours that lie hidden beneath the black. The whole is painted quite coarsely and does not appear to be very hyper realistic, although from a distance it does create that impression. The painting is supposed to look 'painted'. I painted the work quite quickly, in the span of about a week. The toughest parts were the whites because they had to literally glow against the black, otherwise they would look like empty spots I had forgotten to paint. Aside from the black, it is undoubtedly the square format that most affects the impact of the painting on the viewer and myself.

The *Black Plastic* is a painting of a reality that I created in my studio. It is a time when you take steps so as to no longer shy away from yourself and decide to create an environment that reflects what you had in mind. On a sunny day, I completely shielded my studio from the light, taped the windows with black plastic to be alone in my own space, confined in my own black darkroom. Just like my grandfather who shielded his cabinet so as to only experience that reality, and bring to light that which occupied him. To come face to face with the reality of the moment, to see something you had not seen before. Like my father who—with his ear pressed against my body, eyes closed—could experience and see my inner space.

I admit it: the moment I painted the Black Plastic was a dark moment. I never thought that these moments would prove to be so profound. In many ways, the painting has dislodged something, caused something, revealed something. Its darkness has enlightened me, and for just a moment I was able to look around myself, away from my navel. In my mind I see another such moment: how as a child, after apparently having asked the wrong question, I had my head pushed into the soup by my grandfather. Green soup. In a similar way, I felt drawn into the paint by my own painting, thrown back upon myself, hurled back in time. All the way. My eyes shut.

The painting the Black Plastic only found its place at the end of the ride, in the Cabinet Devriendt, although it was both the starting point and the cause of the research. Sometimes a painting is a story that can be told backwards as if one were reading the story from beginning to end. Its ancestry also became my ancestry. I was lucky because, through my ancestors, I could think ahead in reverse. You dig into your past and discover artefacts that are suddenly more relevant than anything you have seen and created so far. A future past.

My father told me that, through my research, he has rediscovered his father. He saw something he had not seen before. Knowing is seeing, apparently. That is what the research is about, a curious longing mixed with an inquisitiveness that creates a clear view on something. Being an artist is something that appears to have originated outside of the self, or before the self even thought of becoming or being an artist. Perhaps my grandfather became more of an artist and I have now become more of a doctor.

Lucas Devriendt. 2007. Black Plastic Polaroid (Polaroid)

Lucas Devriendt, 2008. Black Plastic (oil on canvas
with video projection, 200 x 200 cm), PRS Europe 2015.

Harold Fallon
Metarbitrariness?

AgwA architecture office was founded in 2003 in Brussels by Harold Fallon and Benoît Vandenbulcke.

As many others, the office was almost immediately projected in the arbitrary realm of a deconstructed architectural field, with a vast amount of masters to look at, with infinite technical possibilities, and with landscapes that are continuously reshaped.

Are there still relevant ideologies to follow or is architecture recentering on individual practices? During 9 years of intensive practice (2003–2012), the work of AgwA in Flanders, Brussels and Wallonia has embodied a permanent research on these issues.

6 main projects retrace AgwA's journey for a coherent architectural approach beyond the issue of arbitrariness, of which the inner design processes became an underlying condition. Three of them are illustrated below.

In its ambition and in its development, AgwA's work shows particular resonances with the writings of the French poet Francis Ponge: literary ambition, actual texts and (the entire) writing practice become are dimensions of one single oeuvre.

Vertigo, AgwA, 2007 — © M.-F. Plissart

AgwA was founded two years after the partner's graduation. We did not undergo a long training period at a Master's office. We found ourselves immediately projected in the arbitrary realm of a deconstructed field, with no Master to follow, but instead, a vast amount of masters to look at. Through our projects, we are in a process of definition of an attitude in the field of architectural practice.

Philippeville, model with no roofs, AgwA, 2008

What we aim in our work is not an hypothetical new universal design method. It is rather an attempt to understand "how the world operates" and to make use of this (and perhaps only this) in an architectural practice, thus overcoming the problem of arbitrariness. Quite a challenge!

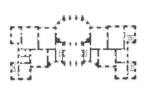

Vaux-le-Vicomte, 1661

"It is the mathematical beauty, to which the matter of things is added, challenged by sensibility and brought to reason."

("pour un Malherbe", Ponge, 1965, NRF, p25

In the end, it could all be about the formulation of hypotheses which are specific enough and generic enough to provide a strong identity to resolve any degree of complexity to respond to local and global constraints and potentials. Theses hypotheses can address different issues like spatiality, program, structure or materiality. Once formulated precisely (after an explorative process of variable length) there is a point in which these hypotheses can simply be applied or built.

Touring Lanaken (images published on www.agwa.be between 2008 and 2010)

A small model of a tower is playfully but seamlessly photoshopped in a wide range of very different contexts. Is architecture still a local issue? Is everything possible everywhere? What is our role as architects? Are we, architects, doomed to irrelevance and relativity?

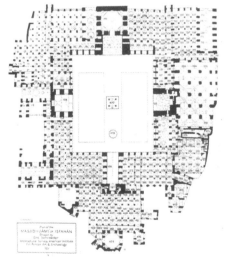

Great Mosque of Isfahan, plan by Eric Schroeder, 1931

I stood still at Foucault's proposition at the end of his book "The Order of Things", which he does not develop: what could the possible "disappearance" of man mean in the history of thought?
    The question can be transferred to creative practices and more specifically to architecture. Is an architecture possible in which the architect retracts from his creative omnipotence and centrality? How could this happen?
    Instead of the provocative assertion of man about to disappear from its central position in the understanding (and making) of the world, I would propose that man could be repositioned: it's position can be redefined.

Pont du Gard, around 75 AD, print by Clérisseau, 1804

"Indeed, they are utilitarian monuments, like the Pont du Gard"

Ponge about Malherbe's poems, and also his own, in "pour un Malherbe", Ponge, 1965, NRF, p125.

Metal, AgwA, 2009 — © M.-F. Plissart

"Anyway, failure is never absolute"

"Le parti pris des choses", F. Ponge, p181, Gallimard, 1941

Metaphorical specificity, Vertigo 2007

Theming of a new ride, Walibi Belgium theme park

While the European cities are gradually getting shaped like theme parks through historicist decorations, politically correct facadism and passeist regulations, what specificity has been left over to theme parks? Perhaps they could respond to this situation by proposing realistic spaces instead of heterochronic projections? Theme parks are in essence heterotopic places out of space and time. Now that cities project themselves in so-called better times, and while housing gets sprawled in pseudo rural styles, may theme parks become the last places of concrete reality?

We proposed to reveal the attraction in its nudity, instead of being packed in an outdated decoration. Its technology and engineering should be exhibited and not camouflaged. Reality without shame. What we actually designed is no theme at all. The attraction's station and queueline are enclosed in a light and industrial translucent skin, revealing the technicality of the attraction while preserving some mystery and untold presence.

Projects can be identified through the concise formulation of an hypothese, that defines their specificity. This specificity is metaphorical in nature. Such hypothese can address the program, the relationship to the context, or even be external to the architecture itself, but always refers to architectural features. This metaphorical relationship can be concrete or abstract in nature. It can address typological, material, spatial issues.

If such an hypothese about the project is enounced with sufficient precision, it becomes the red line that will help to maintain the intrinsic qualities of the project, disregarding the difficulties, contingencies and necessary flexibility of the designing and building process.

The attraction's queueline is enclosed in an industrial translucent skin, revealing the technicality of the attraction and preserving some mystery and untold presence.

Collages are a way of constructing and injecting a reality into another one. In the case of the Vertigo, the collage fixed some parameters of the equation, and keep freedom for other dimensions. This allows the project to evolve through the design and construction process without altering its quality.

A. In the first sketches, the skin of the vertigo was given a quite arbitrary shape. Openings allow contact between the inside and the inside.

B. During the design stage, the openings were adapted to fit needs of the project: entrances, exits, emergency and technical accesses, shape of the existing structure, modulation to the size of polycarbonate panels.

C. The structure becomes the "filling" of the project: it coexists, but its shape is not designed or dictated by the project.

D. Last minute input by the theme park's direction: "You don't want us to develop a colorless theme park, do you?"

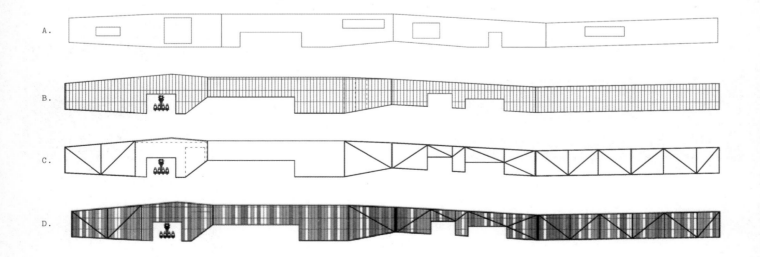

A.

B.

C.

D.

Flexible Structural Principles, Metal 2009

Refurbishment of a workshop in class rooms, sports hall and housing

The building, which has preserved the qualities of space and light of the period of its construction, now houses a sports hall, an after-school homework programme, and three moderate-rent apartments. This mixed development meets the requirements set out in the «neighbourhood agreement» urban-regeneration project of the district.

We decided to preserve as much as possible of the powerful modernist architectural structure. The two apartments are conceived as a totally independent structure hanging over the roof. As the existing apartment is already conceived as a bridge-structure, the new ensemble induces a horizontal stratification of heterogeneous parts contrasting strongly with the surrounding houses.

In order to reinforce this contrast, and also to match sharp financial criteria, the facade cladding of the new apartments is realized in transparent polycarbonate, that is also used in the large glass roofs and façades.

The project focuses on structure and skin topics: archeological preservation, transformation, and resonance of new structural elements with the older ones. These structural strategies are all ruled by the understanding of the structural behavior, instead of the structural design. In consequence, a coherent diversity is made possible in appearances and materialities.

Instead of constraining, expensive detailing and structural design, the definition of flexible structural principles make it possible to adapt to different situations, and to address the design and the construction process with ease, while preserving the intrinsinc quality of the project. Such principles are typological in nature. They allow coherence and diversity at the same time.

The existing building consists of large concrete frames on the first floor, that liberate space from disturbing vertical structural elements between the two neighbouring walls. On the second floor, similar, smaller frames provide zenithal light to the level below, and provide lateral views to the second floor.

This principle of large beams freeing space completely, becomes the red line of the structural approach. It is a very simple, flexible principles, that doesn't give indications on the shape, design, or materiality of the structural elements. In consequence, it gives freedom in the solving of local issues and situations.

A variable set of strategies was developped around this single principle.

First, the structure was cleaned in its original situation. The exterior elements, some of which were discovered during the works, were painted black in order to avoid expensive concrete restoration works.

Second, two beam were modified by the integration of a new staircase. One beam was cut and the scheme of loads was modified. These beams are supported by new elements in black concrete.

Third, the structure is extended with a variety of structural solutions, like simple steel beams for the façade cladding and the realization of a two levels Vierdendeel beam on the front elevation.

Metal, AgwA, 2009 © M.-F. Plissart

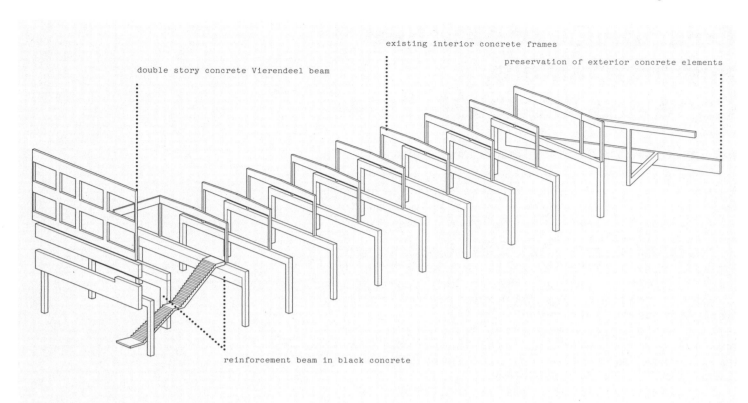

double story concrete Vierendeel beam

existing interior concrete frames

preservation of exterior concrete elements

reinforcement beam in black concrete

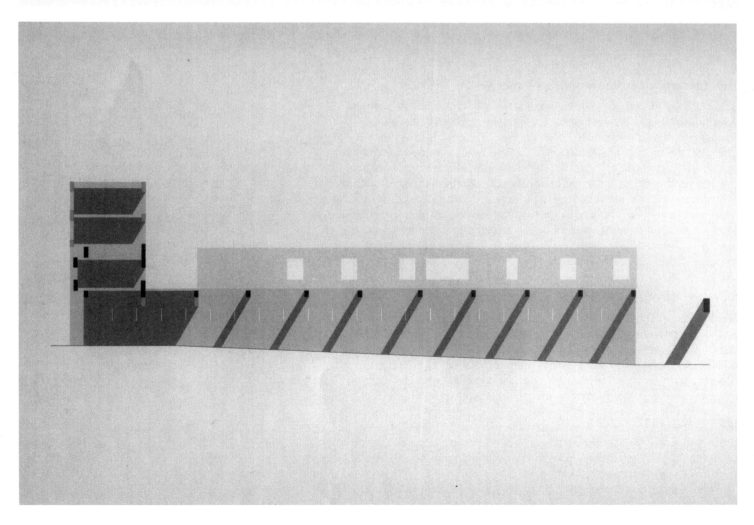

Coincidence of structure and architecture, Carré des Arts, 2008–2014

Retractile covering of the Carré des Arts, Mons, Belgium

The covering of the Carré des Arts ins Mons is a project between roof and tent, is intrinsically technological, and seems to escape the traditional field of architecture. Consequently, the project is about the definition of an attitude towards theses aspects. A common ground had to be found for structure, technique and spatiality.

1. manutention / The first option is an «unconstructed» structure. While the roof is merely textile and has to be rebuilt each time, the only permanent structure are anchoring points on the floor and the roof edges. The Carré des Arts becomes essentially potential, as any future possibility is opened through the chart of anchors.

2. articulated structure / In the second option, is a made-to-measure one. The articulation of the textile structure itself allows to cover partially or totally the square. Permanent rails on the facades guide the mechanisms that fold and unfold this accordeon-like roof.

3. retractable roofs / The third option is the catalogue-based one. A network of slender beams chart the sky above the roofs themselves. The defined «tiles» receive prefabricated retractable roofs, which are fully ready-made and automatised. A wide range of uses is made possible from total covering to complete opening.

Coincidence of stucture and architecture

The shape of structure addresses the physical constraints. It can also integrate other dimensions of the project, like spatiality, rainwater, integration of technological or constructive elements. Instead of cladding the structure with decorative skins, let the structure absorb the architecture, and the architecture match its structure as much as possible. It is a mutual search for coincidence. This questions the tradtionnal Semper (servant structure) vs Viollet-Le-Duc (dominating structure) dual field.

We do not attempt to beslave structure to architecture or vice-versa. Instead, there is a negociation between architectural and structural design, aiming at the blooming of each. The issue is to define the rules and to manage the space for this negociation.

Opening divergent possibilities and paring back

For the covering of the courtyard of the Carré des Arts in Mons, we proposed three projects at the competition stage. The three intentions at the competition stage were based mainly on their materiality: membrane, timber/steel, inflated structure. Their architectural consequence towards the existing building were also evoked: anchored in the building, independent structure modifying space, totally disappearing roof.

During the first stage of the design process, these three intentions evolved into a large collection of possible projects. It was a process of pragmatization of ideas: the zeppelin evolved into balloons suspended by cranes or into self stable, inflated mushroom shaped structures. Each possibility was also referenced carefully.

Then, we did not choose "the best" solutions. Instead, we grouped them into overlapping families. First, an attempt was made according to materiality (tensed membranes, inflated structures, hard structures). As this prooved not to be very helpful, we organized them by what we

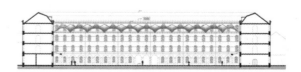

Carré des Arts, AgwA, 2008, sections from the feasibility study

called "use value", which then were distilled into three feasible projects, of which two were completely developed. As these lines are being written, the membrane roof is under construction.

The seriality of the design process in the Carré des Arts is a fundamental way of designing at the office. When developing prohjects, nothing is given at once. Possibilities need to be opened in an almost disinterested way. Things needs to be worked and reworked in order to converge to a point at which "it fits", meaning that we grasped what the project was about, that the essential features of the project have been made conscious.

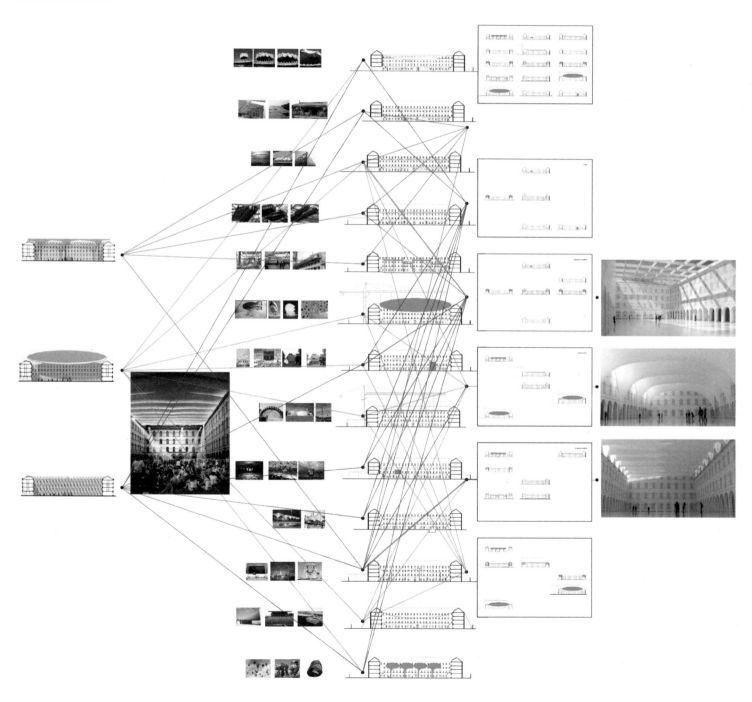

three conceptual proposals at the competition stage, addressing different material and spatial typologies

referencing of existing solutions ...

...compared to a wide range of possible realistic interpretations of the conceptual proposals

regrouping of solutions through the filter of materiality and through the filter of use value and constructive nature (catalogue products vs meade to measure)

extracting three feasible projects combining the three spatial typologies of the competition stage with the features of the three typologies of use value

Spatial genericity Philippeville, 2008

Competition for a school restaurant

The restaurant is located at the center of the school campus. The restaurant is a central place: both the heart of the campus' life and regeneration. The building is conceived as an irreducible set of rooms with different sizes, heights, and uses inside a square footprint. The building is flexible and accessible: it is a place for all. An open, light wood structure fits the room's dimensions. Isotropy and porosity as key themes.

The genericity of a spatial development depends on its independence vis-à-vis the type, and possibly of the number of its subspaces, consequently increasing the level of its abstraction, and thus its capacity to absorb diversity and unexpectedness while establishing a powerful identity.

Spaces can dissolve in the geometricality. They also can simply be juxtaposed, maintaining their original autonomy. These two compatible strategies can be combined to different degrees. Spatial Genericity lies in a concurrence of arithmetics (distinction, quantification) and geometry (relative position of elements in the whole) organized by common rules.

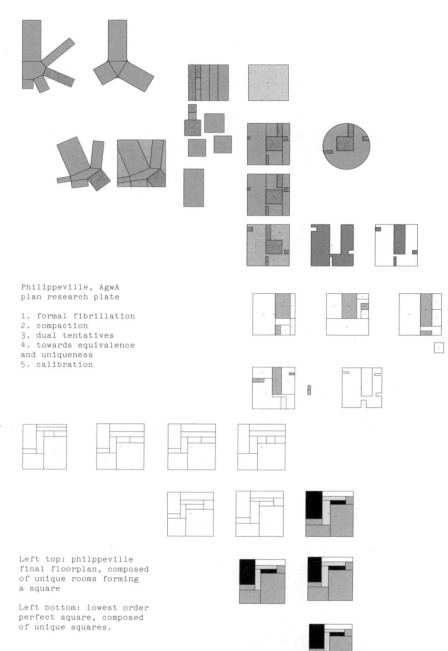

Philippeville, AgwA
plan research plate

1. formal fibrillation
2. compaction
3. dual tentatives
4. towards equivalence
   and uniqueness
5. calibration

Left top: philppeville
final floorplan, composed
of unique rooms forming
a square

Left bottom: lowest order
perfect square, composed
of unique squares.

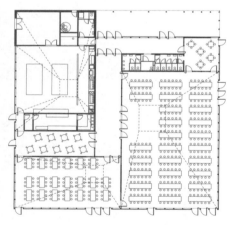

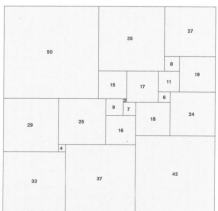

Arnaud Hendrickx
Substantiating Displacement

Differentiation in Practice

Arnaud Hendrickx has segued from being a practitioner designing and procuring daring houses in a recognisably Flemish whimsy manner to being a practitioner academic who is tailoring his designing to the research collaborations that arise within academic institutions. This reorientation has been accomplished but not without some regret for the challenges of procuring in particular. He relishes a tale about how one house with large clear spans was fabricated in steel in Rumania and shipped from there up the Danube and along the Rhine for less than the cost of local manufacture. The adventure of the steel seems more exciting to him than the resulting cantilever, which in actuality jostles with other cantilevers less romantically inflected by their hidden histories.

More than in most places exceptionally creative architects operate in a narrow defile in Belgium. There are twice as many architects per head of population as in the neighbouring Netherlands, and much work in corporate Brussels is bundled up in the practice of a few major corporate practices. Another pincer is encroaching on small practitioners, as part time teachers are progressively required to get PhDs and become, in the jargon of university administrators "research active" — in wilful ignorance of the integrated scholarship1 that actually constitutes productive work practice. Where others have found a path to practicing and teaching, Arnaud has chosen a path that aligns with his love of the unusual, the romantic and the dangerous. His practice has become one that is situated in galleries, and one in which the clients are artists and curators.

Danger? One breakaway design projected live wires along a plank into space. Another created the illusion of an upper level walkway between gallery spaces, passage being impossible except in the mind. Spatial reconfigurations of galleries to suit specific exhibits followed, though the insertion itself became a figure on exhibition in the space. Another project recreated the spatial form of a Greek amphitheatre, but in a gallery and with a manner of access that closed after the audience entered, locking them in hermetically to the amphitheatre fragment.

In the demonstration project that concluded his reflective practice research with us Arnaud presented his various, meticulously charted, authorial personae to an audience seated on a raking set of polystyrene plinths, set in a gallery containing representations of his key works. His audience became an object in the gallery, as curated as any of the set designs. The glee with which he observed their slow journey to the white plinths set on a white base was as evident as it is when he recounts the tale of the house that came by barge. Arnaud is at home in his difference.

Substantiating Displacement

'Substantiating Displacement' is a reflection on my architectural practice by the making of new projects. It substantiates (establishes by evidence) my displacement from the centre of architecture to a more liminal position in the overlapping field of art and architecture. This methodological displacement reveals and questions the operational tactics and conceptual frameworks I work with(in), by actively engaging with mediators (among others art & artists) in the reflection on and the design and creation of architecture, in order to explore the transitional space between subject and object. In this exploration I consider this transitional space to be the intermediate space of human experience that architecture opens up and in which it operates between our inner reality and an environment exterior to it, between shaping an environment while simultaneously being subject to it, between a material environment and its immaterial capacity to affect us.

This methodological displacement generated a new series of spatial works that uncovered heuristic devices that enable to engage in a designerly way and to substantiate (give substance or form to) three forms of displacement: displacement as motion or physical interaction; displacement as the negotiation between two agents, and displacement as a shift in apperception as the result of a contextual shift. A simple thought experiment might shed additional light on the three distinct meanings of displacement that frame displacement as the subject matter of this PhD:

Imagine slicing off one meter of the Mount Everest, Earth's highest summit, and throwing this chunk of rock into the Challenger Deep, the deepest part of the deepest trench in the sea. This action would entail three different forms of displacement. First of all, the chunk of rock would undergo a displacement in the sense of a movement. Secondly, the seawater and the rock would negotiate a new sea level by an displacement of water. Thirdly, without undergoing any physical changes, the chunk of matter formerly known as the summit of the world would in this new context find its meaning displaced to the chunk of matter that defines the deepest point of the sea.

At the outset of the research project displacement was not the presupposed subject. No subject, only a strict method, what I now call 'the method of good company', was defined. Only by implementing this method, that among other things entailed engaging in a designerly way with a strategically selected group of sparring partners, that the three threads framed by displacement emerged: The collaboration with Gabriël Lester in the exhibition 'ProMotion' (images [1a] & [1b]) placed a focus on Embodied Simulations: creating an environment that provides affordances for physical interaction. The collaborations with Michaël Van den Abeele in the exhibitions 'Isomosis' and 'Bonus Malus' (images [2a] & [2b]) placed of focus on Negotiating Space: conceive an environment shaped by two negotiating agents. The collaboration with Richard Venlet and Michaël Van den Abeele in the exhibition 'Perennial' (images [3a] & [3b]) placed a focus on Conceptual Blending: creating an environment that provides affordances for mental interaction.

Lens grinding

'Substantiating displacement' looks at a general topic through a specific lens. By appropriating the means of expression of architecture in a spatial artistic practice that is concerned with conceiving ways to structure matter in order to explore how this structured matter affects us, a series of four spatial interventions are executed. These actions serve as fertile grounds to grind a precise lens to look at, understand and communicate the specifics of my spatial artistic practice. This grinding departs from the notion 'intensive differences drive processes' drawn from an architectural appropriation of a conceptual framework from the physical sciences and the philosophic language of intensive thinking developed by Gilles Deleuze.

Glossary

BECAUSE IT'S THERE — 'Because it's there' is a heuristic device drawn from the installation ProMotion. It is a name that is intuitively given to capture its double ambition:
Because it's there also suggests that design decisions for shaping a project are made, just because it's there, in that context, on that site, that the work had to be conceived. It captures an interest in exploring the potential of a spatial composition for triggering mental interaction with the observer and the context in which it is active. An interest in spatial mechanisms triggers a different reading of a space by considering the site as a brief.
Because it's there suggests that an observer interacts with an artifact just because it's there. It captures an interest in exploring the potential of a functional artifact for triggering physical interaction with the observer that is not based on functional needs but on experiential expectations, an interest in spatial mechanisms that trigger movement and other forms of physical interaction by considering interaction as a brief.

A. BECAUSE IT'S THERE #1: FRAMING SPACE — Highlighting a specific aspect of Because it's there, Framing Space wants to capture an interest in site specificity as creating an environment that provides affordance for mental interaction with a site. It refers to the traditional framing of views commonly found in architecture and wants to expand this by including other notions such as: mapping as intervention, strategic positioning (relational negotiation), point of view (isovist), displacing a room, tracing traces...

A1. AUTONOMOUS MAPPING — Highlighting a specific aspect of Framing Space, Autonomous mapping captures the poetic and sculptural potential of analogy embodied in the creation of three dimensional logical pictures of a site.

A2. MAPPING AS INTERVENTION — Highlighting a specific aspect of Framing Space, Mapping as intervention captures the poetic potential that emerges when an artifact becomes a lens through which we mentally engage with a space.

A3. STRATEGIC POSITIONING — Highlighting a specific aspect of Framing Space, Strategic positioning then captures the poetic potential that emerges when an artifact by its careful placement interacts with a space.

B. BECAUSE IT'S THERE #1: PROMOTION — Highlighting a specific aspect of Because it's there, ProMotion wants to capture an interest in appropriating architectural mechanisms for their potential to create an environment that provides affordances for physical interaction. It also refers to architectural heuristic devices as enfilade, vantage point, blind summit, chunking maps...

B1. CONTEXTUAL INHIBITIONS — This heuristic device captures an interest in the spatial conditions that influence our tendency to physically interact with a spatial situation, in the complex system of subjective, social and cultural restraints that filter the affordances that one picks up from an environment.

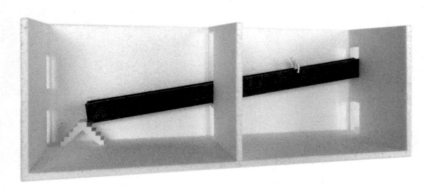

[1a]

The concepts that constitute this lens are formulated in a glossary that was gradually built during the course of this PhD by confronting new insights gained from the new collaborative work with already existing work. I have decided to integrate a large part of this glossary in this publication in its raw form, disconnected from its original context in the thesis. This allows the heuristic devices in it to function in an open way. While they are formulated as descriptions and definitions, in this format they suggest more than they define. They rather function as a cloud of concepts that resonate freely and serve as raw material for the readers appropriation.

An Architecture of intensities

Since space is often considered the basic ingredient of architecture, the notion seems the right place to start a refection on architecture. Suppose we consider two very different containers that have the capacity to store exactly the same maximum amount of tiny marbles. We can imagine an abstract property that is shared by these containers: the space inside them. By expanding this extensive property, it can be understood as an infinite container of all material objects, an absolute space freed from any connection with a particular material object and with a particular observer. But we do not inhabit this absolute space. When we experience space we do not experience an absolute infinite space, where all chunks of space are essentially equal, but a relative space, where chunks differ. Chunks of space are defined by differences, properties relative to our body and to the intensities of fields or forces that are in its proximity. It is in this relative space filled with properties that emerge from intensities the we might identify a place, another basic ingredient of architecture.

Continuing the reasoning initiated before, the identity of a place emerges from the underlying differences in intensities or forces in relation to its spatial and temporal milieu. To illustrate the importance of this milieu, let us try to imagine a place disconnected from any physical context. We might imagine it as a place contracted into one isolated infinitely small mathematical point, or maybe as place that is an infinitely large continuous extension of itself, whatever its properties might be. Nothingness or sameness interchangeable to suggest a uniform spatial context. Without context the place becomes its opposite a non-place. Yet if we would project ourselves in this non-place where nothing ever changes, it would still confront us with temporal differences, differences that originate from before and after embodied within ourselves. The differences we experience are the here and now of the nothingness or sameness confronted with an embodied model of ourselves and the milieu we inhabit based on memories of interactions with different places. As long as we are not a continuously integrated part of this 'contextless' environment we somehow import

B2. INTENSIVE DIFFERENCES DRIVE PROCESSES — This heuristic device captures an interest in thinking in intensities via the notions of intensive differences, nesting of intensities, intensification of extensities, an attractive constellation. Where in physics a difference in, say, temperature drives an actual physical process in which molecules are directly affected, in considering the spatial experience of architecture these differences drive virtual, mental processes that might result in a conative drive that in its place might trigger physical interactions.

B3. EMBODIED SIMULATION — This heuristic device captures an interest in considering the perceiving of an environment as mentally simulating our interactions with the space and by mostly unconsciously doing so we create experiential expectations that might attract us.

B3A ENFILADE — A spatial situation consisting of a rhythmic sequence of aligned spaces functions as a possible attractor for embodied simulation and hence triggers interaction with an observer.

B3B VANTAGE POINT — A spatial situation that affords an advantage (like offering an overview, an opportunity to touch the ceiling...) compared to other situations, functions as a possible attractor for embodied simulation and hence triggers interaction with an observer.

B3C BLIND SUMMIT — A spatial situation that gradually leads to what is expected to give a wider perspective, expected to be a vantage point, triggers an expectation that functions as a possible attractor for embodied simulation and hence triggers interaction with an observer.

B4. CHUNKING MAPS — Highlighting a specific aspect of ProMotion, Chunking maps wants to capture an interest in how actions and movement though space generate mental maps of a space. It also refers to how chunks of space create chunks of experiences that are combined to form a whole where the parts define the whole, and vice versa.

C. NEGOTIATING SPACE — This heuristic device is drawn from the installation Isomosis and captures an interest in creating an environment that is shaped through the negotiation of two agents. Architectural means of expression often expressed in opposing couples (solid / void; inside / outside; load-bearing / being supported, etc.) that can be considered as interacting agents or mediators that structure architectural thinking.

C1. NUANCING DICHOTOMIES — This heuristic device captures an interest in reflecting on and nuancing the seemingly opposing couples in the means of expression of architecture.

C1.1. SUPRA THICK — This heuristic device captures an interest in thickness that nuances the apparent dichotomy of solid and void by inverting Marcel Duchamp's concept of 'Inframince' (Infrathin): more specifically, a thickness that has becomes so thick that it defines a new space on its own. It is a space that one cannot perceive or experience directly, in a single glance, but though 'chunking maps' and combining precepts in order to mentally construct, apperceive and experience its thickness.

[1b] PROMOTION — Gabriël Lester & Arnaud Hendrickx (2009)
— Z33, Hasselt (B).
In favor of motion, Pro Motion combines several works
that either isolate movement by fixing it or that
suggest motion and narration as a progression through
time and space. Cut diagonally through a stripped
space, a balancing ramp defying the laws of gravity
connects the various works on show and directs the
visitor from the ground floor to a small room above
the main space.

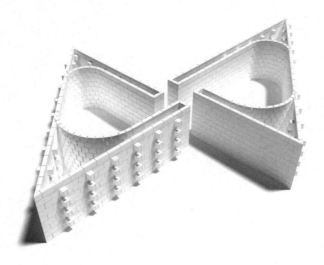

[2a]

temporal differences. Since space and place heavily rely on context and milieu it seems more appropriate to use a term that more explicitly refers to this immersive inside that is simultaneously oriented toward an external milieu: environment.

All of this just say that we can imagine experiencing an environment as the crossing in the present of a vertical 'spatial' axis of synchronicity: the 'here and now' of the actualization—by the specialized cells that we call our senses—of the multiplicity of intensities that the environment gives us (reduction by actualization) and a horizontal 'temporal' axis of diachronicity: the 'here and now' of the re-actualized past and the opening up of the future by inscribing the perceived multiplicity into a network of memories and anticipations (expansion by simulation). So what an encounter with an environment affords us is a matter of the virtual potential of capacities to affect coupled to capacities to be affected. The actualization of this virtual potential entails a reduction of intensities by our senses, while, at the same time, the resulting stream of perception is expanded by inscribing the experienced into our conceptual framework. We could say that, through materiality of the physical environment, something is presented which transcends materiality. An encounter with an environment affords a process of sense making that affects different aspects of our mind: it affects what we think (cognitive), feel (affective) and act (conative). This sense making process can be considered as an appropriation by which the observer constructs a transitional space that bridges the gap between mind and matter.

A designer should constantly be looking for means to address this gap. A possible perspective is that designing entails displacing memories of earlier encounters into a nearby or distant future by equilibrating our conceptual frameworks to imagined novel situations. We construct our conceptual frameworks by internalizing our knowledge of our environment and how we personally relate to it in cognitive structures that originate from action in this environment. Imagining or anticipating a future event entails a mental simulation based on earlier experiences A spatial artistic practice like architecture differentiates space by nesting intensities within these existing differences. By (re)structuring matter it substantiates an environment that establishes differences in intensity of light, texture, color, odor, density and so on. Even when the material substance might only be a bunch of photons or pixels, it is only through this (re)structuring of matter that difference is articulated, it is only through a placement in the world that an observer might crystallize the virtual potential of intensities into a singular spatial experience.

C1.2. EPHEMERAL AGENTS — This heuristic device nuances the apparent dichotomy of solid and void by considering the space-structuring potential embodied in the negotiation of immaterial, atmospheric and dynamic elements like photons or water particles, the usage of a space...

C1.3. TRACING BOUNDARIES — This heuristic device nuances the apparent dichotomy of solid and void by tracking down, registering and redefining the boundary surface (like fences, walls, territorial borders...) that negotiates between two physical or conceptual agents.

D. CONCEPTUAL BLENDING (PERENNIAL) — This heuristic device captures an interest in creating an environment that triggers meaning, turning the environment from a passive container of activities into an active participant.

D1. ADJUSTED COPY (ISOMOSIS) — This heuristic device captures an interest in the poetic potential of creating a replica with a twist, by consciously misinterpreting the source and/or consciously adjusting it to the destination so that a poetic tension arises in the difference between the original and the replica — for example, in terms of scale, materiality, gender, etc. It is a specific form of what in art is generally known as appropriation or borrowing.

D2. POINTER TO VOID (ISOMOSIS) — This heuristic device nuances the apparent dichotomy of solid void by focusing on the poetic and hermeneutical potential of the symbolic void, on that which is consciously absent or omitted.

D3. ANIMISM (BONUS MALUS) — This heuristic device captures an interest in the poetic potential in rediscovering the pre-rational or allowing the post-rational notion that endows non-living things with life.

D4. RECODING CHUNKS (THE CIRCLE, CHIPKA) — This heuristic device captures an interest in the potential to shift meaning, to recode complex chunks of sensory information by means of naming, displacing, juxtaposition.

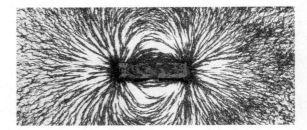

E. INTENSIVE DIFFERENCES — A spatial experience entails variations in sensorial qualities like light, humidity, temperature, color, odor, sound, form... that, through the lens of the conceptual framework of intensive thinking, can be seen as differences in intensities.

[2b]   BONUS MALUS — Michaël Van den Abeele & Arnaud
       Hendrickx (2010), Aalst (B), Netwerk
       The Neolithic pavillion is conceived as an habitat
       for the excentric figures that are portrayed in
       Michaël's paintings and sculptures. It shapes an
       environment where these figures can hang out rather
       than an infractruture to hang them on.

[3a]

Thinking through a medium

It is evident that a spatial artistic practice does not actually produces space; the amount of (absolute) space in the universe is not influenced by the practice. It indirectly tampers with the intensities and qualitative properties of space by structuring its complement: matter. We could say that a spatial artistic practice creates sensory aggregates by structuring matter in such a way that it establishes new differences in intensities that in their turn alter the qualitative properties of a chunk of space. If we also take into account that practitioners of this kind of practice usually do not constructs the material artifacts it conceives themselves, it makes the relation between the subject and the realized object indirect. Since only now and then is an architect also a builder, the most intrinsic activity of a spatial artistic practice is conceiving ideas on how to structure matter so that it creates intensive differences.

Gilles Deleuze answers the question of what it actually means to have an idea in a specific domain like art as follows: "Ideas must be treated as potentials that are already engaged in this or that mode of expression and inseparable from it, so much that I cannot say I have an idea in general. According to the techniques that I know, I can have an idea in a given domain, an idea in cinema or rather an idea in philosophy."

If we continue the reasoning that creative ideas are inseparable from the mode of expression of a discipline, the creative act of conceiving space can be situated internally to the discipline. Through the architect's knowledge of the means of expression, architecture becomes a medium to think with and through. Conceiving space entails an inward focus on disciplinary means of expression and gives it a more intra-disciplinary or autonomous character.

At the same time, when we express an idea, upon perceiving this expression, we also calibrate and expand our (tacit) understanding of the means of expression of the medium we use for expressing it. In the functioning of this expression we gain new knowledge over these means. In that sense, our model of and hence our subjective relation with the means of expression changes. We might make general principles our own, generalize specific insights – in short, we appropriate the means of expression of the medium we use.

Art and architecture have both developed rules and tools to conceive ways to structure matter (rules and tools sometimes comparable and sometimes quite different), resulting in similar and different means of expressing themselves. As a part my PhD I have tried to gain insights into some of these differences and overlaps to see whether this provides fertile ground to recalibrate my personal relation with the means of expression.

For example in Pro Motion the idea of creating expectation in film is checked for its potential and its architectural counterparts to have an architectural idea on how to create expectation.

E1. NESTING INTENSITIES — A practice concerned with making space distinct by creating differences in intensity does this by creating material artifacts, by structuring matter. The spatial context in which the spatial artistic practice places these material artifacts is a space that is already defined by intensities. Experiencing intensities emanating from these artifacts happens relative to intensities that already exist in the context. This makes experiencing intensities intrinsically site specific. In this light a spatial artistic practice can be seen as a practice concerned with making space distinct by nesting (new) differences in intensity inside other (already existing) differences in intensity.

E2. INTENSIFYING EXTENSITIES — One of the modi operandi to create differences in intensity is to implement abstracted notions of space like volume, length, height, width in a relative way. A composition of extensities in which the relation among them or with other extensities or intensities constitutes a quality, and turns this composition of extensities into an intensity.

E4. EXPERIENTIAL DIALECTICS — Only when an intensity is somehow complemented with a variation of the same intensive property can we experience it as a something relative, a quality. When 'high' is confronted with 'low' both intensities are strengthened and the actual experience of both is partly contained in and enhanced by their juxtaposition. This juxtaposition can be implicit, by varying an intensity that we are used to experiencing in a specific constellation (e.g. a living space can be high or low in relation to what we 'normally' expect from such a space) or can be explicit, by actually juxtaposing complementary variations of one intensity (e.g. actually juxtaposing a high and a low space).

E5. ATTRACTIVE CONSTELLATION — This is a structure that embodies a constellation of differences in intensity that subject the perceiver to emotional or psychological influence. These differences of intensities create a dialectic of experiences that function as fields of attraction in the structure.

E6. DISSIPATIVE SCENARIO — One of the modi operandi to create an attractive constellation is scenario thinking. Writing a scenario is often a linear process of describing some kind of path that embodies a sequential progression of experiences over time resulting in a linear experience of attractors. Writing a dissipative scenario entails combining different partial linear scenographies of attractors (cf. labyrinth) to form an open-ended field of intensities that constitute a non-linear scenography of attractors allowing some form of self-organization (cf. cornfield).

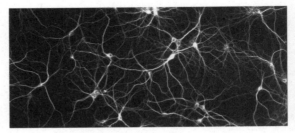

F. CRITICAL STATE — When a constellation of intensities achieves a critical point, a phase transition occurs. In this transitional state properties and qualities change drastically. At the same time this critical state of 'being-in-between' constitutes an ambiguity that affords different things to happen.

[3b] PERENNIAL (27/5/11–8/7/11, Brussel (B), Wiels) a
project by Arnaud Hendrickx, Michaël Van den Abeele
and Richard Venlet, is a comprehensive art piece that
functions as an auditorium, thought of as a salon
and shaped as an event. An autonomous interior that
presented seven artifacts, a lecturing Uranium Lead
clock and a music piece.
The evening program that was offered over the
course over seven weeks included seven carefully
selected events (lectures, readings, screenings
and performances). During the day one could visit
Perennial as an autonomous interior that presented
seven carefully selected artifacts.

Being thought by a medium

The production of a spatial artistic practice is somehow placed in the world, materialized. While most sensory aggregates, like a building or installation, are materialized in an immobile and fairly stable way, the virtual spatial potential of differences and intensities created by this structured matter is dynamic. It only actualizes itself, temporarily, through an observer who perceives, makes sense of, uses and builds a subjective relation with it. In that sense, the spatial artistic practice creates a space of possibilities, a virtual space of potential which always remains not fully actualized.

Every event, every interaction with an architectural object, influences the mental model we have from it and alters our subjective relation with it. The spatial sensory aggregate provides an environment that influences mental processes: it might influence our mood (affective), our thinking (cognitive) and our actions (conative). By hosting our memories it might even shape our being in the world and allow a form of identification that expresses aspects of our self. We could say that the artistic spatial practice produces thinking by creating affects and percepts. In this light, architecture—being an artistic spatial practice—can be seen as a medium that makes us think.

Conceiving space is inwards oriented towards the rules and tools pertaining to the discipline. Perceiving space entails an outward focus towards how an observer might experience space. The activity of conceiving space is characterized by a more autonomous aspect, the activity of perceiving space, by a more extra-disciplinary or heteronomous aspect.

At the same time, when perceiving a sensory aggregate we also consciously or unconsciously build a personal model of the possibilities of the medium that is put to work in the aggregate. It confirms, expands or drastically changes our model of its means of expression. So even when they embody a different mental process (thinking vs. being thought), conceiving and perceiving are mutually dependent and influence each other.

The conceptual framework of Because It's There (initiated by confronting my practice with Gabriël Lester's tendency toward creating a montage of attractions in the project ProMotion and further developed in the reflective actions on this project), and of Conceptual Blending (initiated by confronting my practice with Richard Venlet's tendency toward creating a mental montage in the project Perennial), and further developed in the reflective actions on this project, provide some heuristic devices that have altered my knowledge of how the spatial artistic practice may structure matter that, upon apperception by an observer, establishes an environment that affects our thoughts and makes us physically or mentally interact.

F1. ARTICULATING UNADAPTEDNESS — is expressing the search for a critical state of spatial intensities that allows ambiguity in a structure's being adapted and unadapted. This state of 'being-in-between' allows the occurrence of anticipated and unanticipated events (use) or well-delineated or more gradual experiences (experience). It is situated somewhere between simultaneously considering a spatial constellation as a shape determined by functional or aesthetic rules and as a space of possibilities that shapes the action potential and experiences and enlarges the space for appropriation by its users — between functional solutions and generating new potential for actions. One form of achieving this state is by means of a diagrammatic approach that accepts the fact that a structure is never fully actualized and creates an environment that is never fully adapted, without apperceiver. The diagrammatic approach postpones actualization and in this enlarges the space for appropriation.

F2. ARTICULATING HYBRIDITY — is expressing a critical state between the material and immaterial artifacts of a structure by aiming at generating experiences by making things. An artistic expression is, by the way it implements the means of expression of its medium, in a critical state of hybridity. This means that every expression is a singular combination of a material and an immaterial artifact. It is not possible to explicitly reproduce or describe this hybridity using another medium: it is a tacit quality of the singular combination of both artifacts. At the same time the singular hybrid is to some extent ambiguous, open to interpretation. The creator might conceive with a priority to trigger an immaterial experience of, for example 'symbolic meaning', 'action potential' or 'sensory experience', but when the artistic expression, articulated in a material artifact, is placed in the world it becomes independent of the creator and presents itself to an observer as a compound of percepts and affects that the observer makes sense of in his own way.

F3. ARTICULATING SIMPLEXITY — is expressing a critical state between the simplicity and complexity of a structure. One simple element (a shape or a structuring principle) may possess the potential to create qualities simultaneously on a functional, constructive and experiential level. The informed simplicity of this principle then contrasts with its more complex capacity to solve problems and define spatial qualities. One of the ways to articulate this contrast is by confronting a monolithic exterior with a more fragmented interior that affords many different and unexpected experiences. Articulating simplexity is creating a spatial structure that simultaneously affords synthesis and contrast.

F4. ARTICULATING EFFECTIVENESS — is expressing the fact that a structure is simultaneously efficient and effective. It is a more specific sub-category of 'articulating unadaptedness' that is more directly related to the use of resources: 'efficient' is making good use of resources (quantity) whilst 'effective' is having the power to produce a desired effect (quality). In many quantitative fields that rule our lives, the desired optimum is clearly a high efficiency combined with a high effectiveness. The meanings of these interdependent terms have grown so close to each other that, for many, they have almost become synonymous. However, in qualitative matter like design, these terms are absolutely irreducible to each other. For example an inefficient way of using space might be very effective and hence preferable in some cases. Being conscious about their difference might reveal new ways to deal effectively with ugliness, failure, waste and inefficiency.

Tom Holbrook
Between Furniture & Infrastructure

The challenges presented to society by rapid urbanisation and climate change directly call for the broad synthetic spatial knowledge that lies in the province of architecture and urban design. Curiously, in the face of such challenges, the discipline of architecture seems to have entered a period of self-imposed myopia. In recent years, architecture has lost ground in many of those areas that once lay within the disciplinary realm. The societal value ascribed to the spatial imagination is diminishing, and with it the value of operating as a generalist. The familiar rise of international multidisciplinary firms illustrate a shift towards regarding planning and urban design as a problem-solving activity. The multidisciplinary model privileges the instrumental knowledge of engineering, and the managerial routines of traditional planning and project management. The model depends not on synthesising different sorts of knowledge from within the discipline, but rather the consensually mute operation of diverse specialists contributing to the demands of a particular project without overarching synthetic authorship.

Opposite page: Early research involved the establishment of an archive of the work, and the development through internal discussion in the studio of some general taxonomies, identifying threads between projects and the way that they were drawn

Early research involved the establishment of an
archive of the work, and the development through
internal discussion in the studio of some general
taxonomies, identifying threads between projects and
the way that they were drawn

Generalism

5th Studio—the practice I established with co-director Oliver Smith in the late 1990s—set out to work simultaneously across what we saw as the five scales of design: from furniture, through interventions in existing fabric to the design of buildings, landscapes and very large-scale strategy.

After 15 years of practising deliberately as a generalist our output as a practice was heterogeneous. I was interested in understanding the continuities in the work.

I also wished to understand more fully the bridge we try and make in our work between the strategic understanding of very complex environments and the concrete implications of these decisions on the ground.

Acting as a generalist, which is seen as such a weakness by clients, who prefer specialist knowledge, could be developed into a strength of the practice in an explicit way.

One of the delights of the research was the six-monthly exile to Ghent or Barcelona: the opportunity to discuss the work of the practice away from the familiarity of London's architectural scene. This estrangement demanded a finer definition of terms.

In this context I came to understand how the topography in which we work (broadly eastern England) is so particular and differentiated, encompassing a constellation of ancient cities, new towns and conflicted landscapes, each overlayed on one of the densest accumulations of infrastructure anywhere.

Through looking at the work, and assembling the archive, a very clear thread became evident, composed of projects that addressed highly complex situations over long duration. To address the requirements of these projects the practice has evolved approaches that draw upon different sorts of knowledge.

Through the course of the research I came to understand more fully the diversity of roles that the practice plays on a complex projects. Our role on the Lea River Park—a key project for the practice over a long period of time—has spanned from traditional landscape and urban design responses to strategists ad planners through to acting as political advocates and spatial entrepreneurs.

Understanding how complex projects evolve has led to the development of a range of representational modes, and an acceptance of our pivotal role in the evolution of a narrative, describing the sequence and unfolding of a project over time. This act of long-term taking care is perhaps best described by the agricultural term *husbandry*.

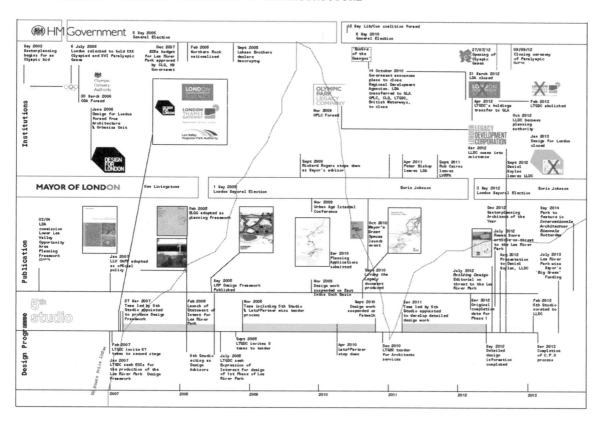

Top: The timeline of our involvement in the Lea River Park project mapped against changing political administrations and institutions.

Bottom: An exhibition of projects at 5th Studio's Cambridge studio, prepared for a visit by my supervisor, Professor Leon van Schaik.

Where We Work

Through the course of the research it has become evident that there are characteristic locations to which 5th Studio are drawn, and that the body of work exhibits surprisingly consistent continuities beyond the trajectories of individual projects.

Almost invariably, the practice finds itself operating on the periphery or along a boundary condition between two worlds: in border country, arriving there often in advance of a client agency or a defined program.

We arrive there with a hunch that the location in question (whether discovered independently, pitched for via competition or other procurement process) has contemporary relevance and is about to become a theatre of activity. Such a theatre is characterised by division: it has physical complexity, infrastructural fragmentation, historical or occluded significance and often a normalised or sublimated underlying violence.

These locations are eclectic, spanning from a littoral ring of trans-national provisioning territories bordering the North Sea, through to the potential inherent in the front arcade of a Hawksmoor College quad in Oxford. They are significant as they are precisely the field of operations on which cities will need to address the environmental challenges facing them in the future.

The Knowledge We Produce

From an instinctive, tacit attraction to location, what follows is a research period that aims to uncover the intrinsic qualities of the place in question, both evident and concealed, physical & phenomenal. This work pays attention to the way the landscape got to be the way it is and how this offers clues to inform the particular qualities of how it might evolve further.

This research towards a 'connoisseurship of place' is always interwoven with an emergent design proposition, and results in a negotiative, discursive narration of how a place could evolve over time towards an environment which is more fulfilling. Such an environment rests on a belief in the ability of rich places to be multivalent: to become, in a key phrase for the practice, more than the sum of their parts.

The roles that develop out of these highly complex projects respond to quick changes in scales of thinking, from the strategic to the concrete and back again. They also respond to the trajectory of the project, from the extended timescales inherent in landscape to the can-do skills of the expedient and opportunistic.

The synthetic interplay of all three modes of knowledge, from the tacit, to the encyclopaedic, to the practical, is necessary for the resilience and value of the work.

The research demonstrates that we have developed our spatial thinking to achieve this bridge between strategy and detail: from the scale of furniture to that of infrastructure. As evidenced through a number of case studies, this approach is able to orientate and bring meaning to highly complex and conflicted sites through sustained and committed involvement. The work is radically contextual, while preserving sufficient buoyancy to act effectively.

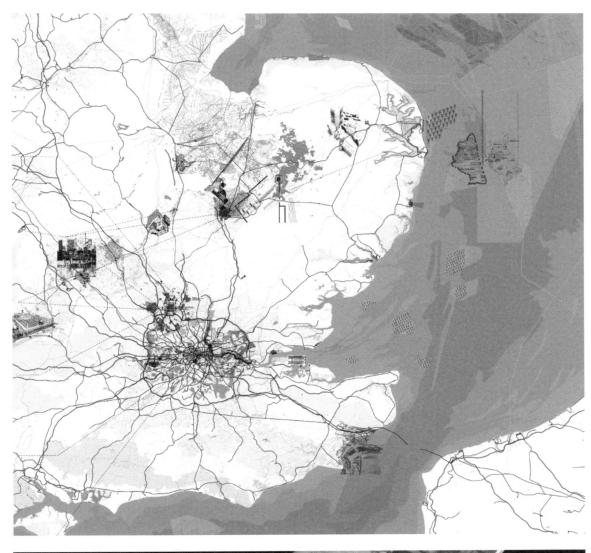

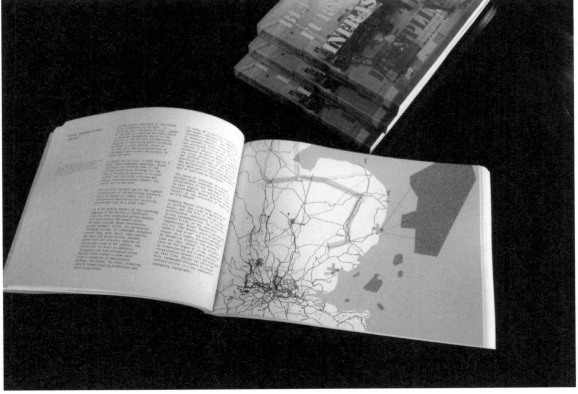

If the model of multidisciplinary consultancy is a consequence of increasing corporate power, the weakening of the social contract matches the fragility of the concept of a vital civil society, the health of which would be signalled by participatory infrastructures and negotiative, agonic public space.

Beginning from these observations I wanted the Viva presentation to make an argument for a generalist spatial design practice, supported by evidence of a particular and distinctive way of working. I wanted to bring the resolution of my PhD back into the life of the city—in particular, the city of Ghent, which has been the location for the presentation of ongoing research over the course of the PhD.

Ghent's market hall emerged as a building during the course of my visits to the city, and on one visit—in June 2012—I met the architects, Paul Robbrecht and Marie José van Hee—and interviewed them for an article on the project for the *Architectural Review* (February 2013).

BETWEEN
FURNITURE &
INFRASTRUCTURE:
E X P A N D I N G
DISCIPLINARITY.

TOM HOLBROOK | RESEARCH CATALOGUE | DOCTOR OF PHILOSOPHY | RMIT UNIVERSITY | 2014

5th
studio

Conclusion: the Duty of Care

Engagement in the research programme has had an unexpected but stimulating denouement: the discovery that much of our work, and modes of working, arise from an unease with the orthodoxies of town planning and the regimes of development. Through a variety of ways, the projects described in this catalogue seek to subvert those orthodoxies, and to find tactics of resistance to allow us to operate despite them.

From that experience has evolved a highly political mode of practice, and the emergent realisation that what is being re-stated through the work is a concern with the nature of professional knowledge and the social contract implied in that.

We have told our clients that, as part of our involvement, we commit to the success of our projects, and the case studies discussed here can be seen as the establishment of regimes of care: a commitment to a place which one could describe as a form of husbandry. I believe that this attitude has profound resonance with the challenges emerging from deep ecological thinking, which looks as much to social justice and ethics as it does to the spheres of technology and management.

The spectrum of knowledge and the innovations in communication developed for a project like the Lea River Park, map precisely onto Leon Van Schaik's tripartite definition of what it is to be a professional: that firstly there is custody of an autonomous body of knowledge that is maintained and advanced; that this body of knowledge is actively deployed to practical effect, and finally that there is a duty of care — a social contract extending beyond the limits of the project commission.

In a number of ways, the body of work discussed in this catalogue has sought to restate the critical importance of synthetic spatial knowledge which should lie at the heart of the discipline. It is useful to contrast this synthetic knowledge to that encountered in the multidisciplinary combines who are so prominent and commercially successful at the scale of work with which we seek to engage.

I believe that it is incumbent upon us to catch up with what is at stake and to restate the value of our spatial intelligence. The capacity of the projects discussed in the research show a way to that end.

CJ Lim
From Smartcity to the Food Parliament: An investigation into the urban consequences of food transparency

The research combines nostalgia and futurism in a narrative architecture to examine food production in urban environments, culminating in the 'Food Parliament' – a transformational tool that reveals London's potential response to the omnipresent energy crisis, and contributes to the discourse around food security and the urban utopia.

We are simultaneously experiencing a global food crisis resulting from climate change, low productivity, government policies diverting food crops to the creation of biofuels, and intensifying demands from an exponentially expanding population. The first part of the research 'Food+' presents an understanding of existing relationships between food, the city and its people, and from that resource develop a multi-programmatic framework to secure and rethink urban community 'wealth', and the reciprocal benefits of simultaneously addressing the threat to and the shaping of cities.

The research explores similar themes of sustainability and transformation of cities initiated in 'Smartcities and Eco-warriors' (2005–2009). The central research component of the Smartcity projects is the establishment of an ecological symbiosis between nature and built form. The stimulus for 'The Food Parliament' focuses on the spatial and phenomenological consequences when speculative design and sustainable planning are applied to cities in attaining food transparency.

The subject area—the future of food production and integration of energy cycles into the practice of everyday life—is one that the non-specialist from the built environment can relate to, especially within a narrative structure. The Food Parliament demonstrates how alternative architectural representation[1] can be employed to communicate narratives and demonstrate urban policies.

The Food Parliament

Over the centuries, there has been an undeniable symbiosis between urbanization and agricultural development. The systemization of food production would sustain the birth and maturation of the city. Food is no less important to the city now as it was then, yet with the advent of industrial and post-industrial economies it has been relegated to the hinterlands, physically and ideologically. The WHO Healthy Cities program has recognized the benefits of urban food cultivation and appealed to cities and their governments to incorporate food policies into urban plans.[2]

'The Food Parliament' reassesses this relationship in an era of unrelenting urbanism and chronic global food shortage, two interdependent phenomena that must reach a rapprochement to prevent an impending catastrophe that is human as much as environmental. It explores the theme of the transformation of cities, and looks at how the cultivation, storage and distribution of food has been and can again become a construct for the practice of everyday life. The scope of the Food Parliament is ideological and polemic, and aims to reinstate food at the core of national and local governance — how it can be a driver to restructure employment, education, transport, tax, health, communities and the justice system, re-evaluating how the city functions as a political and spatial entity.

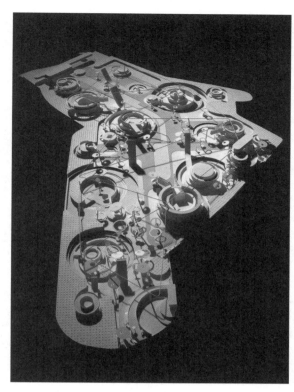

Guangming Smartcity, Shenzhen China (2005)

Parliament examines what the Government of the United Kingdom is doing, makes new laws, holds the power to set taxes and debates the issues of the day. Today, the Palace of Westminster, more commonly known as the Houses of Parliament, covers eight acres (32,400m2). It contains around 1,100 rooms, 100 staircases and 4,800 metres of passageways. From the Victoria Tower at the south end to the Clock Tower at the north, the building is nearly 300 metres long. Over the course of nearly a thousand years of history, the architecture has transformed from royal residence to the home of a modern democracy and has continually evolved, sometimes by design, sometimes through accident or attack.
– www.parliament.uk, 2014

The Food Parliament is the fictional supreme food legislative body for London and its territories. Reimagined here as a landlocked sovereign city-state, it has an area of approximately 3.15km2 over-laid onto the existing city. As a secondary infrastructure,[3] the Food Parliament functions as a holistic ecology: an environmental strategy and food system that is self-perpetuating yet engaged in a symbiotic dialogue with contemporary London below. The main territory of the Food Parliament sits 100m above sea level and traces the outline of the historic City of London, defined by the defensive London Wall built around AD 43 by the Romans to enclose Londinium. Twenty-eight new vertical service-circulation cores, a network of appropriated satellite parks, disused sites and streets named after influential food sources constitute the extension of the infrastructure into the city.

The Food Parliament enjoys similar privileges to that of the City of London with a singular relationship with the Crown, and possessing a unique political status as a communal city. The formally unorthodox, collaborative parliamentary components promote the advantages of decentralization and independence. The Food Parliament has three main pledges: to promote the city as the world's leading international centre of excellence for food sovereignty; to facilitate local communities and individuals in the cultivation, processing and distribution of food within the city; and to disseminate the new notion of wealth.

The functionaries of the United Kingdom's supreme legislative body are transfigured into tectonic analogs responsible for tabling and implementing the new acts of parliament. Each tectonic analog, steered by Erskine May's 'Parliamentary Practice', uses spatial relationships to reframe the spaces of

1 There is a long history of strong interaction between comics and the city. Drawings in newspapers and magazines by Heath Robinson undoubtedly form people's perceptions of cultural, social and political patterns.

2 K Morgan, 'Feeding the City: The Challenge of Urban Food Planning', International Planning Studies, Routledge, 2010

3 The speculative multi-use infrastructure of the Food Parliament also evokes the spirit of unbuilt utopian projects from previous decades, such as Buckminster Fuller's domed-over city project, published in 'Utopia or Oblivion: The Prospects for Humanity' (1969), which outlines a provocative blueprint for the future in which the needs of all humanity are met.

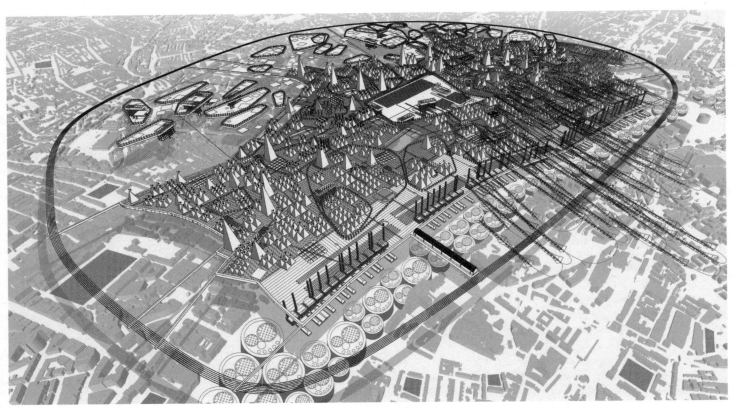

food consumption and production, analysed through historical precedent, function and form. The characters are not human, but anthropomorphic totems that perform duties running in parallel to their real world flesh-and-blood counterparts.[4] There are 646 'Members of Parliament' (MPs) regulating the city and responding to the manifold food issues created by urbanization. 'Mr Speaker' is the authority on irrigation and cultivation, the 'Red Briefcases' function as food repositories, and 'The Table of the House' is London's urban communal banqueting room. Simultaneously, the historical and geographical resources of urban tectonics of London are appropriated to fuel the processes of the second city. The River Thames performs the duties of 'The Lord Mayor' by collecting urban organic waste and feeds it back into the agriculture above, instigating a waste-free cycle.

The vaults of the regional bank Credito Emiliano hold a pungent gold prized by gourmands around the world – 17,000 tonnes of Parmesan cheese. The bank accepts Parmesan as collateral for loans, helping it to keep financing cheese makers in northern Italy even during the recession since World War II.
– A Migliaccio & F Rotondi, 'Parmesan as Collateral for Bank Loans', New York Times, 2009

The Food Parliament propagates sustainable capital as part of the new economic model in food governance. The city's green micro-economy is rooted in establishing shared accountability, and is premised on the adoption of food as the local currency standard of London. Food is a commodity that is in increasingly short supply in the real world. World agricultural production has declined with severe natural global disasters and rapid urbanization of arable land.[5] The rural is becoming urbanized through the migration of urban and peri-urban areas, and the appropriation of the rural for the burgeoning city. Simultaneously, food-producing nations are imposing food export restrictions,[6] and constrained access to sustainable energy and water are further inhibiting affordable food. Given the failures of our debt-based monetary system, the fragility and unsustainable nature of our agricultural practices, and the social exploitation orchestrated by vast unregulated corporations, a reserve currency backed by the tangible asset of food, although improbable, is not illogical.

With the Food Parliament comes a new green religion. The green ascription is protecting more than just food; it secures ecological and social wealth for the city by expanding the commonly received notion of wealth to include fresh air and water, natural daylight, green space and reduction of greenhouse gas emissions. Urban sprawl and old building stock are synonymous with climate change issues including air pollution from transport and the relentless increase in energy consumption, resulting in negative health impacts. The new infrastructure of the Food Parliament sets out an optimum environment for the city below to prevent the problem of increasing summer air-conditioning and winter heating. The innovative renewable energy technologies of the city silently coexist alongside nature, harvesting solar, wind, bio and hydro energies, and recycle organic municipal waste for urban agriculture. Zero carbon deer-pulled carriages, 'The Department of Transport', have replaced all London buses and taxis. In the past, London has failed to address the issue of energy consumption, as well as its food sourcing.

Urban agriculture in Africa is a successful form of self-employment for women since the gardens allow women to cultivate while undertaking other household and parental responsibilities. For Ghanaian families, urban agriculture is a significant income-diversification strategy by supplying months of staple food for the family. Despite the socio-economic and environmental benefits, the Ghanaian policy makers and municipal government have yet to re-evaluate their current urban land

The MPs are 100m tall crusaders of the Food Parliament in the form of travelling banquets distributing the 'pies of new wealth' from the Department of Health, thus facilitating the education, nutrition, food sovereignty and social wellbeing of the city's constituents.

Opposite page top: Employing the propositional vehicle of a new sovereign city-state overlaid onto the existing city, the Food Parliament explores how a secondary infrastructure could function as a living environmental and food system.

Opposite page bottom: The Blue Carpet performs as fisheries atop the flat roofs of London's existing building stock beneath Westminster Hall. Each Red Briefcase is a physical urban manifestation of food availability. The bigger the harvest, the bigger the budget; in the good years the briefcases descend to maximum capacity and surplus food is discharged via an overflow valve to ground level.

4 The use of symbolism and narrative structure is similar to John Hejduk's 'Victims' (1986), applying architectonic forms to combine fiction with architecture, 'spinning a narrative in which it is no longer possible to tell what is being designed: the habitat or the inhabitants, the structure or the institution'.

5 The Foresight Report, The Future of Food and Farming: Challenges and Choices for Global Sustainability, UK Government Office for Science, 2011

6 Asian States Feel Rice Pinch, BBC News, 2008. [http://news.bbc.co.uk/1/hi/world/south_asia/7324596.stm]

*use planning regulations to address issues of land tenure to support
urban agriculture.*
*– K Obosu-Mensah, 'Changes to official attitudes to urban agriculture
in Accra', African Studies Quarterly, 2002*

Food cultivation, a typical oversight for most cities, is now at the heart
of all urban planning and urban health initiatives in London. The Food
Parliament has adapted city laws to address issues of land security and
tenure, and declared indefinite free rights to cultivate food on disused
private sites and vacant municipal land. The new micro-economy invites
the English arcadia back into London; wildlife corridors and bio-diversity
traverse car-free municipalities. The infrastructure of the Food Parliament
accommodates the welcome return of locally grown food in London. Land
is legitimately appropriated for bio-diverse green allotments of urban
agriculture, and wild deer graze in public parks in a campaign to restore
nature's civil liberties. Urban kitchens and bakeries will only source food
within a 10 mile radius. Consumerism is no longer the sterile, cursory
experience redolent of supermarket aisles – streets are alive with trade,
gastronomy and ecology. The wetland habitat from the River Thames has
migrated onto the city's undulating rooftops, harvesting fresh rainwater for
aquaculture and irrigation within repeated fish ponds perched on the skyline,
forming 'The Blue Carpets'. Historically, the distribution of provisions to
modern cities is tenuous, relying on transport and storage mechanisms that
are taken for granted but nonetheless vulnerable to natural and manmade
disasters. Here, local fresh food is distributed along a green national grid
without the historical overriding reliance on extensive food miles.

*Sydney Harbour Bridge is the annual setting for bringing 6,000
people in the city together to converse, connect, and most of all share
knowledge about food. 'Breakfast On The Bridge' is a one-day pop-
up event that turns Australia's most famous icon is turned into a giant
'inhabitable food billboard'.*
– N Bryant, 'Picnic on Sydney Harbour Bridge', BBC News, 2009

Novel and unusual learning environments generate a more active
discourse than in classrooms. The infrastructure acts as both an education
catalyst and support network for a safe, nutritious and life enhancing diet
that is agro-ecological, through social inclusivity, community and personal
empowerment. Socio-economic responsibilities are devolved amongst
London's constituents by the 'Members of Parliament' (MPs), developing
social relationships and trust through local food production to boost
individual and collective recovery capital. Social enterprises nurturing food
provenance and safety empower communities. The 'third age' are no longer
sidelined in demographic state policy – pensioners are invited to mentor a
new generation of cultivators with their invaluable food related knowledge
and experience. Food support partnerships may appear modest in scale but
they play a vital role in stimulating the perceptual shift in how city dwellers
think about and procure meals. The Food Parliament can demonstrate
spatial phenomenology in the city, stimulating our eyes, ears, noses, minds
and tongues – vision made real, social capital that can be tasted.

*In Belo Horizonte, Municipal Law No. 6,352, 15/07/1993, set out an
integrated framework for food security to reduce malnutrition across the
city. The policy allows nutrition and food-related programs to have the
same status as traditional public policies in areas such as health and
education. The service offers daily healthy and well-balanced menus
for less than $1.00, and in the process reduced the strain on the city's
health and social services.*
*– C Rocha, 'Urban Food Security Policy: The Case of Belo Horizonte
Brazil', Journal for the Study of Food and Society, Vol.5, No.1, 2001*

Top and bottom: 10 Downing Street — the urban
scarecrow; Red Briefcase — food repository.

Opposite page top and bottom: Department of Health
— the community bakeries producing the 'pies of
new wealth'; Department of Transport — service-
circulation cores .

Previous page: The Food Parliament is an
infrastructure for cultivation, processing and
distribution of food.

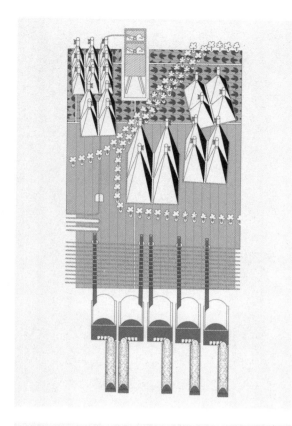

The Food Parliament firmly believes in 'prevention rather than cure', and has invested in a local food distribution system and nutritious diet plan. Through 'The Department of Health', the infrastructure communicates with its constituencies by employing gastronomic festivities, and disseminating nourishment and knowledge on wellbeing. The service also educates urban cultivators in methods of permaculture, composting and the use of biological controls. Permaculture enables the city to have a sustainable high-yielding ecosystem and increased biodiversity. The vertical allotments, 'Westminster Hall', transform London's skyline[7] providing city dwellers with a 'green health center' to rediscover the meaning of hand to mouth existence. The popularity of the garden rekindles mankind's natural bond with food, nature and society, offsetting contemporary introverted pursuits in digital media with real time.

And the LORD God made all kinds of trees grow out of the ground – trees that were pleasing to the eye and good for food.
– Genesis 2:9

And the LORD God commanded the man, 'You are free to eat from any tree in the garden…'
– Genesis 2:16

Prior to their fall from grace for eating from the tree of knowledge, the fruit from the Garden of Eden provided Adam and Eve with food aplenty without having to toil for their sustenance. Since humanity's earliest days, we have yearned for access to fresh healthy food. Yet, James Lovelock believes that we will need to resort to genetically modified crops on a global scale in order to stave off catastrophe and has advocated the synthesis of fermented food from air, water and trace chemicals as the future.

The Food Parliament, a fertile plain over London with lush cyclical farming systems and self-sustaining permacultures, and busied by pollinating insects, is a provocation. The physical absurdity of the infrastructure intends to raise serious questions about the priorities of our governing bodies and to engage individuals with issues of food sovereignty and climate change. However, the principles that underlay its premise and the justification for its existence are both real and urgent, if we are to avoid wholly synthetic foods that will definitively sever all connection between our sustenance and us.

7 The Food Parliament drew architectonic inspiration from the imaginary London skyline of 'A Tribute to Sir Christopher Wren' (1838) by Charles Robert Cockerell, which brought together Wren's major buildings into one vast urban landscape.

Reflection on the Food Parliament

Everything you can imagine is real
– Pablo Picasso (1881–1973)

The ambition of the research lies in its ability to manifest government policies and scientific facts in relation to food into architecture and urbanism, converting dry data into an impossible but speculative design, whose aesthetics capture the public imagination. Research of this speculative nature is not common in the context of contemporary architectural practice, and even less so in the planning of cities. Through the research process, my contribution to knowledge is formed around the following findings:

→ The Food Parliament is a transformational ecosystem tool to regenerate community and city from an architectural perspective that is design propositional as well as critical theoretical thinking. To engage in an innovative discourse on climate change and city planning, governments and stakeholders must take into consideration food transparency and employ speculative designs of ecosystems.

→ The Food Parliament addresses sustainable issues relating to food transparency at an urban planning scale rather than via ad hoc interventions in pockets of vestigial land. Holistic large-scale sustainable infrastructure for food cultivation, production and distribution can contribute to new urban consequences and policies while simultaneously addressing food politics and limiting environmental impacts.

→ The Food Parliament employs symbolism and a fictional narrative structure to create sustainable architecture, cities and environments of spatial and social impact, in addition to alleviating food security with the use of poetics as well as technical exposition. The investigation signals a legitimate spatial symbiosis between architecture and urban planning, with symbolism and narrative.

→ The Food Parliament is a communication tool showing the role of food in the creation of social capital through the unorthodox aesthetics of its allegories and most significantly through the comic nature of its representation. Visual narrative of the built environment has a vital role in presenting the urban consequences of food transparency and engaging the public imagination in negotiating issues of climate change.

→ The Food Parliament is a multi-disciplinary demonstration of sustainable design, combining architecture, planning, geography, hydrology and environmental engineering to develop a holistic model of an alternative urban form – in effect, the 21st century hybrid version of Ebenezer Howard's Garden City and Buckminster Fuller's Manhattan Dome, in the sky.

A designer's greatest influence lies in the visualisation of an alternative reality that can be shared with society. Visions of the built environment whether or not they are accepted are reflections of society and have a powerful influence on the public consciousness.

Mr Speaker is constructed from a modular system of irrigation pipes and sprinkler heads, which drifts through the green parks harvesting morning dew.

Paul Minifie
Design Domains

It seems important, as a practitioner, to be able to provide an account of a project that has a demonstrable correspondence to identifiable attributes of the artefact as it stands alone. This is perhaps not such a pressing concern to a critic who may seek to locate a project within a broader context. To a practitioner however, an account is most useful when it can be used constructively to inform a means of making. A forward mapping is necessary for an account to be constructive. Perhaps more interesting is the question of the backward mapping: from the artefact back to the operative concerns of the project. Although often left implicit, the possibility and implications of these constructions and reconstructions are one of the subjects of this work.

Domains, Traversals & Injections

A Practice of Architectural Transformation

This is an account of a series of architectural projects that have been completed under my direction in the offices of MvS Architects (previously Minifie Nixon Architects) over the last decade. The projects range from small theoretical projects through to several more substantial constructed projects. It begins by introducing several concepts used in the later projects' description, moving to an account of each project.

As a practising architect I have a different mode of access to my own works than I do to that of others. It is not possible to fully and critically examine or locate my own projects from outside, freed from the intentions of their author. Instead, the project accounts here try to outline the constructive concepts and methodological traversals involved in their production.

Many of the projects have been reactivated by this process of reflection, with the project outcomes folding back into their genesis to suggest future development that might activate latent themes and methods. It is this glimpse of a deeper and more consolidated future practice that has been a key motivation in undertaking this work.

I am of the first generation of architects who has worked with computers as an integral part of everyday practice. Seen from one perspective these projects reflect an examination of the workings of computation, and comprise a speculation on how those workings might re-propose architectural themes and transform architectural effects. Put loosely they propose that operations and methods intrinsic to computation can reformulate, in positive and sometimes unexpected ways, closely held patterns of architectural thinking.

This kind of investigation, as an architect, into computational methods also reformulates the usual intentions of that computation. Seen from that vantage, computation is no longer directly about instrumental issues of problem solving, optimisation or connectivity. Rather the methods of achieving these things are selectively picked over and re-purposed to illuminate architectural concerns.

It is important to state that these projects make most sense in the context of a commitment to the discipline of architecture, whatever that means, in all its protean depths and breadth. Projects are finally of interest in the way they intervene in the domain of cultural concerns that can be plausibly said to constitute the discipline of architecture. An examination of concepts from mathematics, computing, and occasionally economics and biology are means to architectural ends.

Terminology from these other fields is sometimes used in the descriptions of projects. Often these terms are used because they best describe a concept that has no easy equivalent in the architectural lexicon. Many architectural terms are so overdetermined, so overloaded beyond their definitions that they no longer have utility. It is hoped that importing and re-purposing the occasional term can help provide another perspective and evocation to architectural actions.

Although I often refer to architectural themes in a general sense, the particular conception of these themes as a bounded group susceptible to transformation by propositional operations is most likely a located one, common to a group of Melbourne architectural practitioners and one 'pole' of the RMIT practice community. While I only briefly discuss the particular accents and tropes of my local milieu, I acknowledge that some of the

The presentation an exhibition of these works took place at the October 2010 PRS.

matters I discuss, even though seeming quite general, might well carry a singular kind of sense from that local context.

An important counterbalance to these sometimes tribal discursive interests lies in the lived life of the buildings: might an aware inhabitant of a proposed building reasonably apprehend and respond to the concerns from which the building emerged? Although not a direct subject of this discussion, constructed projects from our office try to directly and generously engage with an interested public. In the attempt to express the process of a building's becoming, we seek to make that thinking an intrinsic attribute of the building's operation.

It seems important, as a practitioner, to be able to provide an account of a project that has a demonstrable correspondence to identifiable attributes of the artefact as it stands alone. This is perhaps not such a pressing concern to a critic who may seek to locate a project within a broader context. To a practitioner however, an account is most useful when it can be used constructively to inform a means of making. A forward mapping is necessary for an account to be constructive. Perhaps more interesting is the question of the backward mapping: from the artefact back to the operative concerns of the project. Although often left implicit, the possibility and implications of these constructions and reconstructions are one of the subjects of this work.

To be able to address these questions, I have attempted to sketch a model that delimits possible actions, and provide an explanation of both how these actions are undertaken and how a resulting artefact might relate to things beyond itself. Attempting such a thing is on one level absurd: it can never plausibly account for the broad phenomenon that is architecture. Perhaps though, in its oversimplification, it can capture some of the operational logic at work in the projects.

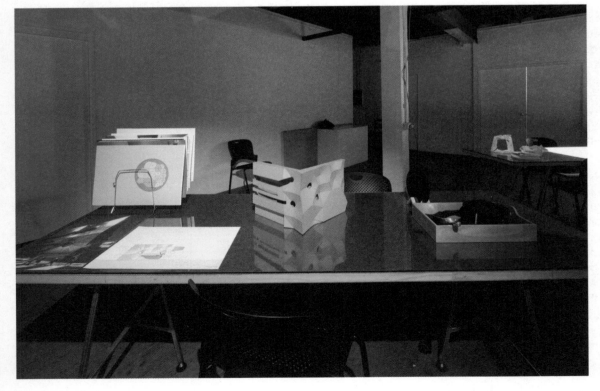

Acknowledgement and thanks for the generous support, continuous insight and unfailing guidance of my supervisor, Leon van Schaik.

Drawings and models by MvS architects, photographs by Peter Bennetts.

Domains

A design domain contains an internally consistent set of elements and operations that can be combined to construct building instances.

This description of the place from which architecture comes is deliberately sparse. In it's reduction it tries to capture how the intrinsic qualities of matter and information provide both the mechanisms and limits of what can be made. At various points throughout the project descriptions I refer to design domains as being constituted by particular relationships of information that can cause arrangements of material things. For example in the description of the Centre for Ideas project, I discuss how the relationships inherent in the Voronoi tessellation can lead to an ordering of building elements that is quite different from and incommensurable with the kind of arrangements that might derive from working within a Cartesian gridded space. I offer the Barcelona Pavilion as something of a straw man in exemplifying an instance of the later. Cellular automata, energised surfaces, and aggregated economic decisions are examples of other structured relationships I later characterise as constituting design domains.

The notion of internal consistency is important. It suggests that only some elements and operations can make sense, but from those, more complex structures can be assembled.

A design domain is a neutral place of potential things. There are a hyper-astronomical number of different potential instances that might be produced by a given domain. It is not until an instance is realised from the domain that it can posses specific appreciable qualities.

Traversals

A traversal is a particular sequence of operations within a design domain that leads to the realisation of a specific building instance.

An analogous architectural concept is composition. Elements are bought together in accordance with an underlying rule system of the design domain into a particular and complete set of relationship with one another. A traversal is where architectural disciplinary skills come into play. Specific traversals bring to the fore a particular assemblage of building qualities and attributes.

The series of energised surface projects show how alternative groups of operations can make different sets of formal qualities available to architectural consideration. A more specific material example of a traversal is given when discussing the design decisions involved in resolving the Centre for Ideas facade.

It is this different set of qualities that emerges through a traversal of a design space that enables a project to posses a valency – that is, the ability to form plausible associations and connections outside itself.

Injections

An injection is a mapping between elements and properties of a building instance, and some object or phenomena external to it.

Such a mapping might occur through reference or association. The choice of the golden fabric for the Costa surface structure in the Australian Wildlife Health Centre(AWHC) can serve as an example. The gold colour shifts possible associations away from that of an abstract reading towards a comparison with domed structures found in other architectures. Similarly, the choice of a reflective material for the Centre for Ideas facade enables an understanding of the building as being not fully materialised, its shimmering being suggestive of the presence of a virtual realm in which the building may still partially reside.

Mappings might also be established through patterns of use. The proposed pattern of atomised and interrelated activities posited in the Volute project may serve as an example. Or the mapping might take place through an affective or perceptual impression, such as when first apprehending the ceiling of the AWHC.

This pattern of potential correspondence relationships latent in the project is ultimately enabled by the properties of the constituent design domain, and the specific instance realised through it's traversal.

It is difficult territory for an architect to attempt a definitive reading of her own project. Certainly it feels hubristic to try. Further, there is a fear of creating a strained closure which by extension will function to constrict the expressive scope of future projects. By using the terms valency and mapping I am trying to allude to the specific ability of a particular building to establish relationships beyond itself, rather than detail exactly what those relationships might be.

While the sequential nature of this exposition suggest a linear development, the experience of designing in this model is in fact iterative and unstable. Design domains cannot be known until an attempt is made to traverse them. Many are rejected as non-viable. A rich and coherent injection only emerges in a fragile stability after many compositional refinements.

It is perhaps constituent of our projects that we favour an injection supporting multiple mappings. Further mappings are preferred that can destabilise the context of the thing to which a connection is made.

Streaming Houses

Strange Procedures and their Misuse

And the Tigers were very, very angry, but still they would not let go of each others' tails. And they were so angry that they ran round the tree, trying to eat each other up, and they ran faster and faster till they were whirling round so fast that you couldn't see their legs at all.

And they still ran faster and faster and faster, till they all just melted away, and then there was nothing left but a great big pool of melted butter round the foot of the tree.

From a Banned Book

The architectural pilgrim at last visits, perhaps from Australia, the canonic building previously only known through the blogs and texts. Let's start in Barcelona. Video camera in hand she moves through the space, eye on the screen, carefully keeping the verticals parallel to the frame, and in a moment of recognition, captures the corporeal affirmation of that drawing where the cruciform column floats autonomously in front of the texture-mapped lushness of the onyx wall. She moves forward among the glass walls, un-present but denoted by their steel frames — they trap the cowering female sculpture in their congruent golden (but never gold) rectangles. More walls, travertine and olivine, the constant white ceiling plane overhead, then... she is back to where we started... but that can't be all, so again... and another go, one more time, in case there is, as surely there must be, something more.

The data from this camera sits as an inert block. When rendered to a screen for friends at home, successive layers of the block are sectioned at precise intervals to represent the visual field of our holidaying architect. Streaming House cuts the data another way. By regarding our block of data as congruent in structure to that gathered by a CAT scan machine, we can establish boundaries around the summed appearances of the structures within the pavilion. Columns, walls, roof, floor, sky and surroundings views become separate volumetric entities, distinguished from each other in the same way as organs are in a tomographic scan. If the motion path is a closed loop, the volume can be bent to join start with end and so form a closed and continuous torus, making a kind of spatial accelerator.

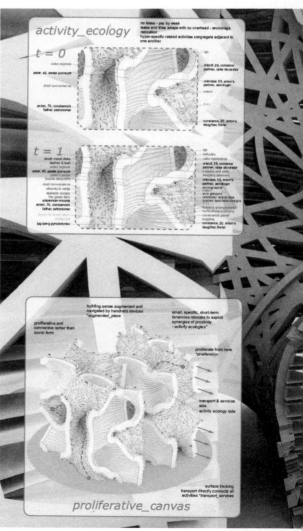

A kind of strange procedure is thus invoked, based on a misapplication of a medical imaging technique. Digital data and procedures of this sort tend to be motivated by imitating some aspect of the world. This mimetic intent and the procedure itself can be uncoupled as a 'found technique', analogous to the found object.

The modern pavilion is wrenched from its pretty siting between idealist Cartesian space and a world of mechanical production. It seeds the procedure by providing a sequence of views as we walk through. Isosurfaces are then made to locate structures within this sequential stream of images.

The result is a transformation; a derivative of the Miesian function drawn by the traversal of the architectural pilgrim. This idea of 'making' contains and connects concepts of motion, perception, visibility and an architecture past. The project tries in this way to educe a kind of sense for living now, or for living soon.

Barcelona done, the next stop for our pilgrim is Beijing.

Manifolds

The Volute Counterfactual

This is one of a series of studies exploring architectural surfaces whose shape are determined by their surface energies, but unfold their architectural implications in different ways.

If not otherwise coerced, things will find their own shape, one that minimises their energy state. Water tends to droplets in a vacuum, and a plane in a millpond. An elastic membrane held in a frame will hold its shape in an equipoise of tensions such that its surface area is minimised. In contemplating any point on such a membrane, it becomes clear that the surface curves in two directions, both into and out of the surface. In a minimal surface, this curvature sums always to zero, that is, the mean curvature at any given point is the same as that of a flat surface. Its shape is held not by the frame, but by the surrounding area of adjoining membrane. It is possible to have a membrane of a shape such that it can link to similar units in a way that maintains the zero mean curvature condition at their boundary. These units can fill space continuously without edges – a triply periodic minimal surfaces. Many different configurations of these surfaces have been described and have terrific names: Gyroid, Mantra, Diphenoid, Starfish, Fischer-Koch S-surface and so on. They are strictly minimal, but in a rather baroque kind of way.

Volute investigates the connectedness properties of such surfaces. Topology is an extension of geometry that describes objects in terms of their pattern of connection. To this way of thinking, a cube and a sphere are congruent, but a sphere and torus are not. Different underlying surfaces, therefore, support different patterns and possibilities of connectedness.

Volute proposes a 'counterfactual' whereby vertical transport moves freely in two dimensions across the outside of an 'energised surface' building, under the guidance of some novel personalised command and control mechanism. A smartphone perhaps.

Cities are tyrannised by their ground planes. As we move through the streets, we can respond spontaneously only to what presents itself within our field of vision. Connections between activities and events are largely limited to adjacencies on the plane. Volute takes this planar surface, allows it to billow and be aerated into a continuous foam.

What takes place in Volute? First, lets atomise any broad concept of function into highly specific actions and events. Then postulate that the viability of a particular activity is enhanced by relationships of proximity with other complementary activities. Volute at time $t = 0$ is randomly seeded with activities. At $t = 1$, more activities have come into being, nurtured by their adjacent complementarities. At $t = n$, new synergies continue to occur between adjacent activities. Volute is teeming and seething with activity

Volute describes an alternative kind of building armature, one that supports an ecology of novel and differentiated activities, each with radically different properties of almost dendritic connectivity. Each node can fully exert its trophic influence on it's neighbours, converging to a dynamic equilibrium existing somewhere between the flickering of lives and the staidness of buildings.

Centre for Ideas

Victorian College of the Arts

A plane is perforated by a series of holes. The holes may be distributed randomly. Dust accumulates, breeding. Soon some dust starts to flow through the holes. Beds of particles gathered in this way are only partially stable. At their edges, some will fall away until the edge reaches a certain constant critical angle to the vertical. As the dust accumulates, its edge surrounding each hole will be conical, with an angle corresponding to the critical angle for that kind of particle. After some time, the cones around each hole intersect with one other. When all the cones have fully intersected, it is no longer possible for the plane to accumulate any more dust. Which hole will a given particle of dust now fall through? It will fall through that hole closest to where it lands. So the boundary of each cone, defined by its intersections with its neighbours, defines an area of the plane which is closer to the hole at that cone's centre than any other.

The Voronoi tessellation is named after Georgy Fedoseevich Voronoy who, in 1907, formally described a division of metric space into regions that are closest to a set of features on that space. Our accumulating dust cones constitute an algorithm, a process that can be used to establish the Voronoi tessellation of a plane. In this case it is an algorithm that uses the physical properties of matter (the coherence or adherence of dust) to make a calculation.

We have some intuitive familiarity with Voronoi tessellations. They are found in natural phenomena: the cracking of dried mud, ice crystals, zinc galvanising and so on. We know them indirectly from the fluctuations of cell phone signals or our interactions with distributed elements within cities such as fast-food chain outlets. Their more instrumental applications are myriad, such as by the pioneering epidemiologist John Snow, in his map of 1855, which used a version of a Voronoi diagram to localise a cholera outbreak to a particular London water pump.

Architects are sometimes fast and loose with the term space. Often it is used with reverential emphasis as a way to not talk in detail about the formal qualities of a building. Instead one can talk of a charged or aura-like quality generated in some unspecified way by the building. If pressed, some version of a Cartesian grid might be called up, describing an invisible but regular and oriented inscription that architectural elements locate themselves against. The Centre for Ideas project explores an alternate design domain to the Cartesian grid, one conditioned by the logic and relationships implicit in the the Voronoi division of space.

If the Voronoi tessellation conditioned the set of operations that comprised the CfI's design domain, then a credible traversal of that domain was required to establish a buildable instance within the architectural realm. As the design developed, hierarchies emerged where parts of the building were emphasised over others. The stochastic nature of early facade studies gave way to those that were almost figural.

Any number of successful traversals of the Voronoi domain are possible. A design domain, by dint of its own internal content and structuring operations, has the ability to form sense-connections with concepts and entities from a wider cultural space. Mathematicians use the term injection to describe unique mappings from one domain onto another.

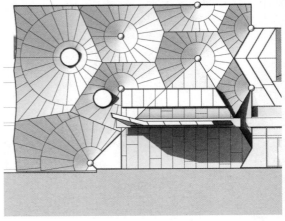

Centre for Ideas
West Elevation

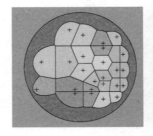

Analog model of Voronoi
Tessellation

Australian Wildlife Health Centre

Healesville Sanctuary

In our work we find it useful to explicitly consider design techniques, as it is around techniques that the other stuff of architecture organises itself. Design techniques establish a domain of possibility in which a building comes to be, and be apprehended.

A technique can be understood as something that defines the properties of elements, their qualities and the relations they can enter into. These elements need not be material things, but, to make sense in an architectural context, they must be able to have a material instantiation.

A building can be understood as one of many possibilities consistent within a given design domain (think of the vast populace of the Miesian domain). Many of the significant architectural values of a project come about through specific decisions made within the parameters of the design space – decisions about composition, materials and so on establish emphasis and value.

The Costa surface is a "complete minimal embeddable surface of finite topology". It is an element that has the smallest surface area for its constraints, could continue without boundary and does not intersect itself. Until this surface was discovered by Celso Costa in 1982, it was conjectured that the only surfaces with these properties were the plane, the helicoid and the catenoid. The Costa surface was initially discovered by using methodologies of experimental mathematics, whereby computers are used to investigate a large number of cases within a particular problem space prior to deriving formal proofs.

The Costa surface is difficult to comprehend at first sight. The patterns of connection within its surface, and the spatial flows and partitions it creates are confounding. There are architectural instances of its sibling surface, the catenoid, which offered some clues in finding a place for it to reside in the architectural ontology. The catenoid is an efficient shape for cooling towers, some of Gaudi's surfaces of revolution use the shape, Leonidov used them in some projects, and Shukov built several remarkable catenoidal towers.

The Russians may have been interested in making a break from historic forms, but the catenoid and Costa surface also have strong radial symmetry, something it shares with domes among other more normative architectural objects. Finally, it being a minimal surface allows it to be constructed using a membrane stretched between three straight forward ring beams.

The AWHC is a working animal hospital, with an interpretive program inserted. Visitors to the sanctuary needed to see and have explained all the internal workings of the centre. We thought of the building as being a regular hospital, but prized open to enable a new interpretive organ to be inserted. The confounding sectional qualities of the surface leads to an engaging ambiguity within the internal space as to whether it is enclosed or open to the exterior. The radial symmetry of the ring structure and the billowing layers of the roof were maintained as dome like – a connection reinforced by the choice of a gold coloured membrane material over the more usual purist white. It is, perhaps, a new kind of dome under which to celebrate the contemporary secular theology of environmental consciousness.

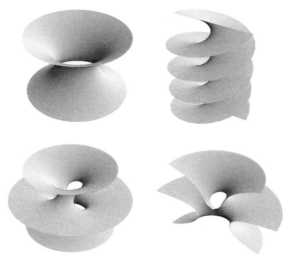

Cloudnets

The Forces Bearing on Sites, and their Intersections

Imagine a very large town, at the centre of a fertile plain which is crossed by no navigable river. Throughout the plain the soil is capable of cultivation, and is of the same fertility. Far from the town, the plain turns into an uncultivated wilderness which cuts off all communication between this state and the outside world. There are no other towns on the plain. The central town must therefore supply the rural areas with all goods, and the town, in return will obtain all its provisions from the surrounding countryside.
– Johann von Thunen 'The Isolated State' 1826

Cities are complex, emergent entities. That is, their large-scale phenomenal qualities derive from a myriad series of small scale rational decisions made at the level of individual sites. These small scale decisions attempt to find the 'highest and best expression' for that particular site. Each site is conditioned by it's relationship to the form and use of all other aspects of the city. For example, to transport infrastructure, the size of it's neighbours, its proximity to retail and places of work. Cities develop iteratively. As each site finds it's best use at a given moment, it changes the potential value of other sites, enabling them in turn to be transformed in use and form.

Architects intuitively understand that every site, which is a particular location for a building, posses a potential value quite specific for that site. Further, certain uses realise more value than others. This value related to location and use is fundamental in shaping the building, for the building responds to this field of forces determining potential value to realise and return an actual return. A given building channels potential values, represents and makes them material.

It is clear that these kind of factors are drivers for the movement of people from rural to metropolitan areas. Doug Saunders in his book *Arrival City* describes the improvements in health and wealth that follow. He also describes how cities consume fewer natural resources per capita than rural populations. These same drivers lead to an increasing complexity within cities. The diversity of goods, services and production inputs relate together to create an increasingly complex matrix of potential values. The field of urban economics contains important insights about how cities are organised and structured. Concepts such as congestion modelling, search costs, production inputs and land value as an expression of travel times all say important general things about the potentials inherent in the spatial arrangements of a city.

If spatial economics describes the potentials of value and possible uses at general locations, CloudNets attempts to capture these insights in their specifics at a more local scale. A city can be modelled at a specific level as a series of nodes, connected spatially to other nodes. To determine the state of any particular node, the condition of other nodes can be examined and responded to. As changes to a node affect it's neighbours, this response is repeated iteratively. The importance of the state of adjacent nodes is weighted in various ways based on proximity. Aggregate properties of all the nodes can be determined and so used to, for example, optimise for particular overall properties. Over a number of generations, the system may converge on a stable state, or, more often, will continue to change developing increasing levels of local complexity.

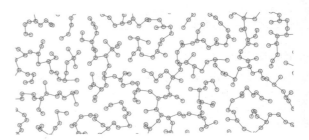

The graph extends over a plane, abstractly, representing potential inhabitation. The first point of inhabitation is deliberate, the rest follows. We define connectedness of a node as the average distance to all other inhabited nodes. That distance corresponds to an average travel time, and so cost which forms a basis of comparison to the physical difficulty of making taller buildings.

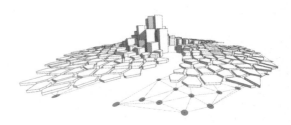

Cloudnet is an examination of the fundamental forces that shapes cities. The premise of Cloudnet is that cities are driven by a desire for connectivity. The richness of urban life derives from exchanging with as many other people as possible.

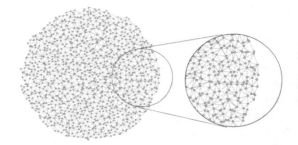

The Cloudnet is modelled by the relational structure of a graph. A plane is understood as being covered by randomly placed, but equally distributed spatial locations — nodes. The connection between each node and its immediate neighbors are called edges. Nodes have a weight which represents their height. Edges have a weight which represent their length.

Cloudnets describes a city as a spatial graph of connections. Costs are assigned to building taller buildings, and travelling between nodes on the graph. Agents incrementally choose where to build based on a balance of these costs. Different city forms result based on patterns of connectivity between nodes.

The underlying graph can be shaped to examine the effects of geography on city growth. Examples might include a river, a large central, or a bounding constraint such as being an island or an enclosing mountains.

Vivian Mitsogianni
white noise PANORAMA:
Process-based
Architectural Design

white noise PANORAMA: Process-based Architectural Design[1], offers a series of propositions at the core of which is an examination of process-based experimentation in architecture. Though a reflection on one approach to working in this way—based on my projects including those completed in my practice M@ STUDIO (primarily with Dean Boothroyd)—I consider the complex array of questions and issues that are associated with working in this way.

I argue that contemporary process-based work is built on an inherited foundation of ideas that are often considered to be naturally linked to this way of working and that despite an evolving of these methods in contemporary practice, these fundamental assumptions continue to be maintained; are rarely specifically acknowledged and can be seen to constrain this type of practice. The persistent, underlying assumptions about working in this way are not an inherent property of this type of practice. I demonstrate that they are simply properties which have grown to be normative values in contemporary work compromising the introduction of other possible approaches. I argue that the reasons one might use these processes might be different – away from these traditions and through my design projects demonstrate an expanded series of concerns for process-based design work. The differences in my design approach have occurred as a result of both incorporating my critique of the field into my own practice as well as developing a series of parallel investigations that inform this practice. These parallel investigations are undertaken as projects that consider; forming propositions for the contemporary civic project in Australia; the use of 'vision devices and systems' in the design process as well as the operative potential of architectural ornament.

1 The *white noise PANORAMA: Process-based Architectural Design* (PhD by project RMIT 2009) text has been published in part in various formats prior to this publication.

white noise PANORAMA:
Process-based Architectural Design

I initially began working with process-based design methods because they offered the potential for the discovery of conditions, arrangements and effects that could not have been produced without them. As my practice developed I became increasingly critical of what I saw as the more problematic aspects of this type of design practice in the wider field, which I felt was becoming a confused terrain with questionable claims, sustained problems, and in some cases, had become what might be called a 'process style' or 'process aesthetic'. The problematic aspects of this area were compounded by the poor quality of available information, processes were rarely published with any clarity although they were often accompanied by in depth explanations. Critics commonly evaluated the processes within the architect's terms and often building propositions were critiqued in relation to the success or otherwise of the process itself rather than critiquing the building on its own terms. The discourse was also overwhelmed with the anxiety to claim that the processes were not 'authored', which was a central discussion in this type of work.

In reflecting on the wider field while undertaking design projects and leading design studios, I began to notice certain evolving tropes, traits and underlying assumptions the most obvious being an overwhelming focus on form—defining the formal envelope or armature—as being the entire project, often this work is stripped of referents, detached from program, site, materiality and particularly socio-political engagement which then forms a very narrow view of what architecture is and can contain. A lot of the issues that I was starting to identify were so completely naturalised in this practice to not even be considered a necessary point of discussion or debate.

'Process-based' design, refers to the approach whereby a process—consisting of a series of actions or operations—is choreographed in order to initiate and develop architectural designs (sometimes known as rule-based, procedural or generative design processes). We can trace a lineage of this type of practice through the early projects of Peter Eisenman and Bernard Tschumi, then through Diagram Practice (as an attempt to break away from the restrictions of linear processes), Greg Lynn's work through the 1990's and various contemporary practices including digital scripting processes. While there are broad variations in this practice that mean that it can't be called one particular method, there are nevertheless certain shared characteristics; involving designing the process as a starting point with a series of rules or actions being choreographed; there is often an adoption of techniques or systems from other disciplines and a translation of these to architectural technique.

I was able to make observations on the wider field precisely because reflection on my own projects had revealed significant differences. Being curious to follow the origins of these differences led to seeing and describing the field in a different way for example the 'context and argument' section focusses on the specifically architectural trajectories through the field. By way of one example—the passage on Eisenman avoids the typical discussions associated with his work; Derrida, Deconstruction and Diagrams, and traces a trajectory of ideas through Eisenman's mentor Colin Rowe, that involve very particular attitudes to architectural history, form and social conditions[2]—which eventually lead Eisenman to the rationale of needing to compose processes that are 'self-propelling' and eschew intervention from the architect and their unavoidable cultural prejudices. I trace this work through Eisenman to contemporary practitioners showing how the groundwork for the rationale for process-based work becomes very much tied to and ingrained within an ideological framework for the use of a process-based approach itself.

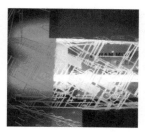

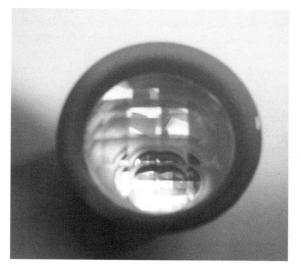

Top images: laser etched plans.

Centre image: process image, raw results of process, produced by photographing colour coded precedent through the prismatic lens (bottom images). Federation Square Melbourne Architectural Design Competition (1997), Project Credits: Vivian Mitsogianni + Dean Boothroyd

2 A key source for this passage was Peggy Deamer, "Structuring Surfaces: The Legacy of the Whites" in Perspecta # 32, no. Resurfacing Modernism (2001), Brennan, Anne Marie (Ed.): 90–99.

I identify the recurring tropes and traits in relation to this practice and outline the compositional and formal prejudices present in process-based work that often originate from an unacknowledged set of architectural concerns. There is in fact nothing in a process-based approach itself that dictates to what end its will be used. The reasons one might use these processes might be different — away from these traditions and default assumptions.

In addition to undertaking and reflecting on a series of design projects and experiments, the methodology of the research involved an examination of the Australian context engaged with by the projects, a substantial examination of the last thirty years of process-based practice in the international context as well as reflection on the 7 white noise PANORAMA design studios that I ran at RMIT. As a design architect and educator I am primarily interested in the use-value of these approaches. The examination of the design studios considers questions of judgment in relation to process-based practice and provides a reconsideration of rigour in relation to these practices. Insight is offered into the consequences of undertaking certain actions over others—in the design process—for example what might we do if our process is poorly constructed and illogical but the outcomes are interesting and useful? How might accidents be handled? How do we avoid getting a mess at the end of the process from which we need to 'translate' to architecture? How much does accuracy matter? When does this approach hinder rather than assist design? Notes are also provided on typical considerations: How do you judge? Authorship; the anxiety of selection — or how do you choose and where for you stop; and notes on common and recurring traits observed in the design studio and wider practice, such as building the diagram, building data, aestheticising science, and why 'radical' process does not necessarily equal radical architecture.

Uncertain Conditions and The Blurred Figure Ground

A number of what would initially appear to be unrelated contexts were brought together through my projects. On the one hand there is the questioning and critique of process-based practice from the inside (from someone who is operating in this area)—on the other is a deep interest in a number of threads in the constructed environment in Melbourne which contain highly specific trajectories of ideas and questions—that I wanted to contribute to.

The Federation Square Competition[3]—an early project—was motivated by a concern for the changing nature of the Institutional or public project in Australia through the 1990's when government agendas of de-institutionalisation (which saw the dismantling of large institutional projects) saw attempts to "demystify" public architecture and increasingly the use of domestic scale and imagery for the public project or alternatively the use of commercial vocabulary.

In the projects a series of iconic terms were used to describe the various qualities and conditions that were desired. Two terms apply to the investigations in this project – or what the processes were designed to fascilitate; the first is 'uncertain conditions'. Initially, the idea of 'uncertainty' was a simple metaphor for the unstable role occupied by the public project, and a desire to use this operatively to claim a difference for the public project. How to build uncertainty later became a series of architectural investigations. The second term, the 'blurred figure ground', seeks to re-examine object and landscape, figure and ground relationships (creating uncertainty between building and plaza for example by treating them as part of the same system) and investigating the architectural possibilities this might offer (particularly for public space and organisation). In the Federation Square Competition this investigation was employed towards generating the 'low flat monument' or how the civic project can

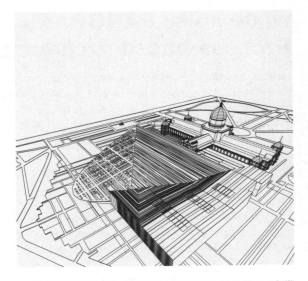

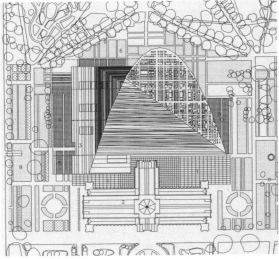

Top image: aerial view.

Bottom image: roof plan. Museum of Victoria Architectural Design Competition (1994) Project Credits: Boothroyd, Larionoff, Mitsogianni, for Joyce Nankivell Partnership Project Team: Vivian Mitsogianni, Dean Boothroyd, Michael Larionoff

3 Federation Square Melbourne Architectural Design Competition (1997) Project Credits: Vivian Mitsogianni + Dean Boothroyd

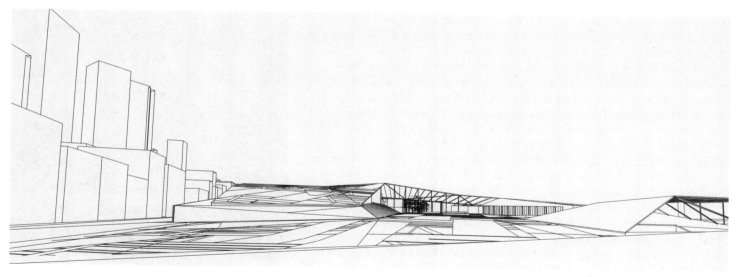

Top and bottom right
images: view from plaza.

Bottom left: aerial view.

Centre: plaza level plan.

Federation Square
Melbourne Architectural
Design Competition (1997)
Project Credits: Vivian
Mitsogianni + Dean
Boothroyd.

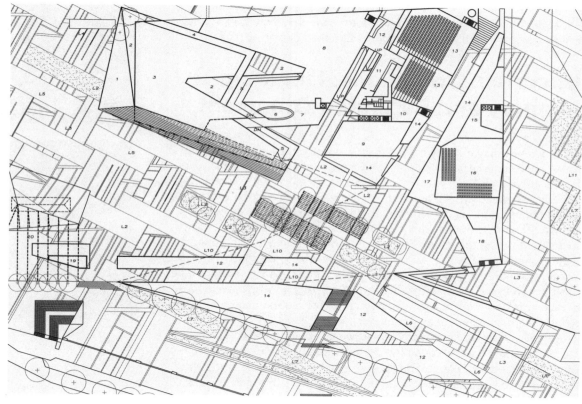

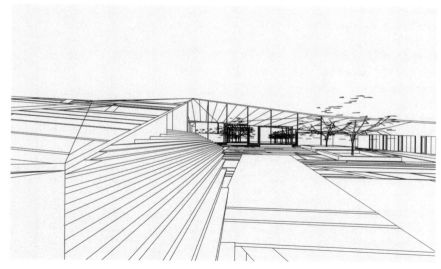

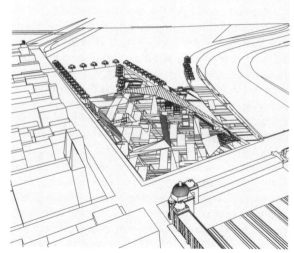

have a presence without necessarily resorting to scale, to see if the postcard image or aerial view could be counter pointed by an experience of the space that was more fragmented and detailed.

The experiments in this project involved the use of a prismatic lens which – simultaneously multiplies, superimposes and shifts whatever is viewed through it. The outcomes were used both as an organizational device in the project and to achieve a system for excessive ornamentation. The selection of the device was influenced by Jonathan Crary's description of 'kaleidoscopic vision'[4] in which he attributes certain qualities to the effects it produced such as "fragmenting iconicity and disrupting stasis". The process-based explorations were developed to assist with achieving these types of conditions which provided a way of judging the performance of the processes that weren't merely tied back to the steps in the process itself. The idea of "uncertainty" was explored in an earlier project for the Museum of Victoria Competition[5] through the appropriation of a strange attractor as a precedent (a symbol of uncertainty) although this approach resulted in a "science-duck", a representation of uncertainty, a 'built diagram' or illustration of the appropriated device rather than using the behaviour of the strange attractor to inform core architectural relationships which is a core characteristic of a process-based design approach.

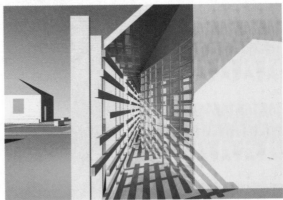

Uncertain Conditions: Lingering Memory and Saturated Ornament

A desire to find a differentiation for the public project also led to a series of façade experiments which were tied to investigations around 'saturated ornament' and 'lingering memory'. 'Lingering memory' is a term that evolved from early operations in which I would appropriate an existing banal, or standard cladding system and through the processes test the extent to which the resultant outcome could contain lingering memories of the original. The interest here was to operate away from collage to consider techniques where the internal composition of the appropriated material would be altered. The aim was to preclude the ability to extract the original imagery from the new façade – which while not necessarily recognisable as attached to the original (that is directly quotational) would make full use of its embedded relationships (window to wall to mullion and so forth), rather than becoming abstract pattern.

A series of projects were developed which take the banal built fabric in a context and through the processes rework it towards a type of standardised exceptional. This part of the work owes a debt to two Melbourne practices, the first, Edmond and Corrigan, refocused what was considered to be appropriate imagery for Australian Architecture and where that imagery was to be found, it wasn't the stereotypical view of Australia focused on 'the dessert' or 'the bush', but that which surrounds us in Melbourne's suburbs, an amplified celebration of the ordinary or the "difficult coded knowledge"[6] of a place. I was also interested in the work of Ashton Raggatt McDougall who throughout the 1990's explored Australia's role on the supposed 'fringe'[7] in an operative way, experimenting with techniques through which to deliberately misunderstand and misread imported architectural precedents, for generative effect and in aid of critique. The work of these two firms involved highly politicised reactions to questions of Australian identity through its architecture and a debate about what was considered appropriate. They also dealt with the public project in Australia seeking to imbue it with a type of heroic potential working with very modest budgets and steering away from default commercial language. The investigations around and desire for 'saturated ornament' in my projects came out of this attempt to counter the retreat of the public project to the anonymity of the office building. An apparent excess of ornament also allowed the projects to appear more significant than

4 Jonathan Crary, Techniques of the Observor: On Vision and Modernity in the 19th Century. Cambridge Massachusetts: MIT Press, 1990.

5 Museum of Victoria Architectural Design Competition (1994) Project Credits: Boothroyd, Larionoff, Mitsogianni, for Joyce Nankivell Partnership Project Team: Vivian Mitsogianni, Dean Boothroyd, Michael Larionoff

6 Peter Corrigan quoted in Richard Munday, "Passion in the Suburbs." Architecture Australia, February/March 1977 edition, p52

7 see Howard Raggatt Masters by Project (RMIT) "Notness: Operations and Strategies on the Fringe" in Fin De Siecle? And the Twenty-First Century Architectures of Melbourne, Leon van Schaik (Ed.) 111–72. Melbourne: 38 South Publications, 1993.

Left page images: New Interpretative Centre and Mary
McKillop Shrine Design Competition (1996) Project
Credits: Vivian Mitsogianni + Dean Boothroyd

Right page images: Façade Experiments on Saturated
Ornament and Lingering Memory — using existing
'found' precedents. Project Credits: Vivian
Mitsogianni, Winnie Ha, Nicole Shiau, Li Chee.

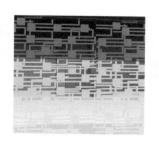

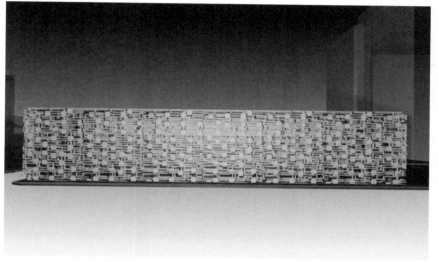

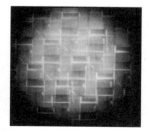

their modest budgets, allowing them to punch above their weight (Mary McKillop Interpretative Centre Competition is a key example).

The experiments used vision devices and systems as their basis. "Vision devices and systems" is a loose term that describes any element that can possibly be related to altering perception or a condition of viewing (this can be as broad as a system/mode of notation, mechanical or digital device, or an "impossible view" – an image that cannot be seen by the eye alone such as satellite, or microscopic photography).

Uncertain Conditions: Building Interference

In the Queensland Gallery of Modern Art Competition[8] process-based investigations revolved around what I referred to as 'interference'. In the project, interference manifests itself as the idea of uncertainty or dissolving the clarity of the view through the façade, and through a peripheral interference, or a noise in the visual field. This peripheral interference is caused by the wrapping of the building with a surface that, at a distance, provides noise and differentiation for the public building, but from within the gallery itself provides a permeable wall that allows for multiple part glimpses through the space and beyond to the wider arts precinct, the river and the city. The process that led to the façade involved the use of a moiré system (in science interference—or noise—is considered a flaw and the moiré is used as a measure of deformation). The process essentially facilitated the generation of a façade system that could adjust to a number of circumstances like a type of gradient as well as a layering of surfaces. In this way the building endeavours to operate as a kind of visual blur within the wider landscape. The primary view from within the plaza was not necessarily of the building itself but the frame of the collapsed horizon of the 'hill', bridge beyond and sky. The attempt was to partially dissolve the building into our peripheral vision which is marked by the modulated cladding system—the blip or glitch in the visual field—intended as a moment of noise and differentiation for the public project. This project shares the concerns of previous projects; an aspiration for an architecture that is affective – with its excess of detail, uncertain presence and that eschews clarity offering instead lingering memories of what might be known and perhaps what is yet to come – a projective memory.

Below Images: Building Interference: raw end results of process tested at a range of scales and opacities.

Right Images: Queensland Gallery of Modern Art Architectural Design Competition (2001), Project Credits: M@ STUDIO Architects. Project Credits: Vivian Mitsogianni, Dean Boothroyd, Joseph Reyes, Mark Raggatt + Nicholas Hubicki

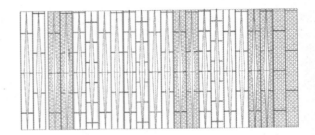

8 Queensland Gallery of Modern Art Architectural Design Competition (2001) M@ STUDIO Architects: Project Team: Vivian Mitsogianni, Dean Boothroyd, Joseph Reyes, Mark Raggatt + Nicholas Hubicki

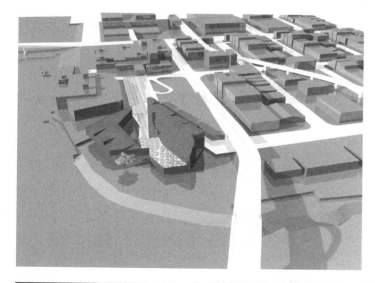

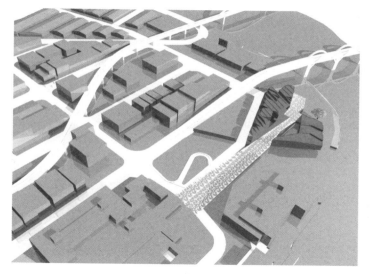

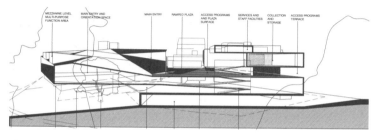

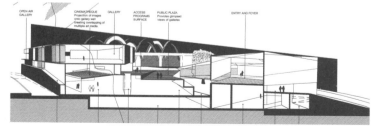

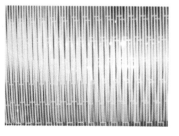

white noise PANORAMA: shifts and propositions

Through the examination of projects, major shifts in my understanding developed including a change in my attitude to authorship. Whereas in the early stages of my practice I had described a process-based approach as delaying authorship, I came to realise that a process-based approach involves authorship from the outset because the design of the process is intertwined with the design of the project even if certain aspects of a process-based approach allow for what we might describe as 'less authorship' of particular arrangements in a project, or for the potential of unexpected outcomes. In my projects, I came to observe that the processes are set up to achieve particular conditions and this involves authorship and composition in the first instance. I have argued that this is the same for wider process-based practice although this aspect has been rarely acknowledged or discussed. In addition, there was a change in my approach in regards to what happens at the end of the process itself. I realised the need to be more iterative if the processes were to be useful rather than limiting. This increasingly iterative practice emerged from an understanding of the relationship of process to architectural project, and my weighing of the project's value as higher than the accuracy of the process itself.

By reflecting on my own design projects, I recognised that a series of parallel concerns mediated the use of the process-based experiments—instead of being isolated formal experiments, they were imbued with the burden of performance—which is to say that the processes needed to behave in particular ways, establish particular types of relationships; the outcomes needed to achieve particular things and this provided an armature for judging the projects that was not just tied to the success of the process itself.

A process-based approach need not default to an exclusion of the banal, the ordinary and referents. Examining the projects themselves including their misadventures away from the 'official and agreed' versions of what one can and should be doing when designing has the potential to open up the possibilities for design and design processes.

In contemporary practice digital scripting processes and other practices using software automated processes pose similar fundamental questions to the ones I have outlined. Although the scope of the PhD focuses on process-based design the discussions are relevant to contemporary architectural design in general given the many overlapping considerations. The viewpoint offered has implications for how the discipline has traditionally understood what is involved in process-based architectural methods. The examination can be considered topical as it coincides with a moment of profound potential and a time when several hybrid practices have arisen directly from the lineage that I describe. An understanding of what is involved with practicing in this way based on the position offered through this research has the ability to expand the potential of process-based practices and the fundamental ways in which they are understood.

Above images: "LIGHTBOXES" showing 3 layers of laser etched acrylic from white noise PANORAMA: Process-based Architectural Design final presentation re-installed in The Nascent Present Advanced Architecture Exhibition, State of Design Festival, 2009 curated by Paul Minifie. Project Credits: Vivian Mitsogianni, research assistants: Joey Azman, Melissa Thong, Molly Hibberd, Nicholas Pratt, Florian Kaiser

Stephen Neille
Speed_Space:
Architecture, Landscape
and Perceptual Horizons

Introduction

Carol Burns notes that "in architectural design, the demands of relating buildings to a physical location are necessary and inevitable; the site is initially construed and finally achieved in the architectural work." It follows, that in order to achieve an architectural project as a work of site we must attempt to understand both the mechanisms of building and the actual characteristics of a physical location. The question is; how can the complexities of any defined site be recorded and modelled to bind disparate elements into being — to model more accurately the wholeness of perception that often drives architectural thinking?

The argument commences with the Rambler's Gallery, and the findings that gave it form. The route along the Goldfields Water Supply Pipeline is considered as an experiential sequence, a necessarily linear sequence that is held in the mind as a series of parts. What is however 'recalled' or remembered (or imagined) is a new constellation formed by the journey.

Speed_Space is structured and presented as a coiled sequence — Expanding, Tremoring and Contracting. Beginning with the Rambler's Gallery, it stretches out to collect and observe the sequence of towns and landscapes. The preliminary research, the recording of the sequence, is informed by text, and the reflections on the thesis are bound into minor projects. These stages are recorded and noted until a tremoring occurs, (after John Sallis) a recoiling at the limit. The tremoring marks a key perceptual moment and sees the beginning of the 'configuration of the project' as the contribution and summary of the thesis. What is designed is a material model of the duality of sequence and constellation. The spatial and sensual markers that are the towns are laid out in a line abstracted from the actual journey. The town figures are coded into conical segments that can be coiled up into a truncated icosahedron, in which the overlapping and reconciling and editing of the total into a single, holistic memory is modelled.

Part 1, Section 1, Beginnings

The Rambler's Gallery is presented as a demonstration project designed to relate building space and form to a physical location. The morphology and topography of New Norcia was used to structure the design of a proposed art gallery. A constellation of independent pavilions are carefully situated at a bend in the road where, from a particular point of view, using anamorphic projection they are perceived to come together as a single building describing a lexicon of spatial types. The project gathers the location and remakes the site; it embodies the architectural preoccupations that gave it form, the findings include:

→ constructed landscape: acknowledgement that the landscape is not given, but produced; it is not of nature but of fiction
→ constellation: that relationship between parts and site is critical to the formation of the minds picturing of the project
→ rambling and body: in rambling we construct mental pictures of the world, the body works as an information exchange system formatting cognition and perception — we feel what we think we see
→ the architectural double skin: operating to structure the interior figure and the exterior at the same time, and recognising that beauty in architecture may have something to do with the necessity to do this
→ spatial types: recognising spatial order from linear to centric
→ making: giving form to thinking through the joy of making.

The Rambler's Gallery is carefully considered and articulated. Yet with all its technique and discipline it stands comfortably within the recurring field of masterly architectural production. It emphasizes the architectural object as a physical go-between that draws on cultivated architectural knowledge and responds to the physical location — the site — the constructed landscape — the 'world as found'. The arial photograpgh shows the town of New Norcia as a constructed landscape that is not given, but produced; it is not of nature but a fiction.

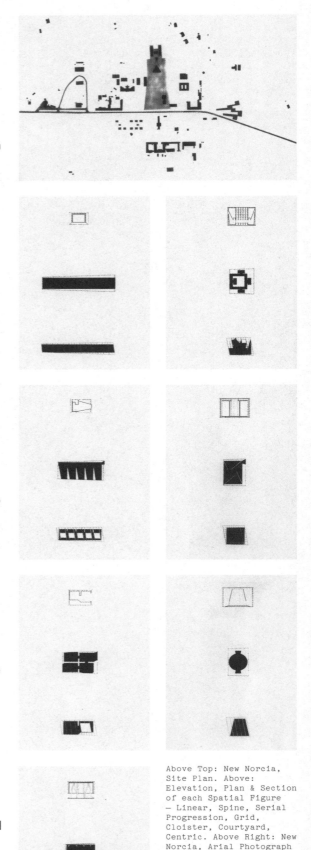

Above Top: New Norcia, Site Plan. Above: Elevation, Plan & Section of each Spatial Figure — Linear, Spine, Serial Progression, Grid, Cloister, Courtyard, Centric. Above Right: New Norcia, Arial Photograph (Battye Library) with Gallery. Right: Rambler's Gallery Model: Each Pavilion holds a spatial figure constructed in Jarrah timber.

Part 1, Section 2, Stretching Out

A performance of place, describes how the research stretches out from the Rambler's Gallery, seeking to investigate the world-as-found, to investigate the site context that is asserted by so many to play a determining role in the outcome of new architectural work. The research begins with wonder, it follows an intuition indicating that something imminent remains hidden in the shadows of the world-as-found, as if aspects of the physical context in which architecture operates still remain unclear. Issues of the constructed landscape needed to be clarified and revealed so that new intelligible beginnings could be made. What is it about, and what could be revealed so as to provide a closer approximation to truth? What aspect of reality could be exposed in such a way that it may affect our experience of architecture and landscape, affect our poetic intelligence? What kind of exposure might affect our re-imagining of site and therefore lead to the achievement of new architectural work?

A linear system, the Goldfields Water Supply Pipeline, was identified and used as the site for an exhibition of theoretical works. Speculative projects were cretaed for each of the small towns that are connected by the pipeline and intertwining road and railway lines as they stretch across the Wheatbelt landscape of Western Australia between Perth and Kalgoorlie. The project was documented and presented as 'Big Journey/ Small Buildings: Inhabiting a Drawn Out Landscape'. When reflecting on these projects and the Rambler's Gallery an intimidating and haunting sense arose that something is absent in the work. In considering the model photographs used to represent the Rambler's Gallery and Big Journey/ Small Building projects a limitation is noticed in the way the projects connect with the actual characteristics of the physical location. Something is missing within the picture; the architectural object is there, but the context itself is almost absent. It appears that in the excitement to reveal architectural intentions some projects may have been over abstracted.

In this situation the site—the physical location—which is an underlying and founding ingredient of architectural making, is diminished. It is as if, in the closing moments of presenting each project, something indescribable was found hidden in the already constructed world, something unfamiliar and formidable, something that could, if detected and exposed, shake the very foundation principles of the architectural project itself; as if the actual conditions of the location, so exposed, could destabilise the whole effort and therefore cause us to feel differently about what we think we see. The problematic reality of the physical locations were perhaps just too difficult and therefore left out.

Part 1, Section 3, Closer Observation

The research focus turned to the close observation of this extensive and pervasive site, a site that may be considered as a major part of Western Australia's greatest single site project, the Wheatbelt. The Wheatbelt developed as a result of the need for economic growth and development; it was constructed rapidly and is a typical example of late 19th century and 20th century expansion. Within that enormous overall project, it was recognised that to observe the whole environment was impossible and therefore the study focused on the series of townsites that have been constructed along the Golden Pipeline. Aerial photographs describe the various geometric configurations of the towns situated within the greater Wheatbelt setting; they provide a snapshot of the new landscape that has been constructed over the last 100 years or so.

The Wheatbelt landscape moved me. It moved me because of its ability to record the passage of time and to physically describe itself. Its capacity to maintain the markings and traces of human will that shaped the location are extraordinary. The sense of overbearing land exhaustion is evident in its surface. It records our continuing need to build human habitat and our continuing lack of regard for a land undergoing collapse.

Wundowie. Aerial Photograph, Department of Land Administration, WA. Facing Page: Noongar. Aerial Photograph, Department of Land Administration, Western Australia. Colour-Scl. 1:25,000
Date: 23/04/94

Meenar. Aerial Photograph, Department of Land Administration, Western Australia. Colour-Scl. 1:25,000
Date: 29/10/94

Wyola Station. Aerial Photograph, Department of Land Administration, Western Australia.

Nangeenan. Aerial Photograph, Department of Land Administration, Western Australia. Colour-Scl. 1:25,000
Date: 28/10/00

Walgoolan. Aerial Photograph, Department of Land Administration, Western Australia. Colour-Scl. 1:25,000
Date :03/5/1994

Bodallin. Aerial Photograph, Department of Land Administration, Western Australia. Colour-Scl. 1:25,000
Date: 03/05/94

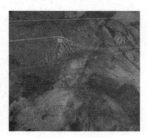

Karalee. Aerial Photograph, Department of Land Administration, Western Australia.

When considering our habitat, the relationship between buildings and landscape, we cast ourselves adrift within the very space of our existence. We open up a method of spacing and distancing that must consider, at the same time, the ground on which we live, and the objects and spaces that we construct for our own purposes. The American poet William Carlos Williams said it so well when he stated …'my surface is myself'.

Part 1, Section 4, Weakening

The research began to indicate that the aspects of site: building and location are in fact much closer together than we may think. It was noted that location and buildings combine to form site and that any particular site is part of a larger system. When you look at any location from a distance you realise that it is really part of a larger site, and from a great distance we realise that 'the earth' is the one site that we have. Site is pervasive, it is everywhere and a lot of it has already been constructed, we have now helped to construct the atmosphere. When considering typical sites or locations anywhere: cityscapes, landscapes, or the Wheatbelt towns described here, it can be observed that an advanced state of degradation and fatigue is occurring in many parts of this thing we call site. Working with the theme of regimes of care and the idea of weaker actions, a Sanctuary Park; Wheatbelt Common was designed between the intertwining lines that define a journey through the Wheatbelt. Rather than inserting more objects in the landscape, a new configuration of landscape is proposed within the existing system. As one passes through the landscape a purposeful pendulum is set-up between constructs; the wheat-fields replacing 'cleared bushland' and 'cwhereand the new bushland generated from 'remnant bushland'.

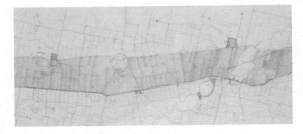

Part 2, Tremoring

Movement at the limit, describes a point at which I was overburdened with the enormity of the project, by the significant fatigue and degradation evident everywhere in the project. I felt that I had come to a movement at the limit, a movement that the American Philosopher John Sallis calls 'tremoring' – the experience of limitation in which man recoils from exceeding nature. With this tremoring came the onset of a discerning paralysis issued in as a result of reflection under the recoil. I read Lyotard's writings on the sublime and moved slowly at the limit, not wanting to move as usual, but to move and act differently, more carefully in the face of the enormity of the fatigue witnessed in the research field. Here came the compulsion to not make more, as usual (Type 2) projects in the landscape, but rather to create a demonstration project that works in the realm of poetic intelligence, as a (Type 3) perceptual model.

Part 3, Section 1, Looking Back

Making sense at the limit, is the beginning of a coiling back, the beginning of the configuration of the final model as the contribution and summary of the project. When encountering site, we rarely, if ever, experience the overall big picture. Generally we perceive site through a whole series of connected locations, as moments, as bits and pieces, as separate elements like the separate Wheatbelt towns connected by a thread of road. While investigating these towns I wondered if a perceptual model could be created to bind the identified parts into being and form a new entity, a new entity that merges the various locations together into a new site, a doctrine of scattered occasions that combines configurations from various locations into a new fabrication which constantly reveals the characteristics of the bigger picture.

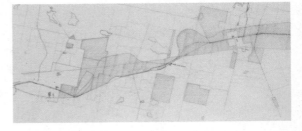

Photographic images recorded and captured the towns as moments in a sequence (like pearls on a string). They represent the experience of the site as a sequence, as a line. However, this is not how the towns, as a part of the greater landscape, are remembered. The total experience of the towns as one travels past, and through, is much greater. The towns gather as a whole, they are bound in the mind, they blur, they are remembered differently. A series

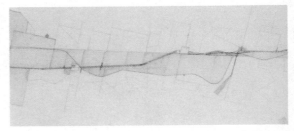

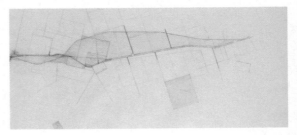

Wheatbelt Common details 1–6. An intertwining linear network; highway, pipeline and railway, are used to create identifiable boundaries between which new landscape is grown using remnant vegetation sourced from towns. Individual lots are bound to create a national park or reserve.

Right: Bodallin — one of 32 'weak' images capturing each town from the road, combining photographs looking ahead, behind, back and front. See Gianni Vattimo, weak philsophy and belief.

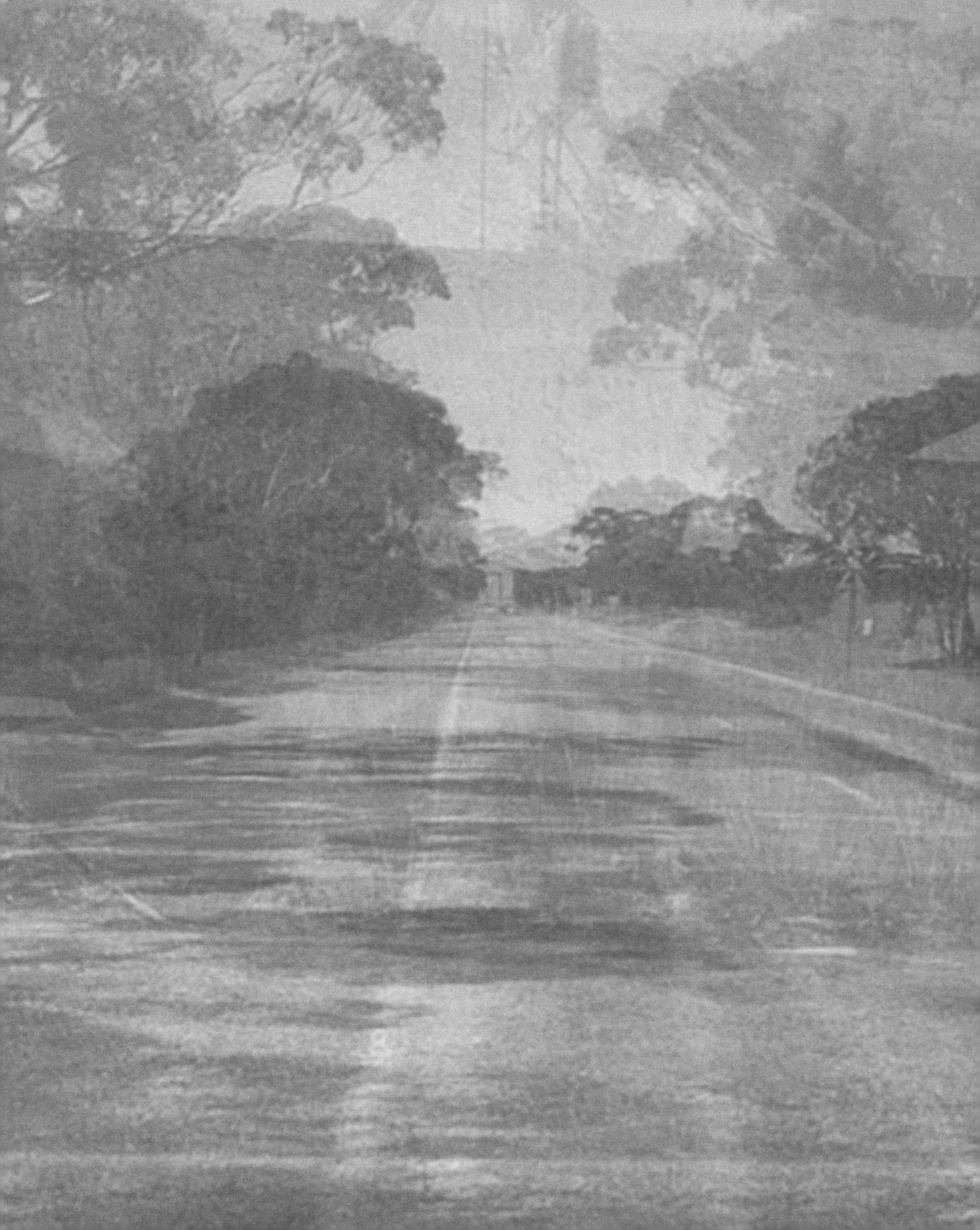

of 'weak images' were created to describe this experience. The string and pearls were gathered together forming a loose ensemble that more accurately described the one big site. The ensemble resembling a loose sphere seemed to present the individual moments (town images) as a whole, as a singular form that constantly presents new horizons as one moves their position relative to that of the object. A spherical polyhedron was unravelled and each component of the polyhedron imprinted with an image of a town located in the sequence provided by the water supply pipeline. The towns, imprinted onto geometric segments are rebound to form a new continuous surface of parts; the line becomes an object; the sphere becomes a perceptual model.

Could a perceptual model act as a muse, as an instrument that may, when experienced, prompt speculation about the recurring conditions of fatigue evident in the site? Such reconsideration may help trigger shifts in perception, shifts that acknowledge site degradation to be a state caused by our mismanagement, shifts that cause useful change and a careful reconsideration of the relationship between building and site. Could such a model cause a tremoring in our perception, a shudder that saw us recoil from the experience of exceeding nature? Could we turn away from our typical buildings that perpetuate our comfort in domination? Could a muse help to reveal a terrifying beauty that exists around us, within the project of our actions: the site? The research attempts to visualise the critical apex of our time, it seeks to disclose the fact that we are making the physical conditions around us and that we are helping to accelerate the condition of fatigue within the very thing that we treasure most – site.

Part 3, Section 2, Gathering

Presenting at the limit. The realisation that we in fact 'make ourselves' is framed as an aesthetic moment, captured and presented as a model that could prompt us to think again, to act differently, to act gently, quietly, and carefully. In the Wheatbelt project Speed_Space tries to reveal that when small moments are bound together they can instigate grand caring conceptions. The sphere of images is powerful, it binds parts into a whole, but the perception of the sphere remains on the surface. The experience of site—the landscape—is greater, of more consequence, more spatial it is three dimensional. The model must gather space. The spatial, double skin characteristics discovered in the Rambler's Gallery are applied to the polyhedral system; each town is inscribed as a spatial figure into a hexagonal or pentagonal cone, the sequence of cones are bound to form an entire system. A new geometric perceptual model was invented.

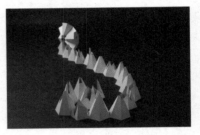

Part 3, Section 3, Coding

The potential in pieces, parts or moments are like a doctrine of scattered occasions. Each part of the model is documented as an occasion; containing the town plan as figure, town image imprinted onto the unfolded cone, aerial photograph, the town figure within the sphere and the location sequence of each cone as one follows the organisational linear sequence.

Part 3, Section 4, Speed_Space Model

Speed_Space is a new perceptual model, a 'Theatre of the World', a muse. Ultimately it reveals a specific intelligence gained in architectural spatial experience, one which recognises that it is our state of mind that must change if we are to build more carefully in future, that coded perceptual models in architecture can help us to feel differently about what we 'think we see'. Speed_Space is like the unsuccessful Wheatbelt towns that never became what was intended, it reveals that our surface is our self, it is a constant reminder of wholeness that is built out of the transitory and fragmentary landscape of experience; a doctrine of scattered occasions. It is a tribute to those who change their minds about current strong practice, who will weaken, who will 'give up' present strength. It is a monument to care and change, to loss, to becoming again.

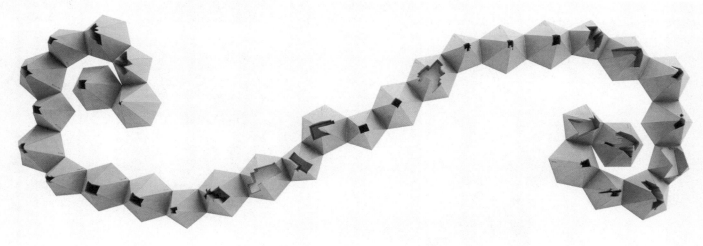

Conclusion

Speed_Space is a work of imagining, commenced by stretching out from an identified beginning, it works to prompt speculation, searching, collecting and reflecting; and by working at the limit, it creates a perceptual model that coils and uncoils into the world as found, presenting a new spatial model for generating poetic intelligence in response to the already constructed landscape, a model that shows architectural experience to be more like a self-made constellation acting as a force of imagining rather than a sequence of facts collected together. The project demonstrates the aim to create a more accurate model of architectural experience. What you take away is not the sequence, but the self made constellation.

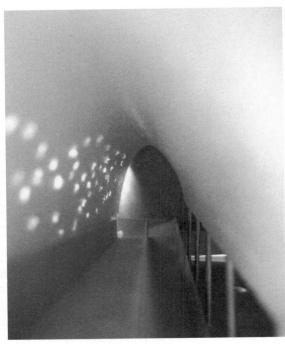

Afterword

A conclusion is a beginning. In pusuing ongoing project based research, the work of imagining, speculating and building continues through the architectural practice Pendal and Neille. Our approach aims to establish lucid and beautiful architecture that can touch the imagination. The furling and unfurling of experience through movement excites us, the inner world of rooms intrigues us. New architecture happens as a result of sustained thinking and doing, of making again and again, of trawling the familiar and unknown in order to gain heightened experience of the world. In practice the familar is edited and bound, making whole-new-worlds as a collection of intense rooms and atmospheres. Similiar to the Speed_Space model, the Carine House diagram (below) is used as a key that collects a series of spatial moments selected from recent projects (right). Combined, these images serve to demonstrate how poetic intelligence works... a perceptual binding into being.

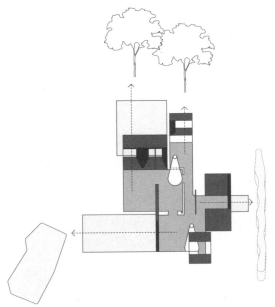

Top. Vaulted Interior, Grey-Smith Institute for Art, Perth, National Winner About Face 2008.

Centre: Living with Portal to Garden, Claremeont House, 2009—11.

Bottom: Living Room with black Bay Windows to Northern Garden, Carine House, 2011—13. Left: Diagram, Carine House.

Deborah Saunt
Orbits and Trajectories:
Why Architecture must
never stand still

I will explain how my doctoral investigations of the work of my Studio **DSDHA** and the way in which it is made are specifically informed by a mode of practice which is founded on a conversational process that, whilst structured, is dynamic. "Orbits & Trajectories" best describe the nature of the way our architecture is both understood and designed.

I have carried out a parallel investigation of the evidence manifest in the work itself as well as the processes involved in its creation, and specifically investigated my own role within this practice.

Evidence within the work

"Push-Pull"

A sense of "push-pull" is embodied in our city making and buildings. The PhD has revealed an overarching search for a kind of New Beauty founded on design values that stand for a sense of public good that aims to improve human conditions and that allows paths to cross, encouraging shared encounter and engagement; resulting in places which foster conversation and exchange. These are designed in a way that is responsive to place and environment, have an economy of means, and generate specificity. This architecture is designed to create a response, and to be responsive, and to engage with the wider world. An architecture that answers back, that is almost awkward in its modernity and that tries to embody imperfect contradictions;

→ solid, three-dimensional but best understood through movement;

→ ever-changing when experienced yet creating duration and persistence over time;

→ preoccupied with physicality and of matter being "made" (in terms of materiality and craft) yet irreconcilably connected to people, emotions, beliefs;

→ above all it is shaped by values and culture. And somehow being "authored" whilst so clearly being the product of collaboration.

Processes of making

A sense of "push-pull" is also found in the way DSDHA has evolved its practice. DSDHA is a place where ideas and people collide, a choreography of chance and purpose.

Through analysing the way we work, our influences and the work that we make, characteristics have been revealed that we are part of a tradition of "creating socially-minded architecture", that we never make the same building twice, and that every project is underscored with a research agenda. In order to arrive at this architecture we find the need for reflection, of bringing self-awareness to the way one choses to practice. Underscoring the process is the need for agency and participation.

Until recently, the "practice" and "academic" sides of DSDHA were parallel endeavours, whereas now a new consciousness has informed bringing them together to create a culture of the studio which, like any design is authored. In particular, the way we collaborate has evolved via our design methodology. This is based on workshops, using research as a driver to generate moments of resistance or collisions where agency pushes design forward.

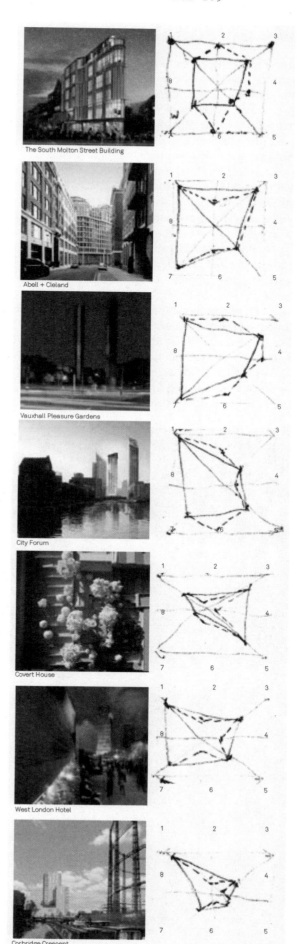

The South Molton Street Building

Abell + Cleland

Vauxhall Pleasure Gardens

City Forum

Covert House

West London Hotel

Corbridge Crescent

My personal roles

Individually there has been the revelation that one must always try "to act upon an idea" and "insert oneself into the project at key points to ensure its potential. These "design actions" impact directly on the outcome of the process. This sense of individual action and self-belief is key to moving projects forward. Speaking out, taking the lead, in the defense of this new kind of beauty are qualities to be cherished, and this is why architecture, as well as architects must never stand still.

Discovering RMIT's practice-based research programme coincided with David Hills and I setting up DSDHA. Writing about new Australian Architecture for a UK Journal, led us to a group of young Melbourne architects who were passionate about understanding both what informed their work as well as the way in which it was made.

This was a revelation. Here was a community of practitioners (Iredale Pedersen Hook, Kerstin Thompson and Richard Black) who were open and reflective, sharing frank insights whilst helping to create a specific design culture in their city. Having reflected on their practice, under Leon van Schaik's guidance, allowed them to curate their own future paths with an enviable consciousness and confidence. Despite the distance, they felt like kindred spirits. On the margins, yet critically engaged with key issues and architectural discourse.

We kept in touch as our practices grew, all actively combining research, practice and teaching at the same time. In 2007, we shared the stage at the RIBA's Practice Research Symposium to expand on our own design

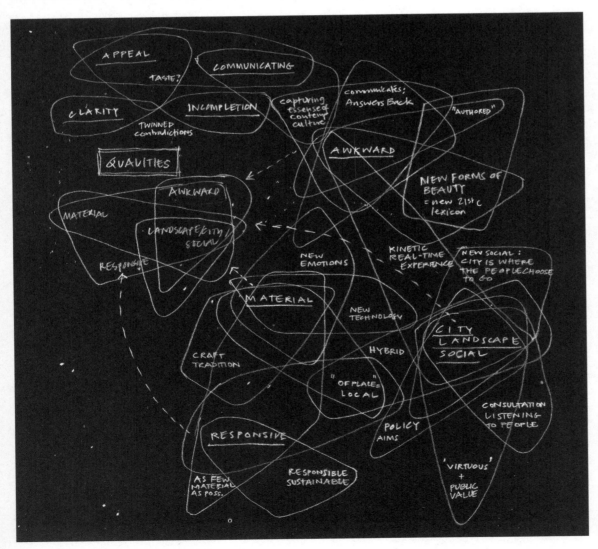

methodology; explaining for example why did DSDHA chose to burn wood to create the carved grotto-like architecture of our Potters' Fields Park Pavilion or testing our own details at 1:1 scale in our wokrshop for St Anne's Sure Start in Colchester?

When, a few years later, I was invited to participate in the programme I leapt at the chance to address the larger questions about why we practice architecture in our own particular way, such as standing in the middle of road, dodging oncoming traffic, just to see a fleeting glimpse of future vista in a yet to be realised urban plan.

Nowhere else in Europe provides the same setting where these core questions can be asked through reflection, as well as through the on-going work of the studio, in situ. Speculating about the origins and recurrent themes of one's work, as well as possible future scenarios, alongside one's peers (such as Tom Holbrook, David Kohn or Andrew Clancy) doing the same thing has been a privilege and a delight, as well as hard work.

My resultant findings have been created mainly through drawings, and focus on the dynamics of operating simultaneously on multiple levels, as if informed by orbits and trajectories which offer non-linear, spatial ways of navigating key issues (such as landscape, city, materiality and environment). Their mutual encounter is influenced by the actions that we chose to take as architects to coalesce our ideas, and make manifest as an act of authorship, created via operations within a collaborative practice.

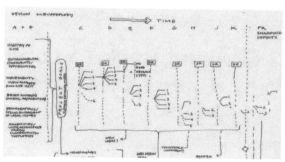

This sense of push-pull is embodied also in the architecture we make and which has been termed for the purpose of this study as "Awkward". Others have in the past described it as exhibiting "dynamic instability". I now call this part of "A Search for New Beauty", as if we try to mediate across scales to make an architecture that is both accessible, and responsive; concerned with sustainability yet engaged with natural phenomenon as a way of enforcing specificity in a networked condition.

Architecture embodies the perfect contradiction; solid, three-dimensional but best understood through movement; ever-changing when experienced yet creating duration and persistence over time; preoccupied with physicality and of matter being "made"; yet irreconcilably connected to people, emotions, beliefs; above all it is shaped by values and culture.

Along side this, Agency is a key consideration – acknowledging that there are roles one can adopt or evolve. I have discovered that I am concerned with the very role of the architect as part of a wider interrogation that asks who should be engaged in making architecture, and how should an architect's education and practice reflect this. Is my having initiated the Jane Drew Prize or the way I teach my post-graduate students to challenge every "rule", related to my contention that today architects must be engaged in agency as a core discipline –questioning the very role of being an architect, and not just the making of architecture. We have to demand more of our talents, to improve conditions for more people globally, whilst remaining personally alert to our own authorship as creative individuals.

Our architecture tries to go someway towards balancing these extremes, without pretending that they do not exist. It is an architecture that answers back and is an act of communication that declares, perhaps, our endeavour to contribute in some small way to making the conditions of being here, right now, as good as they can possibly be; and to not stand back, but to participate.

In the end hopefully the study will be about restating the aims of architecture and to see why architecture must never stand still. The phd is structured in 4 parts. These are:

1. Searching for New Beauty: Orbits and Trajectories
2. Drawing Back To Look Forward: Why Reflect On One's Practice?
3. Interrogating The Evidence In The Work We Make
4. Revealing Actions & Agency In The Way We Work
5. Restating The Aims Of Architecture: Discovering Why Architecture Must Never Stand Still

1 Searching for New Beauty: Orbits and Trajectories

Orbits & Trajectories best describes the nature of the relationships that underscore the findings in the PhD. I have always been drawing the way forward, simultaneous options, laying bare the process, transitory phenomenon orbit and trajectories, kinetic, push pull, trying to find a clear path ahead.

From a survey of OUR PROJECTS and the PROCESSES that underscore them—the archive goes into more detail about the work—from our Olympic Village Housing or our installation for Hermes on Bond Street. And how do we assess a new building compared with an urban framework plan, or a temporary installation?

Speculating on a future architecture for Soho on Silver Street or our West End Flatiron at SMS, to contemporary contested public spaces like Vauxhall Pleasure Gardens – caught between the world city and local needs to small gems—Potters' Fields Park Pavilions—burning timber for the first time in the UK. City making, place making, between public life and private worlds.

From the PhD I can see it has always been moving, not straightforward but Kaleidoscopic, dynamic and kinetic.

2 Drawing Back To Look Forward: Why Reflect On One's Practice?

Asking why we find ourselves practicing in this way is a good starting point – looking at the values that underscore our way of working as a Studio, asking what frames our own aims for the future? The PhD asked the question: Can we even begin to try to understand what one's own backstory, gender or private life might have to do with making architecture and shaping one's spatial intelligence?

Preliminary research uncovered the early influences and interests that helped shape my own sensibilities and spatial intelligence: I have wanted to be some kind of builder from the very beginning, had been fascinated by modernity and also to the idea of an alternative tradition led by people like Denise Scott Brown – where Baroque Gardens and Shopping Centres could be taken seriously side by side.

From the start, we have been researching big issues, and first invited in 1999 by the RIBA to give a lecture whilst teaching at Cambridge entitled "Somewhere between infrastructure and intimacy"

What are the common values and ambitions that we share with our community of practice? Are we part of a tradition? Who are our peers? Who are you placed beside or who do you place yourself next to? Is it the same or different?

Early in our career we had been compared in The Guardian to the Smithsons and had felt unnerved and asked why relate our endeavours to a past generation of architects, not our contemporaries? But I was missing the radical nature of their social agenda coupled with great architecture – which has taken many decades to be re-evaluated and considered more beautiful to a wider audience. This was a revelation and now we are very happy and humbled at the comparison: Alison is personal hero – which I did not acknowledge before. I know now that being part of an architect couple has its distinct advantages – not only for oneself but for the client and the quality of the output.

What is my role in shaping the ethos of DSDHA and the work we make, and in parallel, where, when, and how do I personally influence design within the Studio?

DSDHA have led the design of major educational projects, including a new £33m flagship educational campus in Guildford, bringing together Christ's College Church of England Secondary School with Pond Meadow School and William Bellamy Infants School near the civic centre of Dagenham, to the north of the Thames Gateway.

3 Interrogating The Evidence In The Work We Make

As I said before, I have always been drawing the way forward, simultaneous options; and in fact we may pursue a route then turn back and ask where the decision originated and then trace our steps, take a few steps back and take another look at how to approach it. We don't give up easily and the path is invariably never straightforward. We test several options simultaneously, with a reciprocity between, a dialectic. By also looking at live projects it became apparent that in fact the design sequence was not linear, but more orbital and kinetic.

But before I analysed the process it was key to evaluate the architecture we make and to ask what are our values? So by looking, by focusing on publications about DSDHA, some profound insights into the thematic interests of Studio were offered as tools to understand our work, and in particular Werk Bauen Wohnen's profile by Ros Diamond[1], which delivered an initial overview of Characteristics to answer the questions:
What do the projects mean? What have other people said? So why did it seem awkward or dynamic instability?

I became aware of a potential relationship between what we do and art practice… Work by Ed Ruscha has been an anchor for the research – ever since juxtaposing his Standard Gasoline Station with DSDHA's John Nursery and Children's Centre. His work asks you to take another very careful look at every day, often overlooked phenomena. It reveals a hidden beauty, which has a specific resonance with the work of DSDHA – asking you to reconsider what you are observing, to take a second look.

So I initially tried distilling general characteristics evident in our work, an assessment of 21 projects side by side set against a series of subjective criteria.

- → City-social – eg Potters Fields Park Pavilions – often having an urban quality, meeting bigger goals, for a larger audience

- → Material issues – eg Potters Fields Park Pavilions – testing – blitz burn danger grotto nature

- → Garden-hybrid-veranda – eg John Perry – inside outside, calming super Shelter – scale clash

- → Clarity – eg Christ's College Guildford – crafted, resolved, economic, urban

- → Environmental – eg Olympic Village Housing – sunlight/daylight, wellbeing

- → Appeal – eg South Molton St as a local landmark, but not necessarily receiving awards

- → Recognition – eg Christ's College Guildford RIBA Stirling Prize Shortlist

- → Awkward – eg John Perry, which is an example of awkward, beautiful but unsettling

After distilling general characteristics evident in our work, an assessment was devised to take overview in a comparative manner. The resultant grid of kite-like diagrams shows lopsided projects or projects with only a very limited impact, whilst the 'successful' projects filled nearly all of the respective available fields. Projects in development that were considered problematic as they are small or lop-sided. This lead to a simple revelation:

DH/DS at Versailles
A+P Smithson

John Perry Nursery
Ed Ruscha

1 Diamond, Rosamund.
"Dynamische Collagen"
Werk, Bauen + Wohnen,
March 2010

Not everyone sees our work in the same way, and for some it is not easily understood. We realised maybe that the work is sometimes slightly too "new" and pushes too many boundaries simultaneously, and that as a result people think of it initially as awkward. Incomplete projects cant be judged fully as not experienced yet, as they haven't gained "their own voice", they have not finished being designed as process is on-going.

Case Study 1: The Covert House: Acting on an Idea and Searching for New Beauty

Here the PhD asked that you analyse your work as you do it. This was a project in progress during the PhD and it changed as a result. The first case study is strongly autobiographical, an excursion on one small project and which, like the PhD itself, has been "under construction" for a considerable time. I wanted to see if it could act as a tool to reveal the ways we work and the tools we use and my role within it, and a series of attempts to draw out the qualities of the project over time. It is a project for my own house.

This revealed many revelations:

→ Craft and materiality – making as key component not understood before

→ The process for design review and reflection over time in the studio is a key attribute – our work has to be made public and shared

→ Agency in the way we act on an idea and make something happen that would not otherwise be possible without our own direct personal engagement in the project. It goes beyond being professional and instead is about inserting oneself into the project.

→ Sharing two sides of DSDHA – by inviting on site both our teaching studio together with our design studio it recognized DSDHA as a Research based design studio where boundaries are not cast in a traditional manner.

4 Revealing Actions & Agency In The Way We Work

Looking at our way of working, and my role within this, revealed the kinetic manner in which we make architecture. I further developed a series of "orbit diagrams" to offer a non-linear, spatial explanation of navigating issues and their mutual encounter, helping to explain the actions that coalesce to become authorship, and how this operates within a creative, collaborative practice.

Three simultaneous factors appear to underscore a design's dynamic voyage through the key stages of development:

→ Design Values and

→ Design Actions with

→ The field of Design influences and conditions.

What is key is the acknowledgement that "sparks fly" at special moments of key decision-making. The whole process is buffeted by a purposeful "collision technique" which, in order to succeed, has to be "constantly open to new ideas". This is the manner in which we do it: like Orbits and Trajectories

There were revelations about how I act as an author:

- → via Agency– which I see as design actions as they directly impact on the outcome of design process

- → being there first-hand as a sensibility

- → authoring collisions, as a personal design methodology – via workshop/lab techniques – using moments of resistance to design – and the way as a studio we collaborate, and use research as a driver (theoretical, material, etc) – agency within projects agitating for change, interrogating time and time again.

Also this was manifest in another on-going project which was reviewed to see if this was true.

Case Study 2: Dodging Oncoming Traffic: Operations, Agitation & Actions in The West End Project

This grand urban framework was commissioned in October 2012. It is true city making on a vast scale and carries with it enormous responsibilities and pressures as well as rewards. It proves an explanation of the "field of play" in relation to the scale of the project itself. By drawing the project's design evolution I found that I bring to bear a whole raft of influences from past projects and teaching, fellowships, even speeches / lectures / other projects / new technologies.

Revelations included:

- → How the hand sketch is important for DSDHA

- → How first-hand experience is critical, as evidence of how we insert ourselves into the project;

- → We are present;

- → So this is authorship;

- → The design moves on, changes, gets better (hopefully) at CRITCIAL points, when I act, or others do too, beyong the purely professional.

- → In terms of our practice this review helps reveal other discoveries:

- → Revelation: refusing to be sector specific, scale specific or seeing bigness as having to equate with success.

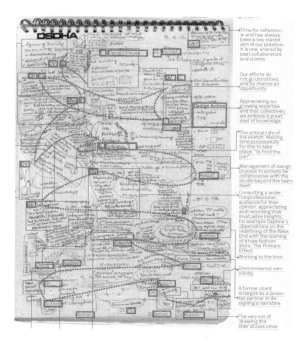

Revelation: my role as a conductor at times to help sort through the chaos.

Revelation: Asking architecture to communicate to a wider audience comes from wanting it to be part of a more egalitarian, non-elitist culture, in which everyone can participate fairly.

Only through this PhD have I realised that I am a provocateur, demanding change for the better, or an agitator purposefully galvanising debate. I am overcome with the need to act upon something, not stand by.

Revelation: By consciously aiming to be a mentor and role model, a promoter of new values, I can help open architecture up to new audiences currently excluded or unacknowledged.

Revelation: Where we find ourselves physically as a studio on purpose: locating ourselves in a specific context in order to be creative. We inhabit the margins, and by making space to create we generate a specific studio culture amongst people who think like us. Where one locates one's self physically, as well as intellectually, is a key action as a designer. I have learnt that DSDHA are in South London for a reason. It is not by accident; it is by design.

Revelation: We are now more aware of our community of practice, of our links to other like-minded people and overlapping fields of research.

We are more situated and confident in understanding the importance of creating one's own culture, developing our own methodologies and being conscious of our vulnerabilities.

Revelation: Fundamentally locating our world within that of other practices – art practice and building, sociology and politics. Better relationships with our clients as we can explain ourselves more clearly, and why we act in our own particular manner.

Revelation: That we can now explain our work as Searching for New Beauty and like Ruscha, it may appear sometimes to be "badly done on purpose".

> You see this badly done on purpose, but the badly-done-on-purpose thing was done so well that it just becomes, let's say, profound. —Ed Ruscha

5 Restating The Aims Of Architecture: Discovering Why Architecture Must Never Stand Still

Afterword

These insights are valuable to the scholarship related to several associated concerns in architecture:

→ Identifying a new trend in architecture – that the new beauty in our work comes from wanting to create relevant and communicative architecture which can engages simultaneously on several levels, in particular with regards to the role of craft and materiality in architecture.

→ That ones' values need to be articulated in order to evolve creatively: which for us is concerned with the public good, of trying to create virtuous work, with an aim to improve human conditions. To foster an environment where paths cross and shared encounter and engagement results, and that places conversation and exchange between people at the fore. To be responsive to place and environment, and to utilise a purposeful economy of means.

→ Developing one's own voice as a creative architectural process by becoming more personally aware of one's role and also conscious of the nature of group collaboration within a studio, and challenging preconceptions surrounding the nature of the role of the architect.

→ The practical concerns of running a creative business – understanding the processes of working across several scales– offering a new scale of diverse practice that goes against the capitalist imperative for constant growth and bigness. This is about the another relevant way to pursue innovation. And also being alert to one's community of practice and one's public behaviours.

→ Gender issues for architecture and the importance of awareness for women as mentors and possible roles within the world of architecture, and the past efforts of women that goes under-acknowledged.

Jon Tarry
Lines of Resistance, Explorations of
Geopolitical Space through Art Practice

This research was carried out through an applied art practice, which involved the interrogation of constructed environmental conditions, through the generation of drawings and the resulting planar extensions into three dimensions. This research used films of the act of decay and active demolition as a means of recording and leading to new, informed understandings of this process. The body of work, which includes drawings, films, and material spatial construction, comes together to disrupt and invert notions of spatial power.

The Introduction referenced a childhood recollection of Martin Creed[1], in which the artist described a mirror in the hallway of his family home – a mirror which his father painted over, thereby concealing or obscuring any person's reflection. Imagining Creed's mirror, with a film of paint on its surface, trapping the paint's reflection in an endlessly repeating cycle in the space contained between it and the silver backing of the glass, provides a symbolic basis for understanding my practice. The research required for this project has been an enquiry into process – the process of carefully scraping away the film to enable a reflexive practice to emerge; one that is informed by a deep and clear understanding of the conceptual drivers and influences within the thinking, and the creating.

The PhD research identified the concept of resistance. Creating works in reaction to circumstance raised questions of embedded history of site. The research 'Lines of Resistance', responded to the way spatial power is formed and undone. The authority given to photographic images, maps, drawings, and three-dimensional forms, including models and computer generated data move into the realm of endless inversion. The doing and undoing.

This research sought to understand the behavioral conditions which indicate the links between political power and geographic space. This position is taken through the creation of artworks, which addresses geopolitical positioning that lead to the formation of disruptive knowledge.

1 Martin Creed, *I Fear This Book*, Thames and Hudson, London 2010

Scope of Research Catalogue

During a biannual research symposium held at the Royal Melbourne Institute of Technology in May 2011, invited critics responded to the question of the Durable Visual Record by discussing the relationship of formatting and archiving. A dialogue followed in which William L. Fox, Director at the Centre for Art + Environment, Nevada Museum of Art, acknowledged that the format durable visual records will take in the future is unknown. Fox's comical suggestion that they might be found etched into rock stayed with me when considering the current acceleration in digital media technology. This raised the question, what would be an enduring format for the PhD record? I thought about taking what Fox had said literally and imagined the PhD document as a rock with weight and potential. During the same discussion, Fox recalled the statistic that ninety-eight per cent of all information societies generate is destroyed within a generation of its creation. The past then exists in elided moments.

Author Jullian Barnes worte, "History is that uncertainty produced at the point where imperfections of memory meet the inadequacies of documentation." (Barnes 2011). This quote prompted thoughts of the petroglyphs that are inscribed onto the surface of many clusters of stones on the Murujuga, or the Burrup Peninsula, in the Pilbara, a region of north-Western Australia. These petroglyphs have been acknowledged as one of the oldest artworks in existence. Who created them, and what their purpose was, are the subjects of speculation and study, and invites a reverence and respect for the indigenous cultures of this country – specifically the Yaburara and Ngarluma language peoples of the area. A landscape of red rock outcrops is edged by sparse vegetation, and one's initial experience is as if the rock art does not exist; as though it is hidden or camouflaged. As the motifs each come into focus, what follows is a realisation of the art's subtle but powerful existence. Seemingly randomly placed on the surface of the rocks are a variety of symbols and images: a hand, a half circle enclosure, a turtle, a fish, a bird and others. Suddenly the entire landscape seems to come to life with these drawings in rock. Adjacent to the petroglyphs is the vast industrial conglomeration of heavy industrial rail and port facilities, also marking this site in a significant, though markedly different, way – through the force and presence of Australian mining prospects. The sites engulf each other in a collision of time and place that seems to merge, to disappear and then be remade, torn apart by questions of exclusion and inclusivity: this is an example of 'resistance'.

Far south of the Pilbara, Perth City acts as a feeder site for the accelerating activities of another resources boom for the State. Etched into the Swan Coastal Plain, the Perth international and domestic airports mark the ground in a way reminiscent of Earth art. It is from this airport, and others around the country that workers in increasing numbers regularly fly in and out of work sites in the Pilbara

I am based in the Perth suburb of Belmont, even my studio is in direct alignment with one of the airport runways. Examining this contrast of contested sites, and the place of petroglyphs and runways in the way they mark the ground, raises questions about what is similar and what is different in the meaning of their marks. The ancient inscriptions carry the power and purpose of the human mark across time, the airport carries an expression of this power, and also of another kind.

Burrup Petroglyphs, Detail, 2009

PhD Exhibition 1: *Migration of Ideas*; Dar Alanda Amman

Remember, View from Dar Alanda Gallery, Jordan

The invitation to exhibit in Amman presented a focus for the *runways of the world* project. The work developed in response to a question of the location of culture in relation to what we term as the geopolitical. Looking at Jordan geographically and historically I decided to make a work expressed through the neighboring regions of Syria, Iraq, Saudi Arabia, Israel, Lebanon, Egypt and the disputed West Bank.

Aerial mapping of the runways of Amman, Damascus, Baghdad, Riyadh, Tel Aviv, Beirut, and Alexandria were translated into hand cut metal templates. Each template had its own container for travel made of timber. The container opened to become a stand for the work and a device for framing it. In the exhibition the works were placed in a cluster in the center of the gallery. While I had explored placing them in a relation to geographic locality this appeared confusing given the density of the gallery space.

A second work was a scaled down air cargo container filled with small canvases. To achieve this I had invited seven artists from Perth to work on small canvases as an expression of exchange and on arrival invited seven artists in Amman to work on the others. These works were displayed together and generated discussion through the act of inclusivity.

The exhibition was unsuccessful on one level but provided a framework for exploration. Scaling down the works shifted them from the sculptural presence and weight that I had been working with. While I rationalized these small works as being about a type of 'Mobili', works which are carried or worn on the body, the work sat more in the realm of jewelry and the domestic. However it was another event, which revealed the most.

When mounting the show I used each work to open conversations with the gallery and visitors; a travel dialogue of sorts. Yet the subject of the *Tel Aviv* (2010) runway received the most attention. I was advised by several artists and curators that this runway may offend some people. Being a visitor myself, I contemplated this. However art is not something to be censored and issues of ethical practice is one that is grappled with, given that art is about challenging values, ideas and creating change. Though I never intended this exhibition to be about propaganda or the tools of state authority, given the political climate I wanted to be conscious of ensuring that it remained as such and at the same time realised it had struck a powerful and sensitive politic.

The solution was to place the *Tel Aviv* work inside a canvas bag and mount it on the wall. I titled this work, *The Unspoken*, of which most viewers enquired about in a somewhat mystified way. What is Unspoken? When journalist Amanda Calvo from the Jordanian Times interviewed me, this subject came up again, only this time coupled with a further question of whether this compromised the work. The runway which re-interprets this concealment by emphasising the discussion of relationship, border and the geopolitical in a way not anticipated yet more revealing. During the interview I also invited the journalist to include this story [See transcript of review]. The National Gallery of Jordan acquired this work for the collection, 2010.

Before leaving Amman, Ala Younis the Curator of Darat Al Funun, the Arab cultural centre for Jordan, invited me to contribute to a project; *Sentences on the Banks and Other Stories*. Ala Younis issued me with a standard blank book, with a map of the world and the text saying 'record your stories here'. I made a hand drawn book with various runway templates that were drawn over in free form. Throughout the book, regulating lines connected each of the runway sketches back to the map of the world. The book is now in the collection of Darat Al Funun. The book was important in that it inspired the later artist book, *Twentysix Runways* of which as with this document has an image taken from Amman Airport Runway as the front cover.

Migrations of Ideas as an exhibition lead to works which are central to the PhD and a subsequent, show titled *reconnaissance*, where the scale of sculpture returned.

JORDANIAN TIMES JULY 4th
Migration under an unseen light

AMMAN – Sculpture, painting and architecture move great lengths in order to convey migration under a light that is often left unseen.

A phenomenon that is prevalent, relatable, and extremely relevant in respect to Amman's ever present mixture of people is portrayed through refreshing and brilliant pieces. Jon Tarry, Ayada Al Qaragholli and Darryn Ansted travelled from Perth, Australia, to Amman for their exhibition "Migration of Ideas".

With an architectural touch, Tarry reasserts the essence of what we know as an airport. Something that is so regularly dismissed nowadays as a hassle and transient space is redefined as the place where those fleeting moments are perhaps one of the most critical movements of this century.

The dissolution of geographical and social borders into a gateway towards an international or rather globalised lifestyle is suggested through exquisite silver stencils of airport designs from a bird's-eye view. Baghdad, Cairo, Amman, Damascus and Riyadh, surrounding capitals of Jordan, are each given tribute through these playful creations that can be dismantled and admired from the palm of one's hand. The stencils appear to form elegant letters of a language that is not spoken but implicitly understood.

It is a challenge to displace the widely accepted negativity associated with migration. However, Tarry does so through his selection of an imperative space allowing a runway that connects one place to another to reveal its true form and value through fine art. With his work on display one cannot help but wonder about the absence of what neighbours Jordan to the west, the contested borders of Palestine and Israel.

Countless of displaced and migrant Palestinians live in Jordan and the absence of an airport in the occupied territories is something that springs to mind. However, hanging on the wall at lengths from the standing three dimensional runway creations is a thick off-white creased bag titled "Unspoken". It is an uncanny piece almost indistinguishable from the wall it hangs from, if touched one can feel a silver structure that dangles from within, hidden from the public eye. Whether it is Tel Aviv, Jerusalem or an airport that has yet to be realised. The extent of his vision, nevertheless, is impressive and admirable.

It appears that the artist has gone through great lengths to design something that is meant to go unnoticed. To a certain degree he has incorporated this absence within his work perhaps in allegiance with the yearning eye. With pieces that are eye catching, versatile, yet so different — the exhibit allows a calming yet inspiring experience.

By Amanda Calvo

Commentary on Review

Amanda Calvo's review appeared in the Jordan Times on July 4th, 2010, entitled, 'Migration under an unforeseen light'. I found the title curious, though appropriate in its suggestion of other ways considering migration. The term 'migration' invites speculation about social construction and the way ideas influence and shape this type of ordering: what is the currency of an idea? How do ideas move around and adapt? Ideas migrate just as people and goods do; ideas are enablers, and an agent of change which can rupture assumptions about what is known. While ideas may be 'apolitical', it is the denial of new thoughts and application that renders an idea 'political'.

I realised during my penultimate presentation at the research symposium in Melbourne 2012, when referring to the adjacent placement of two works, *Baghdad* and *Washington*, in the exhibition *reconnaissance*, that the overt politic in my work was missing the point. While I had thought this was a way to offer other viewpoints hrough juxtapositions, I was actually asserting a singular viewpoint, which was precisely what I wanted to undo. This approach was *engaging* ideologies. From this point onward, my self-critique has involved constantly checking for this integrity. I had at one point been concerned that my work lacked content and relevance, and had become a type of formalist, mannered practice concerned with a cycle of arranging with a political dimension, whereas it now became a means of bringing back content.

Calvo discusses the exhibition in acknowledgment of the airport and the way that new spatial relationships are formed. This spatial potential is free of geographic borders and therefore, the way such borders reinforce social and political power, while airports support this potential by offering ways and means of moving between and across them. While the concept of migration is defined by movement and transition, it has different connotations, specifically where choice and mode come into play, for example, forced migration of displaced peoples and tourist migrations. Dr Annette Pedersen of the Lawrence Wilson Art Gallery addresses this in the catalogue for *reconnaissance*, in her discussion of asylum seekers arriving in north-Western Australia either by boat or by air, both without documents, but the privileges and sanctions afforded those arriving at an airport.

Calvo asserts that airport space is 'imperative'; a space that is required as a function of modern air travel. However, the way it is considered, and meaning extracted from it, as a form for artistic expression, allows for a new way of valuing these spaces quite apart from simply functionality. Referring to my process of transformation, by which an airport runway and terminal is mapped and rendered, Calvo employs the word 'stencil'. This is not a term I had considered in relation to this series, as it implies a simple form of cut out and immediate way of marking a surface. The stencil technique can be traced back to ancient cave paintings appearing around the world, and has enduring applications today for efficiently labelling goods in containers and in depots for transport or storage, and for political protest in street art and graffiti culture. Calvo's observation shifted the way I viewed these works, as I had also been working with stencils in silk screening. Following this, I reinterpreted the manner in which I mark runways onto a sheet of paper. I considered the paper as the ground, or more specifically, as receiving the stencil, just as a runway marks the earth, claiming terrain and defining a space in which to operate and manoeuvre. It was from this point that I developed the *Screed* works discussed further in this chapter, where I discuss how this changed and extended the enquiry.

The work *Unspoken*, discussed above, is a focus of Calvo's review, in which she suggests looking closer and attempting to identify the missing runways concealed from view by a canvas bag hung on the wall. Calvo suggests that the work implied that I, the artist, went to great lengths to make a work intended to go unnoticed, as a reflection of the micro-political climate surrounding specific location of the Jordanian gallery. This suggests a kind of power which exists as a product of anonymity, and absence and erasure. Interestingly, this point affected my approach to work, and now my practice is shifting to having an implicit nature, as opposed to an explicit one that may have characterised it earlier. However, I intend to be explicit about what is being implied, in the sense of leaving the subject open, but requiring a search or enquiry by the viewer.

In summary, like the piece *Unspoken*, the true work is what comes after what has been left unsaid becomes evident. The works created following the *Remember* project *Migration of Ideas* and *reconnaissance*, appearing in Pin-up Project Space show, *Arrival Departure*, can be clearly seen as following on from the feedback taken from the Calvo review, with an informed and refined bodywork.

The Space of Denial

Aspects of art production sit next to words as language that has no voice. Art may often be mute linguistically, and yet there exists no artwork which does not say something or have something said about it. The rock art on the Burrup Peninsula is an unspoken art, its mystery and intention contained in its 60,000 years of existence. In this research project I have been conscious of creating a sense of implicit knowledge in my work, as opposed to making explicit statements. It was a revelation to contemplate how to be explicit about the implicit knowledge in relation to artistic creative enquiry.

One of the exhibitions discussed, *Migration of Ideas*, held in Amman, Jordan, included a censored work, following advice I received against exhibiting a work based on the Tel Aviv airport. An artist cannot control reaction or response to their work and ideas, yet to be able to express a view is integral to my practice. My views are expressed with an inclusive intention, inviting dialogue, as opposed to making exclusive or hierarchical commentary on topical politics. The space of denial encounters the contradictory forces of silence and or being silenced through other means. While what is not said can be as powerful as any stated message, the effects of either silence or non-silence are contingent and case-specific, with context and ethical considerations being paramount.

Concealment of information or knowledge can be misconstrued as withholding and closed, and therefore as asserting a power through secrecy. Equally, however, concealment of knowledge may be a means of preservation, or a demonstration of respect. This complex issue and the challenges it presents were encountered in this project, both in my research investigation and in creating and presenting work. An example of this is the images of the runways, while most are readily accessible on the Internet, mapped by Google Earth, anecdotal responses from people implied that drawing them from above given that airports or effective controlled air spaces, that some the access to the aerial views was covert. This only appeared in one such case when viewing an air force base near a domestic airport, and realising the view of the airbase was obscured in the clouds.

The Tel Aviv runway work was ultimately censored by my decision to heed the advice. Rather than excluding the work from the show, I concealed the piece using a bag similar to those used in sending aide to refugee camps, obscuring it from view. Entitled *Unknown*, the work attracted a great deal of curiosity and enquiry. The outcome of the exhibition, and the inclusion of the work in a different form from its original, highlights the significance and potentiality of inverting notions of power relations. If the reason for self-selecting was based on a consideration of other people's concerns, and that is revealed later as appearing opposite to this intention, then leaving the work out may have been interpreted as a denial of the issue, and therefore continuing the perception of a conflict of interest. This act of representing the topic by an ostensible denial—the creation a new visual context—denies only acquiescence to secretive censorship. Amanda Calvo, in her review of the show for the *Jordan Times* (July 4, 2010) wrote, "it is as if the artist has gone to great lengths to design something that is intended to go unnoticed." This statement informs the basis for understanding the significance of geopolitical spatial power. It does so by having interpreted the power of the work not simply as a non-dominant form, but as a type that oscillates, constantly changing and adjusting, and effectively inverting itself.

Resistance, timber and graphite, 200cm × 120cm, 2012, Jon Tarry

Unspoken Runway, timber and canvas, 120cm × 90cm, 2012 Jon Tarry.

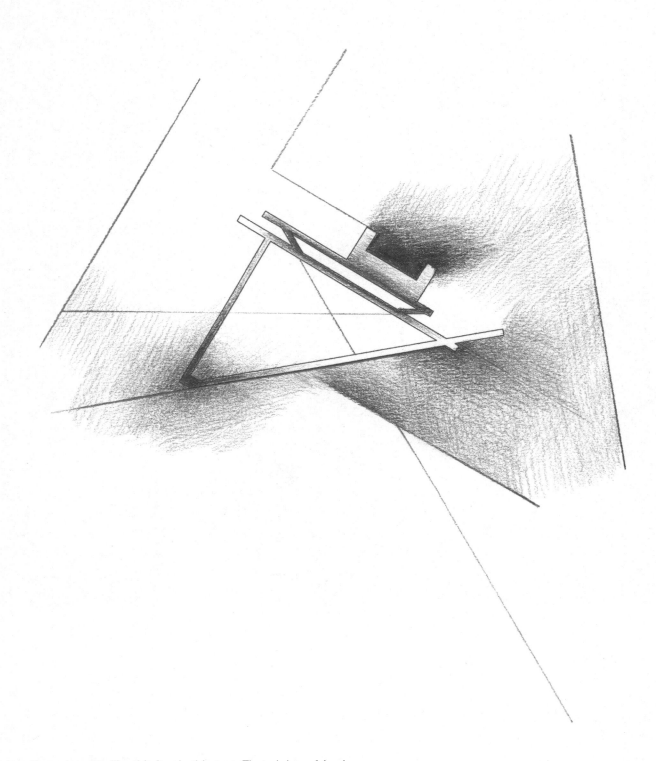

TLV

It's taken there, in print, like this book, this text. First sights of Jordan,
floating in super salt, deep graphite, coloured sea, a distant vision. Later
on the other side, a reflection from the River. Time and out of time.

Branches weave, leaves fall, winds rise.

Jo Van Den Berghe
Theatre of Operations, or:
Construction Site as Architectural Design

I will explain how the doctoral investigations of my mental space (Van Schaik 2008), more specifically my childhood discovery of the subsequent (forbidden) spaces of My Grandmother's House (demolished more than twenty years ago), appears to have shaped my spatial intelligence, hence has influenced my past and actual work as an architect.

I have made a reconstruction of this house on parallel but intertwining tracks.

Track one: I have made drawings of the house. Then I have made a first scale model (scale 1/100) of thWe house and the constitutive elements in its immediate surroundings.

Track two: I have presented track one at international conferences with peers and academics.

Track three: I have asked for the expert input of a clinical psychologist who guided me, by means of a series of regression sessions, to better trace, situate and understand my memories of my past spatial and sensuous experiences in My Grandmother's House.

Track four: I have decided to finally make a textual description of the house in poetic prose.

Track five: all the previous tracks have culminated in a second scale model (scale 1/33) of the house and the constitutive elements in its immediate surroundings, in order to better demonstrate and disseminate the research results as part of the final Ph.D exhibition in Henry Van de Velde's University Library in Ghent (Belgium).

On the following pages I will first 'set the tone' and insert an excerpt from the poetic prose description of My Grandmother's House. Hence I will reach out into moments of design research, and into places of my architectural practice, which appears to be 'standing on' constitutive spatial and material experiences stored in my mental space, where My Grandmother's House still is real.

Top to bottom:
My Grandmother's House,
investigations: sketches,
drawings, scale models.

(LACE)MAKING, DRAWING, DREAMING

I spent many minutes and seconds in my grandmother's house, and I can recall so many of them.

My mother used to take me to my metropolitan 'there', to that little town in the plain, my personal downtown. I was awarene of the the dense urban fabric, which was cosy. Being in that house, enclosed in so many layers of solid brick masses and volumes, of which almost none seemed to have windows, felt comforting and secure, as if no one could find us there, safe in our secluded kingdom. Coming in from the street I looked into an endless rectangular space like in a Renaissance central perspective, with the vanishing point at infinity. My family used to call this space 'the corridor'.

My grandmother used to make tapestry. It was done on a brownish canvas with a wide mesh, through which she wove little strings of wool, of which she had a myriad of colours. The canvas was stretched in a sophisticated wooden framework, "my métier"[1], she called it.

That day, the hatch of the draw well in the garden was laid open. The pump piping needed a repair. Fascinated and frightened, I looked into the well, my eyes scanning the masonry of the tubular volume of brick that disappeared into the subterranean Depth until it became a lightless spot of mat black that marked its perspectival vanishing point, smeared like thumbnailed charcoal on rough paper. Then I looked up and I saw a tall brick factory chimney, sharply presenting itself against the June sky, proudly standing amidst brick factory volumes forming the south wall of the garden, and all of a sudden, it became clear that a master's hand had precisely cut the oblong chimney volume out of the brick crust of the Earth in order to put it in reverse on top of it, leaving a lasered opening for the draw well to look into the brick Substance of the world. Dark shreds of smoke vertically sprouted from the chimney's mouth to immediately change direction and horizontally hurry their way to the pale blue North.

Reminiscent of the Virgin's grotto in Lourdes, my grandmother got herself installed a grotto for the Holy Mary at the south end of the garden. Below, as high as me (forever a four year old), was the main entrance. I stepped into its Darkness. Two meters appeared to be two times two hundred. I felt the proximity of the massive brick factory chimney behind the infinite Depth of the grotto. My time expanded under a lowering vault. At first glued behind me like resin, my own shadow had soon caught up with me and suddenly was running ahead of time, pushed me gently in the back by scarse rays of light that reached towards the invisible vanishing point in the Depth. Unmeasurable. Humidity and vapour reveiled projection lines constructed by the invisible draftsman. I gazed at a dark wall that was looming in front of me. This must have been the picture plane where my world was projected upon: my silhouette, my time that had come and gone and come, and my future as I wanted it to be, projected on it as an additional layer on the palimpsest of my infant imagination. I have spent a lifetime to find the exact place from where I would be able to decipher the anamorphosis that brought it all together: my remembrance, my shadow and my dream. But still I could not see it. It was soundless and waiting. It smelled like humid moss and molybdenum and fern.[2] In an instant, I remembered a small pond next to the entrance of the grotto, wherein I sensed exploding flag that smelled like the birth of green spring, abundantly rooting in the swampy soil, and a griffin straightly standing in the middle, with the gesture of a defrosted cat, his claws firmly gripping around the rim of his dado, a thin water jet spitting from its mule, and a pair of black eyes that warned the intruder of the grotto for the price to be paid in exchange for a dream. But I was unafraid, a hero back then. I knew that this long

Top: Lace glove (1967) and pattern (1947), Brussels Lace, pencil and black ink on tracing paper.

Middle: My Grandmother's House, scale model 1/100

Bottom left: Etude (2010–2012), Let it Bleed (first version): the draw well, the dormer window and the chimney.
Etude is one of the speculative Ph.D designs in which aspects of my mental space have been further explored and translated in new design procedures.

Bottom right: House DGDR: central perspective.

1 This word refers to the French culture in which Belgium has been drenched, especially my grandmother's generation. Métier, here as the name of the device she was working on, in French also means: skilled craft. In my view, the production of culture goes through skilled craft. Craft is a basic condition of culture, not the mere servant of it.

2 "We see the Depth, speed, softness and hardness of objects — Cézanne says we even see their odor. If a painter wishes to express the world, his system of color must generate this indivisable complex of impressions, otherwise his painting only hints at possibilities without producing the unity, presence and unsurpassable diversity that governs the experience and which is the definition of reality for us" (Merleau-Ponty 1966).

Drawing, Dreaming Etude (2010—2012), Smokehouse,
Foodhouse, Slaughterhouse.

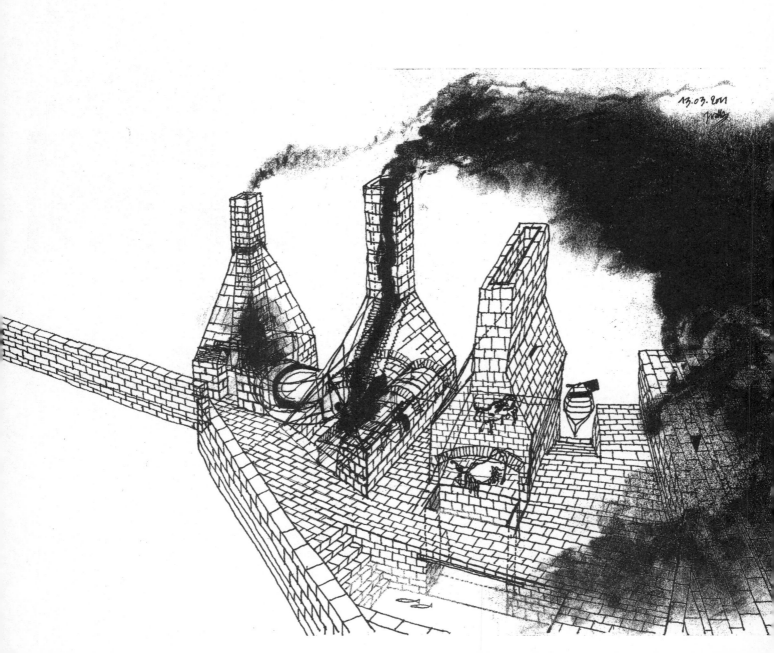

and dark grotto would finally end up in the basement of my grandmother's house, because I believed in it, like grannie believed in the Virgin Mary, and in the Immaculate Conception.

    I had come down to the basement of the house. The stairs, the floor, the massive walls, and the vault, all carefully masoned in brick. A small ventilation shaft transported sounds of female footsteps and sniffing dogs from the sidewalk to this brick subterranean world that reminded me of the draw well in the garden underground: the same masonic precision, the same thick layer of brick Substance out of which the same master builder had cut out a void called basement.

    A secondary brick vault carried the imbricated stairs, and underneath it was a dark barrel-vaulted underworld where succory and asparagus were grown in wintertime, in that cavity where light would never travel. In the back there was a door, and it fascinated me. Although one day I had checked the world behind that door—wooden shelves with bottles of red wine—the almost certain presence of a secret world behind these shelves kept compelling me: could this be the presumed connection with the dark end of the grotto in the garden? My eyes slowly had to adapt to the twilight seeping in from the ventilation shaft. My position was central, and I saw how the perspective loomed slowly in front of me: scarse brownish light falling on the floor and creeping deeper and deeper into the void and onto the feet of two parallel walls, one on the left and one on the right, gradually dissolving into pitch black as my gaze raised up to my eye level, from where an unmeasurable black Depth—where the brick vault must have been—crowned the scene. There, my presumption that had emerged in the grotto would be confirmed: I was looking into an infinite black Depth that was the black humid Depth I had sensed in the grotto, presumingly the other side of the vanishing point of the central perspective, being the point where all the servant lines of the perspectival drawing come together and join to complete the image in a moment of insight and understanding: behind this door in the basement, there must have been a connection with that other enigmatic end, the vanishing point in the grotto, and both vanishing points in fact were one and the same vanishing point, and it was only me observing it from two different angles, one from the vault in the grotto, one from the vault in the basement, and I was instantly instituting the connection between both, with the concept of vault as their common denominator. Paradoxically, in the Darkness of the basement I had found my enlightened point of anamorphosis: my remembrance of the grotto, my shadow cast as another layer on the brownish light on the floor, and my dream in which I connected the loose end of this underground vault with the unfinished business of the grotto.[3]

    In the central room of the house, two concentric arches formed a red brick inglenook big enough to lodge a brown erubescent enamelled coal stove, and a four year old. The TV set had been put in an alcove of a cabinet made by my grandfather. He had very precise hands for wood and metal, like he had ears for music and an eye for photography. He had upholstered the doors of this cabinet with thick sheets of brass which gave the cabinet a golden aura, and the parsimonious daylight reflected in it filled the room with magic, casting mysterious blurs of yellow on the ceiling. The cabinet doors formed a brass wall in the room. Known only to the initiated, like us, one of the cabinet doors opened up like a treasury chest, providing a hidden pass-through to the stairwell to the first floor. This was our secret corridor into the night. The wooden stair was dark and narrow. The landing on the first floor was only one square meter of size. There were two doors: one on the right that gave access to my grandparents' room, one on the left which was the room where we slept when we were lodging at grandma's.

    I was standing at a closed door. The forbidden room of my grandparents. There were other rooms forbidden to us: the basement (too dangerous), the photography studio (I had heard about it), the attic (I had not seen it). These impenetrable spaces have long been solid

Top: House DGDR (1999–2004), sun screen as lacemaking

Bottom: Boathouse (2008–2012): black house as gentlemen's room.

3 Much later, in 2002, I was standing face to face with Leonardo da Vinci's paiting *Saint John the Baptist* (da Vinci 1513–16) in the Musée du Louvre in Paris. Although it is a rather small painting, it overwhelmed me with recognition. It portrays a young man who steps out of an unmeasurable Darkness, smiling mysteriously and pointing at the Darkness with his index finger. Saint John, in the Bible, is described as "a light that shineth in the Darkness".

VOORONTWERP BOTENLOODS RABOES
VERTIKALE DWARSE DOORSNEDE
SCHAAL 1/20

Jo Van Den Berghe en Bart Uvin
info@jovandenberghe.be
bvba y.e.AH-architecten
++32 (0) 474 89 00 36

masses of Darkness, forbidden Substance, a pitch black Thickness with an unmeasurable Depth. This moratorium on spaces has triggered my fascination. The substantiation of these mysterious moratorium-spaces has blended with my clandestine journeys into them. They have constituted my fascination for the labyrinthine.

I guess there was too much light in the room, like there can be in photography, burning away every Depth from the picture. This may be the reason why it took me some time before I suddenly noticed a second door in this room. Strange. Thinking of other houses I had seen, I could not remember rooms in which second doors were needed. The second door was identical to the first door. Was this merely a second entrance I had not noticed yet, and if so, what would have been the hidden trajectory to get there? Or was this a new exit to be explored?

It was an afternoon in late July, it was hot and humid and the threat of thunder was audible in the southern distance. I decided to open the second door carefully, trying to make no sound. I stepped into a narrow and dark new space of about one square meter, right the size and the shape of the first landing I encountered. The rumble in the southern skies was growing, with a diminishing intensity of light. In the mirror above a washing stand on my right I could see a dark velvet curtain on my left. I was afraid of thunder that might jump me in the face if I would open that curtain. So I didn't. I decided I'd rather open the second door in front of me. I stepped into a room of which I did not know the existence. It was almost dark as if light had never been in there, except from one light bulb under which I saw my grandmother, whom I almost did not recognise, sitting upright in her bed. So this must have been the forbidden room, my grandparents' bedroom, apparently accessible by more than one trajectory through the house! My Grandmother warned me that I should not come in there, and that I was a bad boy, and that thunder would come and get me soon! She was reading a book. "Wolfgang Amadeus was not a lightsome man, was he?" she said. I looked around in the Darkness of the room and saw curtains of heavy, almost black velvet that deeply obscured the space. Two mahogany wardrobes, closer to me than expected, loomed up to the ceiling. Their keyhole plates were adorned with bas-reliefs representing candle holders and vases filled with grapes that abundantly hung over their lips. The motif of grapes continued in the brightly sculptured wooden cornices on top of the wardrobes. There, they mutated into angels' heads and feathered wings, and incited by the unchained electrical storm they came into a state of levitation. I was becoming physically unwell, my eye-balls whirling down to meet the floor, where a small carpet looked like long black grass in which the mahogany bed was standing with a high end against the wall, equiped with two lamps shaped like pinkish glass roses. My grandmother looked very old, and everything in this room announced the coming of the Man in Black. The air of a sarcophagus had filled the place. I did not want to breathe it, but still it seeped into my every pore. I could choose between the smell or suffocation. I was too young for this. How could the night come so near to a summerday's afternoon, merely one door away. Wanting to go out, I felt that something very powerful was holding me back, and that this was the price the griffin next to the grotto in the garden had warned me for: "Once you will have penetrated this unknown Darkness and broken the moratorium, you will be contaminated forever, doomed to slip into other unknown Darknesses, carrying torches in order to unveil them, one by one. You will have to repeat your ritual time and again, to instate the Thickness of Substance in order to first insert the unknown dark solids into your world, so that you can explore them, as a powerful antidote to the boredom of your already known voids of light. With most of your colleague architects endlessly repeating their hollow mantra's of abundant light and La Ville Radieuse (Le Corbusier 1924) and so, you will forever feel astranged. A devoted exile in your celebrated Darkness."

Top: Boathouse (2008–2012), Smoke, Water, Air, ink and pencil on rough white paper.

Middle: WoSho/Fashion (2004–2007), lacemaking on the roof.

Bottom: WoSho/Fashion (2004–2007), wooden lock on wooden door.

Opposite: Boathouse (2008–2012), tree growing in.

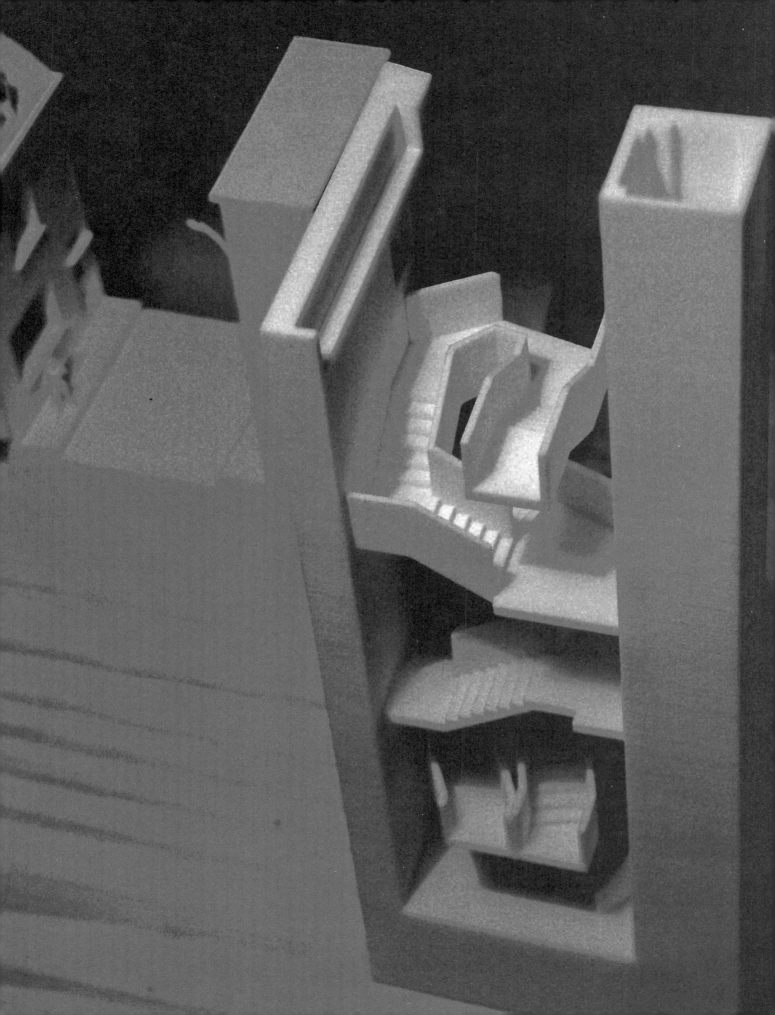

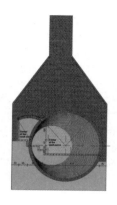

By now, I had not only looked at my vanishing point from one side (the grotto), and then from the other side (the basement). I had finally stepped into it.

So I pulled open the curtain. A seemingly endless steep stair vanished into a distorted perspective obscured by a hollow dark in which I began to gaze. Now I was puzzled: not only two doors, but two stairs as well.[4] I had to climb them to find out, and I reached another landing. Again, two identical doors. Coming from the stairs, doors appeared to give access to a bedroom with more than one door that gave access to identical doors that unraveled my Darkness and unveiled the existence of other stairs to other floors with more identical doors. I was beginning to see a pattern. Standing on that upper landing, I decided not to open the door on my right, for this might be the forbidden room again at the north side of the house, and I was afraid of my grandmother with her spectral white hair, with her old book, with her strange questions about Wolfgang Amadeus's Requiem. "Requiem aeternam dona eis, Domine, et lux perpetua luceat eis"[5] (Mozart 1791).

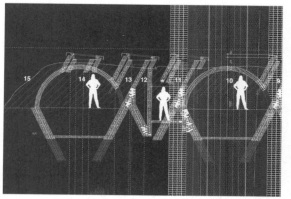

I did not find a second door in the southern attic, like I had found in the bedroom one floor below. Did the pattern begin to fail? High up, I had saw a garret with a television antenna, without finding the access to it. So I walked into the Northern bedroom in the attic, looking for the assumed second door in order to find another stair to bring me to the garret with the televison antenna. I slowly turned around the corner. Yes, there was a door, identical to all the other doors that had lured me into this labyrinth of doors and stairs. It had a doorhandle, a keyhole, and a key. Now I would finally find my stairs to the supreme garret of the house, where I would stand face to face with the television antenna, to see the universe, circling above my labyrinth like Daedalos and Icaros, tracing the Minotaur, finally understanding the complexity of my world in exchange for the price the griffin had warned me for.

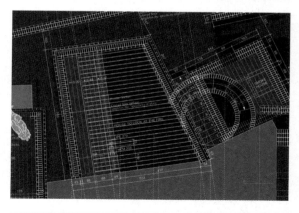

I opened the door decisively, preparing to take my first step on the stair towards the universe. But apparently I had discovered a built-in cabinet. I knocked on the vertical wooden planks in the back of it. This knocking sounded warm and greeting, inviting to interlocution[6], so I knocked again. Pushing them gently, the planks seemed to move a little. My insight emerged: there had to be a hollow in the wall! What if the wall between the southern attic on the other side and this built-in cabinet in the northern attic was thicker than I had thought? Then, the missing stairs should be inside the Thickness of this wall!

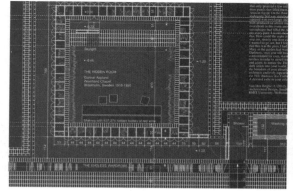

4 Alain Resnais' experimental film *L'Année Dernière à Marienbad* (Resnais 1961) is a cinematographic adaptation of the Nouveau Roman, in which the boundaries between fact and fiction are blurred and the framing of time and space is being put under investigation. The film presents a luxurious Baroque hotel, where a man tries to convince a woman of how (he dreamt how) they had an affair in the same hotel, one year before, something she cannot remember. Another man plays (card) games with all the guests in the hotel, and he wins time after time, as he masters 'the rules of the game', whereas the first man, who tries to turn his fiction (or his memory, or his imagination?) into reality, is being shunned by the woman, who, at the end of the film, leaves the hotel with her husband who appears to be the (card) player himself. Finally, the name of the game is logic and rule, with the discouraging conclusion that the realm of the dream is completely in vain, granted no chance to win in this world of logic and rule, the name of the game (of cards). The gardens, together with the sumptuous spaces and rooms of the Baroque hotel, play a protagonist role, wherein the human characters are their servants. The gardens and spaces of the chateau refer to the 'clarté' of Versailles, in which Cartesian compositions and planned geometry overrule the wandering spirit of the mere dreamer who does not play cards. The film is a fatalistic demonstration of a 'mariage de raison' (based on fact), and how this concept overrules the dream of true love with its own unplanable paths (fiction).

5 "Grant them eternal rest, O Lord, and may perpetual light shine on them."

6 I call upon the world to heed and welcome the words of the poet's uncontaminated language, so as to resist the degrading instrumentalisation of these words by and for the malicious translations by and for perverted institutions. The latter are the real hell of this world.

Top: Etude (2010–2012)
red brick facade, and brick facade.
transverse through the secret wine vault at night.

Bottom: Etude (2010–2012)
plan of the stairs from Smokehouse to Foodhouse.
plan of the secret wine vault.
Opposite: New Stairs (2010) (Ph.D design), scale
model 1/100.

I was standing in the dormer window in the southern attic. My
withdrawal in there was inspired by my longing for some southern light
after I had found the missing stairs in the Thickness of the wall during my
temporary residence in the northern attic with the built-in cabinet. Through
the dormer window I could see the the lowland stretching southwards,
where it swept into a fringe of hills that formed my horizon. This was my first
Emergence of Thickness. From my metropolitan there, My Grandmother's
House in a small town in the plain, I was looking at my local here, where
my home was in the hills. In this moment of clarity, my understanding of
the essence of here and there, and of their co-presence as the anatomic
section of my landscape, emerged.

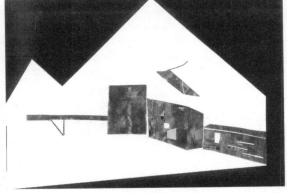

Top: Boathouse (2008–2012), gentlemen's room
(nightview), brass clad furniture.

Bottom: WoSho/Fashion, entrance through the golden
door, the secret corridor into the night.

Gretchen Wilkins
Manufacturing Urbanism: An architectural practice for unfinished cities

Cities emerge through making things, including themselves. The relationship between industrial manufacturing and urbanism is a shifting one: changes in the ways things are made effect significant and tangible change to the fabric and culture of a city, and vice versa. This work sits at the intersection of those practices, documenting shifts in manufacturing for architectural and urban work, and speculating about future urbanism in light of contemporary industry. A series of architectural projects, and ultimately a model of urban-architectural practice are proposed, poised between states of urban and industrial change. Distributed and collective models of design and production are a primary focus and enabler of that work.

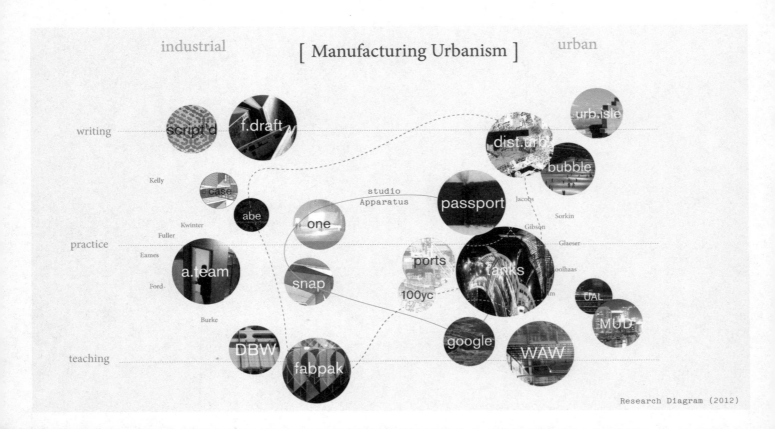

ARCH∧UP
Debate 2010

Utopia – a lofty and necessary goal, or a quixotic distraction from the very real and pressing issues of the present? The unbuilt architectural project may catalyse action, or it may crystallise thought around fundamentally irrelevant concerns. Join us for the final Process event of 2010, when we debate whether:

"The pursuit of Utopia is a waste of architects' time..."

VICTORIAN CHAPTER, V-YAG,
PRESENTS 'PROCESS'
6:30 MON. 6th DEC. @ LOOP
23 MEYERS PLACE MELBOURNE
WWW.ARCHIPROCESS.ORG

Top: Advertisement for the Arch^Up debate (2010)

Middle: General Motors Pavilion, from the New York World's Fair, 1964. As seen from I-94 in Michigan, 2005.

Bottom: Woodward Avenue, Detroit, 2007

1 van Schaik, L. (2008) Spatial Intelligence: New futures for Architecture, Great Britain, John Wiley & Son Inc.

Manufacturing Urbanism
An architectural practice for unfinished cities

Introduction

This work assesses links between industrial manufacturing and urban change, highlighting ways in which contemporary and adapted industrial manufacturing techniques, tools and expertise (labour) come to bear upon urban space, and vice versa. Insofar as industrial and urban practices are perpetually and rapidly changing, their status—and the practices that might be undertaken across them—is continually in flux. This marks a highly productive territory for architectural and urban design work. In this research the coupling of manufacturing and urbanism enables design to harness the surpluses or scarcities inherently resulting from urban and industrial shifts; including building stock and urban space, materials, technical expertise and economic or intellectual capital. The aim of this work is to establish a more flexible and expanded framework or 'platform' for future architectural practice, situated at the intersection of industry and urbanism and predicated on the agency of incompleteness in architectural and urban design.

While this research was developed in the academic and professional context of Australia, it emerges from a legacy of Midwest American industry and urbanism where I studied and first practiced architecture. This context cultivated a preoccupation with the relationship between industrial manufacturing and urban expansion, especially concerning patterns of population migration, distribution and related shifts in economic and industrial development, the effects of which underlie urbanism of this region and those like it. Looking closer at this context directly and comparatively was instrumental to this research in several ways 1) for articulating my own 'spatial intelligence,'[1] and the impact it has on future architectural practice; 2) it establishes a link between the way things are made and how cities evolve; this link becomes the primary driver and trajectory of the research projects; 3) as a case study and precedent demonstrating how conditions of social and economic instability are necessary and productive for urbanity, rather than trying to control, account for or succumb to them. This last point establishes the intellectual and practical foundation for the architectural practice proposed through this work, one which endeavours to operate betweenphases of urban change, between individual and collective work, and between local and remote sites.

The practice includes design, teaching and writing projects, ranging from full-scale architectural interventions to speculative urban proposals. *Manufacturing* and *Urbanism*, taken together, identify modes of working or triggers for design more than preforming the outcomes. This is to say that 'urban-type' projects are often driven by industrial practices and vice versa; and also that investments in practice are not always-already linked to clear material outcomes. More importantly however, this coupling establishes a productively indeterminate space of practice between them, and that is the primary focus of this work.

The following research is structured in four sections. *Urban Practices* presents a series of 'incomplete' urban case studies from three key cities: Detroit, Tokyo and Dubai. *Industrial Practices* documents design projects predicated on technological or economic shifts. *Networked Practices* establishes links between distributed urban networks and industrial techniques. *Modelling a Future Practice* outlines a proposal for future practice, and directions for that work.

Urban Practices
Between industries &
economies

Becoming unfinished

Cities change incrementally, unevenly, and constantly. At specific moments however, acute and dramatic transformation is evident, especially in stages of frenzied construction or rapid de-urbanisation. The aftermath of such change is often characterised by incomplete plans, unrealised agendas and an uneasy ambivalence about next phases or directions of development. These in-between phases of a city's development, even if downturned, instigate new considerations for architectural practice, especially the mechanisms through which it can alter, (re)organise and (re)envision the city. This section of work introduces a context for thinking about these approaches both historically and through a discussion of specific urban practices taking place in acutely transforming (shrinking or expanding) cities. Detroit, Tokyo and Dubai are discussed in detail and are compared to each other. A photographic series for each illustrates this comparison spatially.

The cities and sites collected here are either enduring or enjoying the effects of massive economic shifts, often in connection to the way things are physically produced or manufactured. Post-industrial sites, unfinished urban developments and the under-regulated zones that emerge through rapid or severe economic change offer much potential for design often because of the lack of direct attention to it, and also because there is much less resistance to change. These cities and sites exist between the present and the future in a distinctly palpable and unique way, caught between what they are, once were and what they are expected to become. As William Gibson has suggested:

'Cities in the world that have been great cities in my lifetime have gone through legendary phases in which they offer cheap ground level retail space and cheap live-work space for young artists. New York had it aplenty, London had it aplenty. They no longer have it in the same way. They've become sort of 'cooked', and once a city is completely cooked, it's more like Paris, where the city's business is not to change; but it's not a place that actually welcomes innovation.[2]'

However, in a typical course of urbanisation, predicated on continual growth, liminal or marginal spaces too often and too easily become absorbed into higher valued space as the need for housing, commercial and retail space grows. Unregulated spaces are colonised first by fringe or unsanctioned activities, with higher-end retail and residential development following closely behind. In this manner cities naturally progress from 'uncooked' to 'cooked', from an abundance of inexpensive space to an abundance of relatively expensive space with more predictable (and profitable) uses for it.

However, if the progression of urban development has already demonstrated that it can move in two directions, from nascent to mature and from inexpensive to exclusive, and in reverse (in the case of shrinking cities for example), might it also be possible for cities to remain perpetually 'uncooked' as far as accessibility to space, opportunity for alternative programs, and retaining low property cost are concerned? Economic growth tends to foster the former, pushing these opportunities ever farther from the centre of the city. Economic recession, on the other hand, releases those coveted inner spaces once again. Given the example of late twentieth century Detroit and the many other 'shrinking cities,'[3] it is clear that

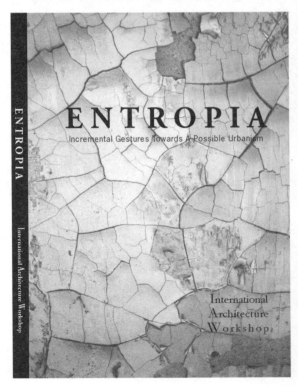

Entropia book cover, Borderlands Workshop, Detroit 2007

Odaiba, Tokyo (2006)

Odaiba, Tokyo (2006)

Abu Dhabi (2008)

continual progression is never fully predictable, nor is the socioeconomic and programmatic exclusivity that comes with such 'progression' wholly desirable. How might cities remain 'unfinished' even as they mature? How might they strive towards completeness and incompleteness simultaneously, given that both conditions have recognisable benefits economically, architecturally, culturally and in terms of productivity?

If unfinished cities engender innovation by nature, as the Gibson quote suggests, it might also be said that cities that engender innovation are perpetually unfinished. Mature cities might remain 'uncooked' provided they find ways to resist the negative or exclusionary spatial and programmatic effects of growth, while it's happening. Many recent tactical urban projects aim to instigate growth in the face of decline. Here however, the proposition works in the other direction too, to seed economic and regulatory resistances to the momentum of growth.

Unfinished urbanism is posed here as an agenda rather than a description of a quality of space. That is, cities should strive to remain unfinished, and to do so in central districts, not just the urban peripheries. The momentum of growth in any major city would suggest that this is impossible, but is it? How might architecture and urbanism embody incompleteness, even if their city is already 'cooked'?

The paradox may be resolved through the mechanisms of planning, or through the subversion thereof. Projects that actively resist full economic, architectural or infrastructural cohesion, or that forego conventional planning altogether aim at this goal. Hou Hanru's strategies for 'post-planning', William Lim's Incomplete Urbanism and SITRA's building prototypes with the Helsinki Design Lab are all examples.

Tactical, provisional or stop-gap approaches to urban development seem most attractive when they are the most necessary, such as during an economic recession or boom. However, the longer-term effects are where their real value lies. Experimental, unofficial constructions and post-planning projects share an agenda toward action and away from analysis, by enacting the process of building for regulatory change rather than the other way around. In this manner they demonstrate the effects of alternative architectural approaches rather than simply describing, analysing or proposing (planning) them. This may be the most effective way to enact change in the midst of an overwhelming momentum otherwise; to resist exclusivity (and stagnancy) during growth or to seed activity (and innovation) during a decline. Of course the pressures in either case are quite different, but the value remains located in the agency of action. In the face of seemingly unremitting change—toward or away from urbanisation—active, material approaches to practice resonate in ways that may not be known at the outset. Regardless of the immediate benefit or function, they act as Trojan horses: smuggleing in greater, longer-term change through seemingly insignificant, ulterior, or provisional modes.

Three case studies are offered to further articulate these approaches in three cities: Detroit, Tokyo and Dubai. Each is presented in two parts: as a narrative essay and as a photo essay. Each tells a story of a site or urban condition poised between what it was and what it is yet to become, highlighting the architectural opportunities and challenges posed within that city's indeterminate and unfinished spaces.

2 Gibson, W. (2012) 'William Gibson in Real Life,' interview with Alex Pasternak, on Motherboard-TV, April 4, Paris. <http://motherboard.vice.com/2012/4/4/motherboard-tv-william-gibson-in-real-life>.

3 Oswalt, P. ed. (2001) Shrinking Cities: International Research (volume 1) and Interventions (volume 12), Ostfildern, Hatje Cantz Verlag.

Material Practices
Reclaiming industrial work

Optimising by-products of change

Cities emerge through making things. As the mechanisms and processes of making shift over time, so do the spaces and practices around them. The gaps between phases of production or lulls in economic or technological activity are not unproductive ones, however. On the contrary they trigger new applications and methods of making as well as producing useful material and technical by-products. Extending the discussion from *Urban Practices*, which aimed to harness new surpluses or shortages within the evacuated city or in the wake of economic recession; this section of work attends to the residual effects and implications of those urban shifts, namely industrial manufacturing techniques, skills and materials. The research focuses on specific material and architectural practices that exploit the gaps resulting from shifts in industry, such as recycling, up-cycling and optimising cast-off materials for architectural use.

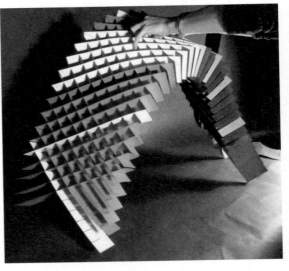

This work is prefaced by a longstanding interest and practice-based experiments around the notion of limits, specifically as they pertain to the material, regulatory or economic systems within which architecture operates. This began with my Master of Architecture thesis—exploiting the restrictive covenants of residential building construction—and concurrent volunteer work coordinating creative workshops in high-security correctional facilities. Previous practices, as a partner of both Ply Architecture and Wilkins + Comazzi Design, furthered these interests, working in collaboration with underemployed automobile fabricators and adapting their techniques and materials for architectural construction. An understanding of material limitations, especially in connection with shifts in local economies, persists here as a central focus. The current research addresses larger urban streams of manufacturing in the context of rapidly growing, receding or otherwise transforming city regions.

The agenda of this research is to establish architectural agency beyond inherent limitations of material or technical resources. Several design and studio projects are conducted and documented in the work. The *Fab-Pak* studio projects interrogate the limits of cast-off or disused sheet material and international shipping logistics through full scale architectural constructions. The *Snap School* project pursues a slightly different trajectory, focusing not on limited resources or residual material but on unitised systems and their capacity for proliferation, variation and reuse. In both cases the value of the process is measured terms of both immediate outcomes – i.e. as urban furniture projects and demountable classrooms in their own right – as well as in broader socio-economic terms, such as educational value or environmental impact.

This approach is particularly informed by engagement with the automotive industry in previous practice, the context of Detroit and experimental manufacturing processes, and by early interests in Henry Ford and Charles and Ray Eames. Detroit, the city that emerged and declined around Ford's industry, is inseparable from discussions about contemporary manufacturing, urbanism and the design trajectories which link them. The shift from the vertical assembly line to the horizontal assembly line to roboticised, distributed assembly networks is one example.

Charles and Ray Eames' experiments in laminated plywood, furniture manufacturing and adapted technologies during WWII are an equally important early influence on my work. Their practice is predicated on experimentation across many scales, material systems and venues for design while remaining committed to producing for clients and the public

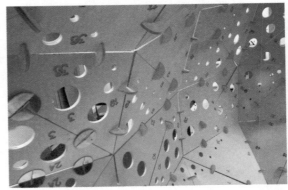

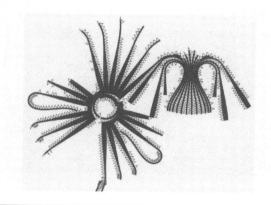

Opposite page:
FAB-PAK studios, student work images:
Left 1—3: Sliceform Project: in Melbourne.
(students: Barzel, Forget, Kulatunge, Litera, Lucas)

Bottom: Plywood Project: (students: Chisiza,
Collins-McBride, Peggans, Holmberg)

This page:
Top: Softcore project (students: McGuire, Wright,
Perera, Macleod, Maehr, L.Chan, X.Li, W.T.So)

Middle: 'unfolding' forms (student:David Christiansz)

Bottom: Aluminium Project (students: Mitra,
Rossetti, Stafford)

alike. This aspect resonates with the earlier discussions in this research (*Staging Practices*) on experimental constructions within and for the public realm, such as Expo buildings and constructed prototypes. It also suggests an approach to networked practice and informs the model for the future practice, Studio Apparatus, which is invested in making, experimentation and collaboration with industry.

Project Descriptions

Fab-Pak Design Studios

A series of studio and elective courses I co-designed and co-taught at RMIT University articulate this research through full-scale fabrication projects using reclaimed materials.[4] Looking to fabrication technologies as a way to bridge the gap between design and execution, this research tested various methods for the digital optimisation of flat sheet materials, specifically those which can be reclaimed from building and manufacturing sites. Focusing primarily on material constraints enabled creative approaches to the reuse of residual building materials in fabrication, also working to reduce the amount of building waste in construction processes. Digital information and scripting processes were embedded into material systems in order to rethink the relationship between input and output in design, especially in the context of sheet material manufacturing, reclamation, fabrication and distribution. Two design studios tested this approach using reclaimed laminate, plywood, aluminium, tarpaulin and foam. The ambition of the projects was to establish new links between digital and material techniques for reprocessing excess off-cut materials, and to extend the limits of these materials as a result.

Snap School

The Snap School was a design entry for the Future-Proofing Schools competition sponsored by the University of Melbourne.[5] The brief for this competition called for ideas appropriate to the design and construction of relocatable classrooms in Australia. Taking lessons from automobile and pre-manufacturing techniques, our proposal was designed as a platform with a series of customisable options. The basic unit was designed as a wedge-shape monocoque system with electrical, plumbing and air services embedded. This allowed the units to snap together in a variety of configurations, being adjustable to various site conditions, school sizes, changes in educational or architectural program brief, or other variables specific to contemporary school environments. Each school or purchaser could customise the shell through an online interface. Users were able to build the classroom online by selecting the size (number of units) and specific programmatic requirements, as well as options for colour, logos, branding, or sun shading assemblies. The *Snap School* was an experiment in applying industrial techniques to an architectural proposition, extending the lineage of unitised or prefabricated building systems, reusing building components and engaging users in a platform for design and customisation.

4 Design studios co-taughe with Leanne Zilka and John Cherrey

5 Wilkins, G., Zilka, L., Cherrey, J., Boden, T. (2011) 'Snap School' entry for the Future Proofing Schools Competition by the MSD Incubator at the University of Melbourne.

Networked Practices
Access to tools

Overview

This section of work discusses the space of practice that emerged between the paralleled interests in industrial manufacturing and contemporary urbanism. These two streams introduced key drivers for these projects, and the approach described here shares and integrates ideas and methods across them. One of those drivers is the relationship between distributed and local practice; including networks of practice, intersections between local and remote sites, virtual and physical space and digital and tangible media. A second is assessing the structure of authorship in creative practices, especially collaborative networks of design. The outcome of this work is an argument and proposal for the incorporation of collective production in architectural practice. It highlights the importance of designing the end-stages of projects and of retaining 'gaps' within project and practice structures. Four projects demonstrate this approach, undertaken through design, writing and teaching.

Argument: the Agency of Incompletion

The space of practice that emerges in my work between the poles of manufacturing and urbanism is not clearly defined. This is partially attributable to its status as a new territory of my own work; i.e. it is impossible to fully know or delineate, yet. However, the indeterminate quality inherent to this new practice is also a deliberate agenda of the work; incompleteness and open-endedness are specifically pursued as productive drivers for creative design practice. To actively resist full completion is to acknowledge that this territory of work is not well defined by nature, and therefore may not become neatly delimited or contained by an all-encompassing strategy ever, even over time. Indeed the value of this approach is predicated on maintaining an opposite approach, one that resists comprehensiveness and closure.

Unlike so many other disciplines, collective authorship and deliberate strategies for 'creative incompletion' in architecture are not immediately obvious, applicable, or widely taught. Indeed the strict regulatory, legal and financial conditions through which the profession and industry operate all but disallow it. This does not mean there is no place to rethink these principles however, or that methods for doing so are already prescribed elsewhere (open source platforms in computation, for example). The challenge for architecture is to structure a way in which completion perpetuates production rather than terminates it, to allow multiple 'completions' within a project's lifecycle.

Perhaps, ironically, the best way keep things unfinished is to get them done. If being 'done' can be defined more in terms of future potential within the work and not a termination of it, then 'being done' becomes an inflection point rather than an expiration point. In this sense, being done indicates the most productive or actionable point of a project rather than the most perfected or comprehensive one. In design practice this suggests that the ending-stages of a project are a key focus, and that these need to be considered (and designed) not as conclusive points but as expandable strategies. This might imply releasing control or authorship earlier in the design process, embedding mechanisms through which others may 'complete' the work or enabling contingency

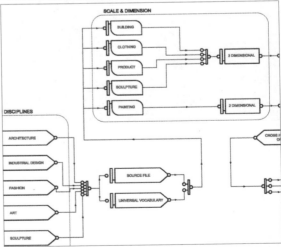

Top: Distributed Urbanism book cover (2010, Routledge)

Below: TankView project
Competition drawings for Portland (2011)

Lower Google Cities design studio poster (2011) and Remote Control research seminar poster (2011)

Drawing: 'scripted' architectural practice (student: Neo Hun Lin)

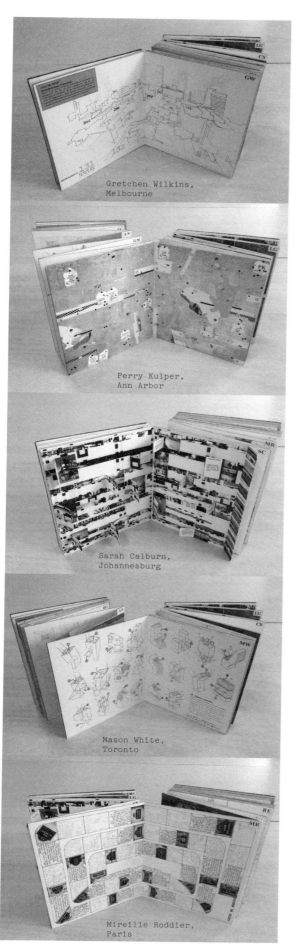

Gretchen Wilkins,
Melbourne

Perry Kulper,
Ann Arbor

Sarah Calburn,
Johannesburg

Mason White,
Toronto

Mireille Roddier,
Paris

and risk rather than trying to control for or eliminate them. The endgame of design is strategised to trigger multiple future openings. 'Creative incompletion' becomes 'creative completion.'

In this work four projects are presented as examples of this conceptual framework. Each captures an experiment with collective approaches for architectural practice and authorship, undertaken through design, teaching and writing.

Distributed Urbanism: Cities after Google Earth (editor, 2010) is a publication that emerged from a symposium and architectural workshop in Detroit entitled Borderlands (2007). The symposium invited architects, academics, artists, industry and government representatives to offer new perspectives and design approaches for the increasingly indeterminate urban and spatial conditions in Detroit. The publication then extended this discussion to contemporary urbanism more broadly and the forces at play within it, inviting twelve authors to provide case studies from various cities or situations around the world. These included Beijing, Mumbai, Rotterdam, Dubai, Hong Kong, Tokyo, Detroit, New Orleans and Arequipa.

The *Passport Project* is a prototype for collaborative practice, a test of multi-authored engagement with questions of contemporary urbanism.[6] The aim of the project was to produce a global document in linear book form, comprised of discrete, individual drawings about local and contemporary urbanism. The project was launched from Melbourne in June 2010 as a book and website, travelling around the world until March 2012. The format of the document, a linear double-sided, accordion-style book, was sent to 24 people in 23 cities sequentially, each asked to produce a 'construction document for urbanism.' Each of the contributors, who were architects, urbanists or artists, was given a two-page layout and two weeks to produce a drawing before sending the book on to the next contributor. The method of drawing was left open; the only stipulation beyond the subject of the brief was that the work was produced in the book provided and that it must respond in some fashion to the work immediately preceding it. As such, the book progressed in an exquisite corpse fashion, becoming a volume of individual, disconnected pieces and yet one collective work.

TankView is an ongoing project exploring the repurposing of abandoned or obsolete infrastructure in cities.[7] It began as a submission for a competition in Chicago, and went on to win, in a different format, a competition in Portland, Oregon. The tanks are designed to act as portals into the local roofscapes of cities, connected globally through digital and physical media.

Google Cities is a combined design studio and research seminar I taught at RMIT University from 2010–2011. The ambition of the combined coursework was twofold: to explore the relationship between virtual and actual cities through program, accessibility, documentation and design, and to explore the tools and techniques by which this form of distributed design and architectural practice could occur professionally and logistically. This was developed through architectural design projects in design studio, and propositional research projects in the seminar.

6 A link to the Passport website, documenting all the work, contributors bios and tracking, can be found here: <www. passport-projects.com>

7 Tank View project was authored in collaboration with John Comazzi

Modelling a Future Practice
studio Apparatus

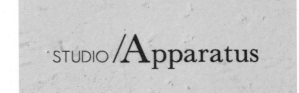

A primary outcome of the work undertaken in this research is the initiation of a vehicle for future practice. *Studio Apparatus*, a new collaborative project launched in July, 2012 with collaborator Anna Tweeddale, is designed to operate as a framework for curating and enacting projects within the space between industry and urbanism. The structure of the collaboration learns from industrial manufacturing practices; it is modelled as a 'platform' incorporating essential elements for practice rather than being organised as a complete, holistic brand. The identity develops from the work of the practice itself and from the collaborators invited to participate. These include partners in industrial manufacturing and urban economics, artists, urban designers, architects, writers and academics located globally. The ambition is to curate and cultivate a practice geared towards a variety of outcomes, such as events, building proposals, urban frameworks, speculative designs and prototypes.

Studio Apparatus will focus on contemporary urbanism and give attention to the types and qualities of sites described in both the Urban and Material work described above. These include post-industrial or post-bubble sites and spaces in the midst of, or affected by, the dynamics of urban and economic change. Key subjects include changes in population, density, infrastructure, ownership, zoning, procurement and parcelisation, as well as contemporary approaches to manufacturing and production and the technologies they employ. At the core of this work are questions around urban policy, urban economics and development. The goal is to initiate urban-based projects that operate strategically through design, and that build upon partnerships already established across other disciplines.

As an Apparatus we imagine the practice in terms of its tooled capacity to make or achieve outcomes, to itself 'do' work. An apparatus is a mechanism or instrument which enables a variety of outcomes. It is designed and constructed in order to design and construct other things. We use this name quite specifically for these connotations, envisioning a variety of types of work it can produce across urban and architectural contexts.

Future Directions

This body of design research, thereby, finishes on the verge of the next. To summarise the findings and developments of this work is to still refrain from final conclusions of how all of the threads tie neatly together into a composite project. My emphasis has in fact been on working towards the opposite, and my practice and research will continue to be developed in this way. The work is newly launched and remains creatively incomplete.

I'd like to acknowledge the insightful and generous support of Leon van Schaik and Pia Ednie Brown, supervisors of this work.
All images and photos are by author except where otherwise noted.

Conclusion

The Practice of Spatial Thinking: Differentiation Processes – Second Edition

Informed by research into design practice conducted over the past 25 years, we explore the ways in which architects and landscape architects differentiate their practices from those of their peers, and consequently find their voices and particular manner of spatial thinking. We focus on communities of practice that have something in common, including a city region context, and have a research-oriented approach to practicing. These practices tend to be interested in questioning the status quo, pushing limits, and being experimenters whether they are in a 'strong idea', a 'strong delivery' or a 'strong service' grouping. We uncover how their design-approaches self-organise, through the early years of their immersion in practice, and how they benefit from examining the process of mastering their discipline. We describe how mastering an approach requires them to encounter other practices, in forging a boundary or horizon of difference with the practices of their peers and thus establishing energising resistances. We uncover specific modes of engagement with design that propel new practice directions, opening up new opportunities for them in new operational niches. We argue that innovative communities of practice arise, or at least tend to thrive when at least three alternative and differentiated positions are actively operating as part of the constitution of that community of practice. We don't limit our analysis to a singular tripartite schema, but move across a series of ways to categorise practices into three different groupings. There is an important moment where we discuss the 'inexact process' of categorising, because 'designers may adopt different stances in different circumstances.' We argue that the exactness/inexactness of any given categorisation doesn't really impact on the vigour of the culture of such communities because what matters most is that enough differentiation occurs. A capacity to adapt and adopt different stances in different circumstances supports innovating practices, and the liveliness of the communities they are part of; though the most important factor in the differentiation within a community of practice is that its members clearly articulate their positions, consequently helping their peers to find the defining boundaries of their own practices. Movement and malleability across position-categories may signal innovation, as can long periods of consistency do likewise. Very often a community is characterised by a high degree of commonality, with differences in a single category, forcing radically different design approaches.

We have developed a tool that enables practitioners to analyse their design-practice moves, project by project. The tool contains a wide range of categorisation 'types', as a way to both understand the differentiation within, while simultaneously taking into account—or incorporating a sense of—the shifts and movements and slippages across categories. The articulation of differentiation, while maintaining a sense of the movements inherent in practice, is a particularly important aspect of this analysis.

Architect Leon van Schaik, who pioneered this research, and SueAnne Ware who was the first Landscape Architect to engage in the research, came to know what they know of the knowing that is designing through their own past practice, but chiefly through in depth conversations with architects and landscape architects. In part this is through the design practice mode that we have pioneered and refined at RMIT, and now being furthered by a consortium engineered by Richard Blythe having been awarded a Marie Curie ITN grant 2013–2016.

For over twenty years at RMIT we have used a form of design review process during the design development of buildings that we have commissioned. Colin Fudge and Geoffrey London have pursued design review processes across the range of government agency commissioning practises. We conclude with this argument: Spatial thinking is the capability that architects and landscape architects develop as they learn their professions. Thinking through situations spatially, and three dimensionally, is the most unique quality that they offer to the communities that they serve. While this learned capacity can be understood in the abstract, it is in no way a neutral or a generic capability. Every human being is endowed with immensely sophisticated spatial intelligence, and for every individual this intelligence emerges and develops in specific places. More and more[1] we better understand how we make our world, and it makes us. This is a different shaping of intelligence for everyone, even where there are broadly shared community experiences doing the shaping. The professions inculcate canons of exceptional works, but these are apprehended and appreciated through the gauze of experience.

Here we have presented a pioneering investigation into the ways in which spatial-thinking is differentiated in the mastering of practice. We see this as a beginning in the better understanding of how practitioners use their spatial-thinking in design. We also see this informing the design review processes that are so central to creating upward spirals in the quality of designing, with peer review processes observed to be at the base of almost all innovative communities of design (Procuring).

Further we believe that when those untrained in spatial-thinking observe spatial-thinking at work in design review processes, they become aware of what is at stake and what good spatial-thinking offers to those who commission buildings, and to those for whom they are commissioned.

1 Malafouris, Lambros (2013) *How Things Shape the Mind: A Theory of Material Engagement*, MIT Press, Cambridge, MA